MEANING IN LIFE

MEANING IN LIFE

A THERAPIST'S GUIDE

CLARA E. HILL

American Psychological Association
Washington, DC

Published by
American Psychological Association
750 First Street, NE
Washington, DC 20002
www.apa.org

APA Order Department
P.O. Box 92984
Washington, DC 20090-2984
Phone: (800) 374-2721; Direct: (202) 336-5510
Fax: (202) 336-5502; TDD/TTY: (202) 336-6123
Online: http://www.apa.org/pubs/books
E-mail: order@apa.org

In the U.K., Europe, Africa, and the Middle East, copies may be ordered from
Eurospan Group
c/o Turpin Distribution
Pegasus Drive
Stratton Business Park
Biggleswade Bedfordshire
SG18 8TQ United Kingdom
Phone: +44 (0) 1767 604972
Fax: +44 (0) 1767 601640
Online: https://www.eurospanbookstore.com/apa
E-mail: eurospan@turpin-distribution.com

Typeset in Meridien by Circle Graphics, Inc., Columbia, MD

Printer: Sheridan Books, Chelsea, MI
Cover Designer: Naylor Design, Washington, DC

Library of Congress Cataloging-in-Publication Data

CIP data has been applied for. Library of Congress Cataloging in Publication Control Number: 2017044801.

British Library Cataloguing-in-Publication Data
A CIP record is available from the British Library.

Printed in the United States of America
First Edition

http://dx.doi.org/10.1037/0000083-000

10 9 8 7 6 5 4 3 2 1

Contents

III

IV

Acknowledgments

Susan Reynolds and Ed Meidenbauer heard my keynote address on meaning in life at the Society for Psychotherapy Integration in April 2014 and immediately asked me to write a book about the topic. I was terrified because I felt that I did not know enough to write such a book. I have since learned a lot, although I still feel that there is much more to know. I am grateful for their encouragement and support. I also thank Andrew Gifford as the developmental editor and the other folks at the American Psychological Association who have worked so hard to make this book a reality.

I am grateful to the following people who have reviewed chapters in this book and given me feedback: Zack Borkowski, Dana Falk, Jim Gormally, Shakeena King, Carol Mishler, Kathy O'Brien, Kristen Pinto-Coelho, Pat Spangler, Eva Suliman, Barbara Thompson, and Heidi Zetzer. I am also indebted to the many family members and friends who have endured endless discussions about meaning in life. In addition, the three undergraduate classes in which we did qualitative research projects on meaning in life were incredibly beneficial for helping me think about the topic. Trying to develop a measure of meaning in life with Kathryn Kline, Matthew Miller, Heidi Zetzer, Kristen Pinto-Coelho, and Ellen Baumann Marks also forced us to think about this construct and how to measure it. A project with Dennis Kivlighan, Shakeena King, and Aaron Borkowski looking at changes in meaning in our clinic also shaped my thinking about psychotherapy. I also thank all the people who participated in our studies on meaning in life and all the people who attended workshops that I gave on meaning in life; without their input, I could not have developed my ideas. I am particularly grateful to the experienced therapists who provided cases that are highlighted in Chapter 7. I also especially want to thank the three reviewers of the book; their comments really helped shape the book.

MEANING IN LIFE

Introduction

Life exists only where there is meaning.

—C. G. Jung, *Collected Works: The Practice of Psychotherapy*

Elisa is a 35-year-old single parent. One day, she asked a doctor for medication because she felt like she was having a heart attack and could not breathe. After a consultation, the doctor referred Elisa to a counselor, who learned something about her story. Elisa had lived in El Salvador until the conditions with the gangs became so dangerous that she was frightened for her children's future. She figured out how to get her family out of the country and into the United States, but she had to leave behind her parents and extended family. She got her children into a safer school, but she could only find work cleaning houses even though she had a university degree. She constantly worried that she would be deported and that her children would be left with no parents. Elisa also worried that her children were no longer speaking Spanish and were picking up bad American habits. She was lonely and worried that she had made a mistake in coming to the United States. Everything seemed to be a struggle, and Elisa felt disconnected from herself and often had trouble leaving the house. She wondered what meaning her life had now.

We all struggle to figure out how to lead our lives and to make our lives meaningful. What can we do that gives us satisfaction and feels like it makes a difference? Do we matter to others? Are we engaged in things that feel meaningful, whether through work or hobbies or family? Will we be remembered when we are dead? Can we make sense of our lives, tie the past to the

http://dx.doi.org/10.1037/0000083-001
Meaning in Life: A Therapist's Guide, by C. E. Hill

present and future, and make meaning of our lives? These are the questions that stimulated this book. In it, I describe how psychology and psychotherapy can address these questions.

Key Ideas in This Book

The key construct in this book is meaning in life, which I shorten throughout to MIL. MIL involves an intuitive felt sense of the experience of having meaning in one's life, the feeling that one matters and is significant; having purpose or goals in life; having a sense of coherence and comprehensibility; and having the ability to reflect consciously about meaning. Compared with meaning *of* life, a phrase which typically suggests a universal connotation for the human species as a whole (as in, "Why do humans exist?"), MIL is a more personal construct (as in, "What meaning have I created in my life?"). MIL differs from happiness (which relates more to pleasure and immediate satisfaction), identity (which involves a more global sense of self), subjective or psychological well-being (which again is a more global construct involving quality of life), and search for meaning (which involves a more concentrated seeking). (See Chapter 1 for more about definitions and Chapter 11 for descriptions of measures of MIL.) MIL can be a focus of personal reflection, and it can also be the focus of psychotherapy, both as an explicit concern in and of itself and as an underlying component of other concerns (e.g., depression, physical health problems, career concerns).

Audience for This Book

There are a number of audiences for this book. First and most important, I want to reach mental health professionals so that they can provide better services for clients who have MIL concerns. On the other side, clients who are interested in MIL could hopefully profit from reading this book so they can be better prepared for talking in therapy about their struggles with MIL. Students who are interested in learning about the theory, practice, and research related to MIL will also find this book useful.

Another audience I hope to reach is researchers. Psychology has had a bias against studying abstract constructs, such as MIL, because these concepts may not always be observable or easily measurable. Hence, more and better research is needed about MIL, particularly that involving measure development as we begin to clarify the construct of MIL and distinguish it from related constructs. We also need more empirical research on how to work with MIL in self-help and psychotherapy, in terms of the markers for working with MIL, how to work with MIL, and the consequences of such work.

Finally, the interested educated person outside of psychology will also hopefully find this topic and book relevant. Given that we all struggle with existential concerns such as MIL, we all can benefit from thinking deeply about the topic. I have tried to write the book with a minimum of jargon so that it is accessible to as many people as possible.

Outline of the Book

In the Prologue that follows, I describe my own journey searching for and reflecting about MIL. The main part of the book follows and is split into four parts. Part I covers what we know theoretically and empirically about MIL. Part II involves applications of what we know to psychotherapy and self-help. Part III is a description of our research program on MIL at the University of Maryland. Part IV includes a concluding chapter in which I draw together what we have learned and reflect on future directions for theory and research.

PART I. OVERVIEW OF MEANING IN LIFE

Prominent psychological scholars have posited that all humans strive toward meaning and that we have a need to understand the world, to know our place in it, and to have purposes and goals (e.g., Frank & Frank, 1991; Frankl, 1963; Klinger, 1977; Reker, Peacock, & Wong, 1987; Yalom, 1980). Similarly, philosophers such as Descartes and Camus have suggested that we have a fundamental impulse to make sense of our experiences (see Proulx, Markman, & Lindberg, 2013). Frankl (1978) even proposed that seeking meaning is crucial not only to well-being but also to survival.

In contrast, some have argued that the quest for meaning is a luxury, a "first-world problem," and that people only turn to thinking about meaning when things are going well (Baumeister, 1991). In this line of thinking, MIL is highly valued but reserved for a few lucky souls (Seligman, 2012), kind of the icing on the cake of psychological well-being (King, Heintzelman, & Ward, 2016).

Heintzelman and King (2014) argued persuasively, however, that MIL is not an esoteric phenomenon reserved for the self-actualized few. On the basis of empirical evidence, they concluded that, on average, people evaluate their lives as pretty meaningful. They suggested that meaningful lives are commonplace and that the things that make life meaningful (social inclusion, positive affect, religiosity, and environmental regularities) are readily available to most people. Heintzelman, Trent, and King (2015) also suggested, on the basis of the empirical evidence, that these high levels of meaning are not just due to people responding because of social desirability (i.e., wanting to look good to themselves and others) but because people feel that their lives are meaningful. Furthermore, the strong correlation between experiences of meaning and positive outcomes (well-being, health) suggests that having a sense of meaning is adaptive (King et al., 2016). King et al. (2016) further argued that the lack of meaning is pretty devastating, given that many tragedies (e.g., suicides, mass shootings) occur when people do not see their lives as meaningful.

Interestingly, the enjoyment of reflecting about MIL seems to vary widely across people. Some of us love to reflect on meaning, to ponder the existential issues about our role in the universe, and to examine whether we are making a difference in the world. We need to feel that we matter, that we are worthy, and that we are contributing in some way to the betterment of our fellow human beings and society. However, we all probably know people who seem blissfully uninterested in thinking about meaning. They seem perfectly content with partying, shopping, watching television, playing games, pursuing hobbies, hanging out with friends, or making money. They do not spend much time thinking about the whys and wherefores of existence. They are not worried about leaving a legacy or doing something important. They are not wallowing in angst; they are just going about living and being.

So, is there a fundamental impulse toward finding meaning in life? Must everyone find meaning? Is all meaning good? Can a person be considered "healthy" if she or he is not willing or able to seek deeper meaning? What is MIL anyway? How does MIL develop? What are the sources of MIL? These are the topics of Part I of this book. More specifically, Chapter 1 focuses on defining MIL and distinguishing it from other constructs. Chapter 2 describes the development of MIL and goes into more detail about the nature of MIL. Chapter 3 describes the sources of MIL.

The large body of research that has been conducted on MIL has been summarized in several excellent edited volumes (Hicks & Routledge, 2013; Markman, Proulx, & Lindberg, 2013; Shaver, & Mikulincer, 2012; P. T. P. Wong, 2012; P. T. P. Wong & Fry, 1998). This research has come largely from social psychology, developmental psychology, and personality psychology and is summarized briefly in Part I of this book.

PART II. THERAPEUTIC APPLICATIONS FOR WORKING WITH MEANING IN LIFE

It is one thing to contemplate MIL, try to define it, and engage in philosophical discussions, but it is quite another thing to think about how to help ourselves or help clients in psychotherapy who are struggling either explicitly or implicitly with MIL. What are the best interventions? When and how should a therapist approach the topic? Are there indications and contraindications about when and how to work with MIL?

Metz (2013) made what he called a bold hypothesis that psychodynamic and humanistic therapy, clinical psychology, and counseling psychology are best understood as "enterprises in search of meaning in life" (p. 405). It is indeed intriguing to think that our underlying endeavor in psychotherapy is to help people in the journey toward understanding MIL.

The purpose of Part II is thus to focus on how to work with MIL in psychotherapy and self-help. In Chapter 4, the focus is on the major theories that have been presented for working with MIL, particularly logotherapy, existential therapy, and acceptance and commitment therapy. I then present in Chapter 5 my integrative theory for working with MIL, specifically describing background conditions that facilitate MIL work, a general three-stage (exploration, insight, action) framework for MIL work, and possible interventions for each of the three stages. In Chapter 6, I describe how MIL is implicated in many of life's problems (e.g., physical health concerns, career concerns, transitions), and I provide more specific ideas for interventions for working with the MIL component of these problems. In Chapter 7, I present 10 cases to provide an inside picture of how experienced therapists work with clients about their explicit and implicit MIL concerns. In Chapter 8, I discuss multicultural and ethical considerations for working with MIL. In the final chapter in this section, I present a self-help guide for working with MIL, similar to that for psychotherapy.

PART III. RESEARCH ON MEANING IN LIFE

In concert with trying to define and understand what we mean by the construct of MIL, it is helpful to try to conduct empirical research on the topic. Struggling to operationalize the construct enough to study it forces us to refine our ideas further. Paying attention to disconfirming data also challenges us to think through what we mean by MIL.

The purpose of Part III is primarily to present the research that my research team at the University of Maryland has conducted on MIL. In Chapter 10, we describe studies with undergraduate students, doctoral students, and practicing psychotherapists about their definitions of MIL, how MIL developed, sources of MIL, and how therapists work with MIL in psychotherapy. These studies helped us refine our definition of the construct of MIL. I firmly believe that this observation step is critical to the first phase of the scientific approach. It is important to go into the endeavor with few expectations about the construct and attempt to learn from others. These studies used a variety of methodologies, ranging from qualitative to survey to quantitative. In addition, we review the existing measures and then present a new measure that we have developed to assess the presence of and reflectivity about MIL (see Chapter 11).

PART IV. CONCLUSION

I conclude the book by summarizing some take-home points and discussing future directions. Thus, in Chapter 12, I discuss the need for new theories about the construct of MIL, new theories about how to work with MIL in psychotherapy, and the need for future empirical research about the construct and about working with MIL in psychotherapy. I hope to stimulate new and exciting work in the field, particularly in terms of the applications to psychotherapy and helping people develop MIL.

Prologue

> Camus (1942/2004) recounts the "Myth of Sisyphus," in which the gods punish the titular rebel by assigning him a miserable, futile, and utterly pointless task: pushing a boulder to the top of the hill, watching it roll down the hill, and pushing it back up (again, for all eternity). More ingenious than an eternity of acute pain or the eternal slumber of death, the gods can imagine no worse torture than an existence with no *why*. However, in truth, the true horror of this fate is felt by Sisyphus only when he thinks to ask *why* and is aware that there is no obvious answer—his fate is "tragic" only in the rare moments when it becomes conscious.
>
> —Proulx, Markman, & Lindberg, *"Introduction: The New Science of Meaning"*

In qualitative research, there is a tradition of articulating biases both to help researchers think through what they bring to the research process and to allow others to put the results within the context of the researcher's biases. With a philosophical existential topic such as meaning in life (MIL), biases are also important because they form the foundation for one's beliefs and theories. For that reason, I present my narrative of how I have struggled with, pondered, reflected on, argued about, and loved the topic of MIL. Come along for the ride!

http://dx.doi.org/10.1037/0000083-002
Meaning in Life: A Therapist's Guide, by C. E. Hill

The Early Years: The Influence of Religion

My parents were devout Christians (fundamentalist, conservative Baptists), and religion structured our lives. We had Bible reading every night and prayed before every meal (the long, rambling kind of prayers that were spontaneous expressions of a personal relationship with God). We spent Sunday at church: First there was Sunday school, then the main service, then home for the big Sunday dinner. Later in the evening, there was youth group, evening meeting, and often singing afterward. On Wednesday nights there was prayer meeting, on Friday nights there were often church dinners, on Saturday morning we had choir practice even if we could not sing in tune, and on Saturday night there were activities for teens. In summer, we went to vacation Bible school. The church was an extended family. We knew everyone, and they knew us and watched over us.

The type of Baptist that we were was hellfire and brimstone conservative. My parents believed in the literal interpretation of the Bible. We were not allowed to smoke, dance, drink, or play cards because these were all instruments of Satan.

As the youngest living child of four siblings (I had a younger sister who died when I was 2 or 3 years old), I was eager to catch up to my siblings and be part of the church family. I got "saved" (i.e., took Jesus Christ as my personal savior) when I was about 5 years old. In the Baptist church, children were not supposed to get saved until they reached the "age of reason" (typically 6 or 7 as I recall), but I was convinced I understood what I was doing and, of course, my parents wanted me safely in the fold.

I memorized Bible verses. In fact, I remember winning a contest because I learned the most verses in my age group. I carried my Bible to school. We were encouraged to "witness" to others and get them to come to church with us and get saved so that they could go to Heaven too. Not too surprisingly, other people did not respond well to our witnessing. But we were taught that we were supposed to be different and stand apart for our values, so there was a certain pride in not fitting in (although it sure did not feel good).

Given this background, you can easily imagine that all our meaning came from God; it was "the" meaning. We were to do "God's will" and to pray to God for his wisdom. We believed that God knew and recorded everything we did and that there would be a reckoning when we got to the gates of Heaven. Although life and behavior are predestined, the big fear was always "backsliding," so we had to constantly recommit ourselves and "come back to the Lord."

We were supposed to read the scriptures and figure out what God's message was to us and follow the teachings, but we were not to question. My father's refrain was "You just have to have faith, baby." If you had enough faith, prayed hard enough, and read the Bible, God would let you know his will. My father would say that we have to listen and let God guide us. His will, not thine or mine. My mother would say that we may give up some things here, but we do it for eternal life. The trade-off for following God is that we get to sit at the right hand of the Father. She thought it all was a pretty good trade-off.

In so many ways, that belief system is compelling. The answers are all there. One does not have to question (in fact, it is better not to), just believe and accept and give it over to God. Meaning is dictated, given, predestined, and ordained. We each have a calling. Life is certainly a struggle because God does test us, but if you believe, you can make it. And God does not give you more than you can bear (remember the story of Job and all he had to endure; he could handle it because of his belief and trust in God).

Another aspect of these early years that I should mention is that we were poor and moved around a lot (we lived in at least eight different places between my birth and fourth grade). Although my father was educated to be a Baptist preacher, he could not find a ministerial or teaching position that paid enough to support the family; he worked in a menial factory job starting when I was in elementary school so he could provide for the family. My mother started working as a social worker at about the same time, although she had only a high school education. With four children in the family, we had very little money, especially given that 20% always came off the top for the church before taxes, with additional money given to Christian charities and any poor people who needed it. I had a lot of anxiety about money, social class, wearing hand-me-down clothes, and fitting into new places during my childhood years.

Questioning "The" Meaning

As a teenager, I started to question many things about religion. Things I had been taught did not make sense. What is the bit about the Trinity? How does that work, anyway? And the virgin birth, the second coming, and Revelations? And God knows what I should do with my life? And if everything is predestined, why are we responsible for what we do? And all that sin stuff sounded pretty interesting. When I asked my father, he told me to go to the Bible for my answers. I did, and came back to him pointing out many contradictory passages, to which he replied, "You just have to have faith, baby." Not a very satisfying response.

And what was it with all the infighting in the church? As a teenager, I recall church members fighting over things that seemed to me as trivial as the number of angels dancing on the head of a pin. Our church ended up splitting into two different churches. There were only 200 members to start with, and now only 100 each—hardly enough to form a viable unit, so of course, they begged for more money from church members. How could Christians be so nasty to each other? I was disillusioned because of these seemingly petty fights. These Christians were not good role models, and I certainly did not aspire to be like them.

In contrast, I remember during high school having great discussions with my non-church friends about meaning of life and religion. What was it all about? What were the other options? As seniors in high school, my best friend and I decided to visit different churches. My parents were fine as long as the first church was Baptist, but they got very upset when we next went to a Unitarian church, and so they forbade me to go to other churches (i.e., they would not let me drive the family car). But despite my parents' prohibitions, I was hooked on reflecting about and debating with others about meaning and life.

Although I was not into studying and schoolwork (somehow my parents never pushed that because they were so busy pushing religion and health food), I read a lot. I was often totally absorbed in books, which gave me a glimpse into other worlds and other ways of thinking. I learned that not everyone believed as we did and that many different religions existed.

I got very depressed and contemplated suicide. Where did I fit? I no longer wanted to hang out with the kids from church because they definitely seemed strange. But I did not fit with the other kids at school either, given that I could not go to dances or parties and would not have known how to act even if I did go. I recall the fantasy of making up a funeral announcement and watching my own funeral from the balcony like Tom Sawyer did.

My mother and I fought a lot—after the older children left home, she turned her considerable attention to me and tried to control my every move. As the time came for college, my mother tried to make me go to a Christian college. She bribed me, saying she would buy me a set of suitcases if I would go where she wanted me to go. I went to an interview at one such school and am pretty sure I got turned down because I said I believed in free speech in response to a question about what should be in the school newspaper.

I chose to go to Southern Illinois University (SIU) because my older sister had gotten a scholarship to go there, although she eloped instead of going to college. It was as far away as possible in Illinois from where my parents lived in Rockford, and I could afford to pay my own way through school (it was a different era when public universities were almost free). My first year there I was miserable. I did not fit in the secular world. I even tried to go to a Christian group for a while, but I did not fit there either. I no longer had a group of people with whom I could relate. I retreated into reading novels.

Nor did I know what to major in. I eliminated all the majors I did not like and was left with psychology and sociology. As a sophomore, I got a job in a vision lab in the psychology department and finally found a home there. I worked there for the rest of my undergraduate time. I also made friends and got a bit wild. I gave up religion, although Sundays felt empty and like I was missing something.

When I met my future husband in our doctoral program in counseling psychology at SIU and wanted to please him, I started occasionally going with him to the Catholic Church. When we decided to get married, I converted. What a culture shock! Whereas the Baptists had all the charismatic pull and guilt-inducing hell and brimstone, the Catholics had their staid rituals and liturgies, a different version of guilt, and little sense of community. Although I converted, I never really "became" a Catholic and withdrew soon thereafter, keeping up a modest arrangement of attending church every month when we had children so that they would grow up in the church and have some foundation of religion.

For many years as an adult, I was blocked and could not think about religion and what I believed. It just felt too threatening, like I would be hit by a lightning bolt if I seriously denied everything I had been taught (I still have a twinge of anxiety writing about this so openly). But religion, especially a fundamentalist Christian belief, and psychology do not mix well in liberal academic settings. I have more or less lived in limbo regarding what I believe. I certainly have abandoned the Baptist Church and the Catholic Church. Maybe I am agnostic or atheist, but I am not sure any label fits well.

What does all this mean for MIL? When I was in the Baptist Church and the Catholic Church, it was easy: Meaning is given to you by God. You "accept" your meaning, your calling, your purpose, as revealed to you through prayer and listening to the still, small voice that tells you what to do.

But what a shock to leave the religious worldview and struggle in the morass and swamps of a lack of meaning. I had to figure it all out on my own, which was difficult because I was so used to the authority of the church telling me what to believe and how to behave. I have come to believe that there is no benevolent or harsh being out there who knows everything I do, think, and even dream. I have only this one life and need to make the most of it. I have to construct my own meaning and make my own choices.

To say a word more about psychology: I picked a field in which I can think about existential issues. Theories of human development, psychopathology, and psychotherapy all deal extensively with the role of meaning. So, in effect, I switched to a new belief in going into psychology and science. It has been about 50 years since I left home for college, and maybe this book is an attempt to finally sort all this out!

Existential Crises During My Professional Career

When, after considerable agonizing, I decided on psychology as my career choice, I felt relieved. Having a goal of getting my PhD gave me something to strive for. Especially coming from a background in which education was not particularly prized, I had to all of a sudden change my attitude toward school and start working. I found that I loved learning, but writing and speaking were major challenges given a lack of confidence, poor education and training, and a lack of affirmation about my scholarly abilities.

Choosing an academic versus a clinical track was relatively easy because my advisor suggested I go into academia first given that it would be easier to move from academia to practice than to move from practice to academia. But did I really want to be an academic? I did not make a conscious, reasoned choice, but I did like research, and I very much wanted to prove I could make it in the academic world. I hated my job for the first 5 years. I was not prepared for the demands of an academic job and did not fit well in the male-dominated high-achieving department. Gradually, however, I accommodated and figured out how to survive and occasionally thrive. And then, of course, I started working toward tenure and the never-ending constant pressure to publish and prove myself.

But every 3 to 6 months, especially during semester breaks and trips to other countries and after completion of major projects when I paused to reflect, I wondered about my choices. Was what I was doing relevant? Was it what I wanted to be doing? Did anything make a difference? I pondered about my research strategies and even wrote about that when asked to talk about my career choices (Hill, 1984). I am rather neurotic (as my family and friends will certainly affirm) and love to reflect and figure things out. Some 30 years of psychotherapy with an incredible therapist helped me struggle to understand what gives me meaning and to get centered and live more in the present moment than dissociating as much and being as anxious.

I should also mention here that having two children (and now two grandchildren and another on the way) provided a good balance to work and contributed hugely to my sense of meaning. They matter to me, and I matter to them. I felt connected to them. I felt I could provide them with better parenting than my parents gave me so they would have a more secure sense of attachment and mattering. Likewise, mentoring students and seeing clients have allowed me to nurture others, an important source of meaning for me.

Other times meaning became central to my life were when my parents and my husband's parents died and when many of my professional heroes died. All of a sudden, I was now part of the older generation (how can this be? I was always the youngest!). Not only was there the loss of loved ones, but these deaths also foreshadowed my own death. What have I accomplished? Will I be remembered? Am I doing what I want to be doing? Who am I?

And another word about my parents' deaths: Their biggest purpose in life was to raise children in their faith. It was devastating for them, on their deathbeds, to realize that none of their four children believed as they did.

Retirement Age

I turned 60 and began feeling my age (bad when you are at a university and students are always young!). Friends and acquaintances started asking me when I was going to retire. I had to think about it. And I am still in that process.

The biggest issue is what would give me meaning if I retired. I feel like I have been able to make a difference with my work on helping skills, training therapists, psychotherapy research, qualitative research, dreams, and now meaning in life. I would not want to give that up. I have started seeing clients again after a few years off; I am liking that a lot, and I think I can make a contribution there. I started a clinic to do research, train therapists, and provide low-fee services to the community, and that feels good. When I think about what I would do if (really, when) I give up my line at the university, I think I would like to keep doing research, maybe do a little teaching, maybe do a little therapy. That is no different from what I am doing now. Volunteering elsewhere does not sound appealing. I have no real hobbies (unless you count playing spider solitaire, walking, and reading novels). I worry (okay, okay, I panic) about becoming isolated. What would give me meaning? I figure I might live another 20 or 30 years, and hoping that my health is good, I need something to do that matters.

I am fortunate that there is no mandatory retirement age at my university and that I have the privilege of being able to make my own decision about when to retire (at least as long as I stay productive). But, of course, that puts the burden on me to make the "right" choice.

And yet, for all this, when people ask me where I get my meaning, I have to pause. I do not have as many goals now as I have had in the past, and I doubt my work actually makes a difference in the large scheme of things. But I do enjoy being engaged and immersed in a writing project such as this book (at least most of the time when I am not feeling frustrated that I cannot quite grasp the construct well enough). I think back to Yalom's (1980) notion that engagement is what is crucial, that when one is engaged, one feels meaning. Perhaps that is the case; when I am involved in something for which I have some passion, I feel like I have meaning.

In conclusion, I want to emphasize how fortunate I have been in my life. I got a good education back in the days when an education was affordable even for poor people, I have had no major health problems, I have not experienced any major traumas, I have a wonderful, supportive husband and amazing children and grandchildren. We have enough money to have a nice house and be comfortable, and we have gotten to travel extensively. I have attained some distinction in my field. Many are not so privileged and have had to struggle much more than I have to survive and to find meaning. Certainly, I have seen my siblings struggle more than I have.

What Can We Learn From My Narrative?

I want to emphasize that my choices are just that: my choices. Others make different choices. Each of us has to come to our own conclusions about what gives us meaning, given our circumstances and abilities.

From my narrative, it is clear that religion can play a big role in thinking about meaning. My parents did not have to think about meaning; they knew "the" meaning of life, and that dictated the meanings they lived by. When I gave up religion, I had to struggle to construct my own meaning.

Family can be a big source of meaning. Having my husband and children and now grandchildren gives me a reason to live. Nurturing them is a big part of my life. Worrying about them, trying to understand them, fighting with them, and loving them are a big part of what makes life worth living.

Transitions can also be big in terms of meaning. Part of the reason I have stayed at one job for over 40 years is that I have trouble with change. Change brings opportunity but also crisis. So, transitions like choosing a job, unemployment, retirement, aging, and death of loved ones cause one to pause and reflect on meaning.

Although only alluded to in my narrative (in terms of my being neurotic), I also believe that personality has an influence on this discussion. I like to reflect on meaning and have since my teenage years. I like to talk with others to find out what gives them meaning. I love talking with my undergraduate and graduate students about meaning in life. Although I find much of scholarly writing about philosophy and meaning to be abstract, pompous, and hard to relate to, I love thinking about existential issues. Others are more content to just live their lives without agonizing, or they choose to give over to a higher power, and they may be happier than me because of that. But for me, the unexamined life is not worth living.

Thus, these strands (religion, family, transitions, and personality) are things that I bring from my conscious awareness into my thinking about MIL. Clearly, people with other stories will bring a different lens to their thinking. If you grew up with money, a nonreligious home, a minority status, differentness due to sexual orientation, or trauma, you probably have different views about meaning. I encourage each of you to think about what you personally bring to the discussion about meaning.

OVERVIEW OF MEANING IN LIFE

I

Definition of Meaning in Life

1

All of man's troubles have arisen from the fact that we do not know what we are and do not agree on what we want to be.
—Jean Bruller (Vercors), *You Shall Know Them*

Most people have an intuitive sense of whether or not they have meaning in their lives. But when asked to define *meaning of life* (MOL) and *meaning in life* (MIL), they often cannot define the terms or distinguish between them. They often have a clear sense of what their sources of meaning are (e.g., relationships, religion, work), and they often enjoy reflecting on meaning, but they cannot pinpoint exactly what MIL and MOL are. In fact, the more we try to pin down exactly what MOL and MIL are, the more elusive the terms feel. As Heintzelman and King (2014) noted, "as clearly important as the experience of meaning in life is to human existence, it remains, in some ways, a construct and experience shrouded in mystery" (p. 561).

In this chapter, I turn first to how others have defined the constructs, and I then present my definitions informed by this literature. Later in the chapter, I distinguish MIL for related constructs (e.g., meaning of life, happiness, identity) to work toward a clear definition.

http://dx.doi.org/10.1037/0000083-003
Meaning in Life: A Therapist's Guide, by C. E. Hill

Review of Current Definitions in the Field

The word *meaning* has two meanings (Janoff-Bulman, 2013). One is comprehensibility (i.e., questions about whether something "makes sense" and whether it fits into an accepted system of rules or theories). The other is significance (i.e., questions about whether something is of value or worth).

MIL has often been thought of globally, as is evident by broad questions on some measures of meaning (e.g., "Taking all things together, I feel my life is meaningful"; Baumeister, Vohs, Aaker, & Garbinsky, 2013). However, Heintzelman and King (2014) indicated that "within the scholarly literature, *meaning in life* and *purpose in life* are often used interchangeably. Most measures of purpose in life include the word *meaning*, and all measures of meaning in life include the word *purpose*" (p. 561). Similarly, P. L. Hill, Burrow, Sumner, and Young (2015) suggested that there is often a conflation between purpose and meaning given that people often just mean purpose when they talk about MIL. P. L. Hill et al. noted, however, that purpose and goals are not the only way MIL can be understood. They suggested that MIL comes not only from goals but also from a sense of self-worth, self-efficacy, and a justification for one's values and beliefs. Moreover, whereas they suggested that purpose is intrinsically centered within one's self and provides a self-organizing aim, they posited that MIL could be derived by perceiving coherence and regularity even outside oneself. Thus, they suggested that meaning could be derived from multiple sources, only one of which is meaning.

Similarly, Janoff-Bulman (2013) suggested that the nature of meaning involves a sense of coherence or a sense that life makes sense and that people can see where they fit into the world (citing the work of A. Antonovsky, 1993, and Reker & Wong, 1988). She also noted that meaning involves investment in valued goal attainment (citing Ryff & Singer, 1998) and the fulfillment of basic needs such as purpose, self-efficacy, value, and self-worth (citing Baumeister, 1991).

Reker and Wong (1988, 2012) suggested three components in personal meaning: a cognitive component that involves making sense of one's experience, a motivational component that involves pursuit and attainment of goals, and an affective component that involves feelings of happiness and satisfaction for attaining goals. For Reker and Wong (1988), the cognitive component "directs both the selection of goals and engenders feelings of worthiness" (p. 234), and the goal striving leads to satisfaction and fulfillment.

Perhaps the clearest definitions of MIL have been offered by Steger and colleagues. Initially, Steger, Frazier, Oishi, and Kaler (2006) defined MIL as "the sense made of, and significance felt regarding, the nature of one's being and existence" (p. 81). Steger's (2012) more recent and more comprehensive definition is as follows:

> Meaning is the web of connections, understandings, and interpretations that help us comprehend our experience and formulate plans directing our energies to the achievement of our desired future. Meaning provides us with the sense that our lives matter, that they make sense, and that they are more than just the sum of our seconds, days, and years. (p. 65)

Recent reviews of this literature (George & Park, 2016; Heintzelman & King, 2014; Martela & Steger, 2016) have converged on three common themes in the existing definitions of MIL: (a) a meaningful life is one that has a sense of purpose (P. L. Hill et al., 2015); (b) a meaningful life is one that matters or possesses significance (Baumeister, 1991); and (c) a meaningful life makes sense to the person living it, is comprehensible, and is characterized by regularity, predictability, and reliable connections (A. Antonovsky, 1993; Baumeister, 1991; Baumeister & Vohs, 2002). Thus, King, Hicks, Krull, and Del Gaiso (2006) proposed: "Lives may be experienced as meaningful when they are felt to have a significance beyond the trivial or momentary, to have purpose, or to have a coherence that transcends chaos" (p. 180). Halusic and King (2013) further clarified that "judging one's life as meaningful might, then, indicate that one has a sense of one's place in the broader universe that is provided by a sense of mattering, of purpose, or, essentially, of one's existence" (p. 46). Thus, according to the recent literature, the tripartite model (mattering/significance, purpose/goals, coherence/comprehensibility) seems to be gaining in popularity as the preferred conceptualization of MIL. For Heintzelman and King (2014), these three aspects, although treated as if synonymous, are potentially distinct. See Figure 1.1 for a graphic depiction of this tripartite model.

New Definition of Meaning in Life

Before conducting research in this area, I now realize as I look back on it that I intuitively had three components to my definition. First, I thought of MIL as being engaged in meaningful activities that contributed to the social "good" (e.g., parenting, research,

FIGURE 1.1

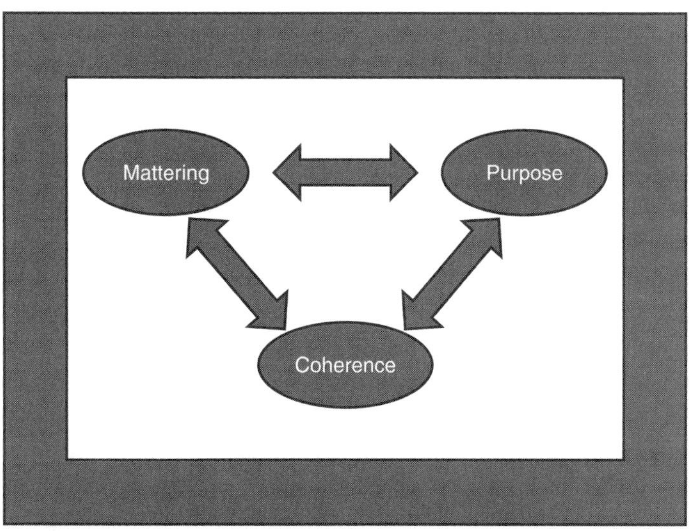

Components of a tripartite model of meaning in life.

teaching, conducting therapy). Second, and relatedly for me personally, I needed to feel that what I did and who I am matters. If I got too many rejections for manuscript submissions or was heavily criticized for my work, I despaired and felt like what I was doing was not worthwhile. Third, a dimension that has always been important to me is thinking about or reflecting on existential issues as a way of understanding my place in the world ("What's it all about?" "How do I fit in?"). I have always valued pondering about life and trying to understand my role in life and trying to choose projects that I considered meaningful. Following Plato's dictum, I strongly feel that "the unexamined life is not worth living." Thus, my sense of meaning came from (a) being engaged in life; (b) feeling that what I did mattered, was significant, and contributed to society; and (c) and reflecting on meaning and making sense out of life.

When reading the literature, then, I was surprised by the components of the tripartite model (coherence, mattering, and purpose) that seems to have gained ascendance. Mattering/significance as described earlier came closest to my personal definition of having meaning. Purpose/goals was also an understandable inclusion for me personally; I could relate especially to purpose/goals earlier in my life when I was ardently pursuing my education. But purpose/goals does not fit as well for me now personally given that I am closer to retirement. Nor does it fit as well for people who are retired and no longer striving for achievement as much. Finally, purpose/goals does not capture a sense of engagement in life, which seems like an important component. Coherence was the construct I probably had the hardest time absorbing as a component of MIL, given that coherence seems like insight to me, and there is such a rich history of psychotherapy being a meaning-making endeavor (see Castonguay & Hill, 2007). After additional pondering, however, and thinking about the definition of meaning as comprehensibility as well as significance, I began to see coherence as an integral part of MIL, in the sense that we need to have a sense that the world is comprehensible.

What strikes me about the tripartite model (coherence, mattering, and purpose) is that these three constructs do not on the surface seem to form a cohesive or united whole; rather, they seem like three separate but related components. In addition, it seems as though some crucial components are missing (e.g., reflectivity, engagement, and an affective component). Another confusing aspect is determining which components are central to a definition of meaning and which are sources or antecedents to meaning (e.g., is belonging a component of meaning or a source of meaning?). The distinction between what MIL is as opposed to the sources of MIL is difficult because some of the components seem to be sequentially related to each other. For example, having a sense of coherence could lead to a sense of purpose, so how is that different from being a source of meaning?

In trying to put my own experiences together with the literature, I converge on suggesting five related constructs that imperfectly constitute the essence of MIL as a cluster of related components: felt sense, mattering/significance, purpose/goals, coherence/comprehensibility, and reflectivity. I thus propose the following preliminary definition: MIL involves a felt or intuitive sense of meaning, a sense that one matters and is significant, a sense that one has purpose and goals and is engaged in life, a sense of coherence or comprehensibility, and a sense of enjoyment of reflecting about meaning. Thus, I see reflectivity as the feature that unites all the components and that all the components are interrelated, but that these components are not necessarily a complete depiction of this elusive construct (see also Figure 1.2).

Borrowing Martela and Steger's (2016) terminology defining MIL, we could say that felt sense represents an affective component, mattering an evaluative component, purpose/goals/engagement a motivational component, coherence a cognitive component, and reflectivity an attitudinal component. Thus, MIL is a multifaceted construct involving affect, evaluation, motivation, cognition, and attitudes.

I next describe these five components individually. Then, I describe possible interrelationships among the five components. The caveat is that this work is theoretical and speculative; empirical work is needed to confirm the components and the interrelationships.

FELT SENSE OF MEANING

As noted earlier, the felt sense of meaning is an intuitive, global felt sense that one's life is meaningful, without necessarily knowing the reason why one feels this way. This construct of felt sense is similar to Gendlin's (1981, 1996) felt sense, which Gendlin suggested helps us become clearer about our emotions when we focus inwardly on trying to experience and then articulating the emotion. Although one might not be able to specify what the meaning is or what gives emotions meaning, one has a sense of having meaning, being grounded, being centered, being in tune with life, and being connected with self and meaning. One might describe this felt sense as being in one's

FIGURE 1.2

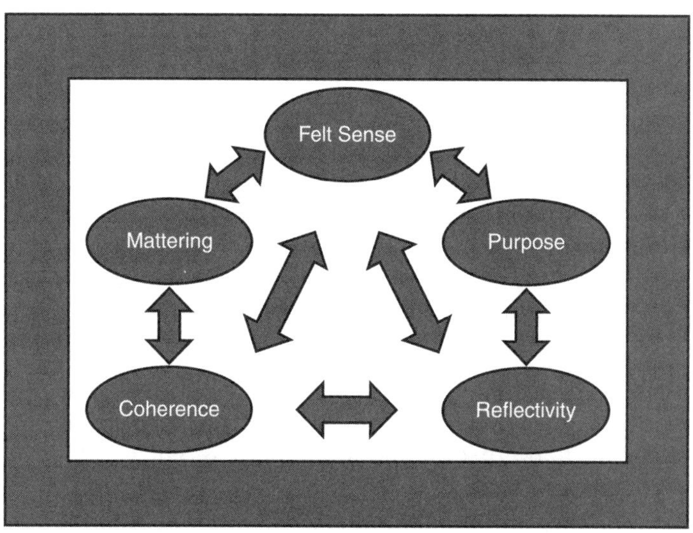

Components of a five-part model of meaning in life.

body, being present, and feeling that life is meaningful. King (2012) described this kind of meaning as intuitive, as sensed rather than constructed (whereas the other components are more constructed). Similarly, Weinstein, Ryan, and Deci (2012) suggested that meaning refers to the intuitive sense individuals have of living (or having lived) meaningful, fulfilling, and satisfying lives. Janoff-Bulman (2013) suggested, "We seem to know a meaningful life when we experience it (or don't), but nevertheless, psychologically it remains a fairly amorphous construct" (p. 203).

This felt sense reflects "being" as opposed to "doing." Yalom (1980) noted that in the Western world, we determine meaning by doing, whereas in Eastern traditions it is more a sense of being. This concept of being also fits with Maslow's (1970) highest level of needs and with Rogers's (1951) sense of self-actualization. Just as plants and animals get their sense of meaning from simply being who they are, we can get our sense of meaning from being who we are (not what others want us to be or what we think we should be). Having a sense of being oneself thus implies a sense of peace and self-acceptance.

Similarly, "judging life as meaningful involves evaluating the contents of mental life for a *phenomenological experience* or a *subjective feeling*, that life is, in essence, meaningful to the person living it" (Halusic & King, 2013, p. 446). Moreover, Halusic and King (2013) suggested that one's judgment of life as meaningful involves one's phenomenological experience or subjective judgment that his or her life is meaningful. And, interestingly, Halusic and King found in their research that this subjective sense of MIL is associated with positive affect, such that we sense that life has meaning when we feel good. People who rate their lives as meaningful are satisfied with their lives (Chamberlain & Zika, 1988b), feel hopeful about the future (Mascaro & Rosen, 2005; Zika & Chamberlain, 1992), have good health outcomes following a serious illness (Chamberlain, Petrie, & Azariah, 1992), have low anxiety and depression (Crumbaugh, 1968), and have low substance abuse and suicide following depression (Harlow, Newcomb, & Bentler, 1986).

MATTERING OR SIGNIFICANCE

If you are concerned about significance, you are wondering whether you matter or whether you have made a difference in the world. Has your existence changed anything? Has anyone noticed? Will you leave a legacy? Do you belong to a community? Is your life worthwhile and of value?

Life worth living is similar to the construct of *eudaimonia*, a Greek word that means living well, successfully, and responsibly (Martela & Steger, 2016), as opposed to *hedonia*, or pleasure seeking. When one experiences mattering, one feels that life has some profound and lasting importance (Baumeister, 1991).

Rosenberg and McCullough (1981) talked about mattering as a universal but often overlooked need to be noticed; feel important or recognized; feel appreciated, needed, or depended on; and feel pride. They noted that people need to count in others' lives and make a difference to others. Schlossberg (2009) was particularly interested in mattering in retirement. She noted that when people retire and feel they no longer matter, it can be perplexing and devastating. She gave the example of a retired social worker who had once been quite prominent in his field but felt marginalized, unappreciated, and unneeded after he retired. Feeling that his time was past was difficult for him.

One way of understanding mattering is in terms of *personhood*. One could wonder about whether one matters or has value as a person: Does anyone care about me? Will anyone miss me when I am gone? For example, one client talked about a father who said that if he had known she was going to be so disabled, he would not have allowed her to be born. Surely, hearing her father's words made this client feel that she and her life were not valued.

This type of mattering often comes from relationships. In fact, Halusic and King (2013) cited research showing that participants spontaneously nominate family or friends as the most important source of meaning in their lives, stating that relationships are an even more fundamental source of meaning than religion. Halusic and King reasoned that if "MIL is a fundamental human need, it would make sense that people would turn to close others to satisfy that need, as people tend to look to their community to satisfy most if not all of their fundamental needs" (p. 449). They believed that people feel they are a part of something greater than themselves when they feel a part of the community, and communities transfer cultural beliefs that give order and provide a sense of predictability. Halusic and King suggested that "people who have environments that support their growth and the realization of their potentials should have more frequent experiences with idiosyncratic sources of meaning and therefore should experience life as more meaningful" (p. 451).

Another way of understanding mattering is in terms of *contributions* (legacy). Thus, people wonder about whether what they are doing matters, whether it is worthy, or whether they will leave a legacy. Thus, one client might feel he has wasted his life by not following his passion and writing the great American novel. Another client might feel that because she is unemployed, she is not contributing anything of value to the world. As another example, American presidents are often concerned about their legacy (i.e., how they will be remembered in the history books).

Clients are often concerned about mattering/significance when they seek psychotherapy. Clients who experience depression and anxiety often feel inadequate and hopeless, despair about their abilities, do not see a future for themselves, cannot see possibilities, and have poor social relationships. They do not feel inherent self-worth, may feel fraudulent or like imposters, and may feel that if people truly knew their inner selves, they would not like them. For example, a client who had been adopted at birth expressed concern about whether she had value. She felt she had no meaning in life because her biological parents did not want her.

Although less research is available about mattering than about purposes and coherence, some findings reflect on the connection of this aspect to the construct of MIL. For example, in a large survey of adolescents, Rosenberg and McCullough (1981) found that self-reports of mattering to parents were positively associated with global self-esteem and negatively associated with depression, anxiety, and delinquency. Furthermore, higher presence of MIL was associated with less suicidal ideation and fewer suicide attempts, suggesting that the idea of having a meaningful life is associated with a life worth living (e.g., Harlow et al., 1986; Heisel & Flett, 2004).

PURPOSES, GOALS, AND ENGAGEMENT IN LIFE

Having purpose or goals means one has aims, something one is currently accomplishing or wants to accomplish in life, direction, and future goals. It might involve a belief that one can make a contribution to the world, whether it be in terms of curing cancer, being a great athlete, being an inventive cook, being creative, being a good friend, or helping others. Weinstein et al. (2012) talked about meaning related to life purpose, a sense that particular goals are important or meaningful to people and that if these goals were achieved people would feel they had led a meaningful life.

Closely related constructs to purpose and goals are engagement (see especially Yalom, 1980) and passion, the idea that it may not matter so much what one does in life but that one is actively engaged in life and has a passion for life's activities. For example, in my world of psychological research, this might mean conducting research that inspires a sense of passion rather than just doing research that receives funding. The person with a passion for what he or she is doing is engaged in doing something that feels important at the moment. Thus, goals are not always for the future but also for the present. Unfortunately, many people are not able to pursue opportunities that align with their passions, and this can create a sense of desperation or despair. Yalom (1980) advocated leaping into commitment and action, citing Tolstoy: "It is possible to live only as long as life intoxicates us" (p. 481). For Yalom, it is not the mad search for pleasure but meaningful engagement. He even indicated that one cannot just search for meaning, but rather if one is engaged in life, one will have a sense of meaning. Thus, meaning for Yalom is a by-product of engagement (see Chapter 4 for more on Yalom's existential theory).

As opposed to the felt sense involving "being," purpose and goals involve more "doing," being actively engaged in pursuing some goals. Having goals and being engaged in life often allows people to feel they are making a difference. The activities are frequently related to career or work but often might involve an avocation (e.g., a medical doctor who starts a clinic in Africa), commitment in the community (e.g., maintaining the community garden, starting or volunteering for an organization for aging in place), or dedication to a cause (campaigning for someone running for president). Furthermore, people might make a difference by doing something they have a talent for, such as art, music, dance, writing, doctoring, helping others, or the ministry.

A person might also gain meaning not so much from what she or he is doing but from the idea of doing it well. My father-in-law worked his whole life at a job in a grocery store. The job itself was not inherently meaningful, but he took pride in doing the job well and felt that it gave him meaning because he was able to provide for his family.

Goals seem to be particularly important at times of transition. In late adolescence and early adulthood, people think about what career they want to have. At midlife, many adults are concerned about whether they are in the best career or whether another career would be more fulfilling. If they stay in an unfulfilling career, they might seek out other non-career-related pursuits (e.g., volunteering, running marathons) to find meaning. At retirement, people often worry about what is next, how they will find purpose without work. They might have to readjust their values to find fulfillment from other activities. In addition, when life does not go according to the traditional developmental markers (graduation, getting married, getting a job, having children, retiring), people are often confused and discontented because they do not meet society's definition for meaningfulness. Furthermore, when one loses significant others to death at any age, one is forcibly reminded about the importance of doing what one loves to do because life is short and uncertain.

Carver and Scheier (1998) proposed a self-regulation model that is useful for understanding purpose as a component of MIL. They suggested that behavior can be understood as a process of identifying goals and working to attain goals. They proposed a hierarchical model of goals with the more abstract higher goals (*be* goals representing ideals) at the top and lower level and more concrete goals at the bottom. For example, the ideal of being a good parent leads one to want to give one's child a good education, which leads to the concrete goal of driving one's child to school. Carver and Scheier suggested that clearly specified be goals (e.g., being a good person) facilitate better identification and pursuit of lower level goals, and only those goals that are highly valued motivate behavior.

George and Park (2016) cited several strands of research supporting the assertion that purpose is an aspect of MIL. For example, on days that people with social anxiety devoted considerable effort toward a purpose in life, they experienced more self-esteem and positive emotions (Kashdan & McKnight, 2013). Similarly, several studies have shown that having highly valued goals or purposes is strongly associated with physical health, mental health, and well-being (e.g., Boyle, Barnes, Buchman, & Bennett, 2009; Matthews, Owens, Edmundowicz, Lee, & Kuller, 2006; Ryff, 1989; Scheier et al., 2006; Smith & Zautra, 2004). In addition, research has shown that the more that goals are perceived to be of value or importance, the higher the well-being and flourishing (Emmons, 1986; Little, 1999).

A related construct is *calling*, or the idea that one's purpose involves a calling (e.g., Duffy & Dik, 2013), as in hearing from some external source about what one is to do in life (e.g., a calling to become a priest). I suspect that whether one thinks one has a calling depends on one's philosophy about the origins of MIL. Those who believe that purpose comes from God, Allah, or some other higher power are likely to think they have a calling (e.g., a calling to become a priest or missionary). If people think, however, that they have to construct their own meaning, they have to decide, on the basis of the best available evidence and their values, what to do with their lives in terms of career and relationships (this would be considered a choice rather than a calling). An in-between position is that people feel that they have talent (e.g., for music, sports, art, helping) and feel an obligation, motivation, or calling to fulfill that talent, although not as related to God or a higher power but for themselves.

It is important to note that goals range on a dimension of mental health. At the healthy end of the spectrum, people have a secure sense of mattering and have chosen (rather than just following another's imperatives) goals that fit their talents, are realistic yet aspirational, and fulfill some social good. In the mid-range, some goals are not necessarily healthy or unhealthy, but are also not particularly life affirming. For example, a person might have a goal of winning the lottery, which is not statistically realistic and also causes them to spend money they might otherwise have used more beneficially. Unhealthy goals might include being a crusader, being so busy one cannot think or feel, or forcing others to share one's goals (see also Yalom, 1980). An example of an unhealthy goal is the anorexic's desire to be perfect, always in control, and not eat; such a person has clear goals, but these goals are ultimately self-destructive. These unhealthy goals are often defenses against living rather than a reflection of living meaningfully.

COHERENCE OR COMPREHENSIBILITY

Coherence refers to the idea that people can make sense or meaning of their lives (past, present, and future), that there is comprehensibility of one's existence, that disparate things hang together and make sense, and that they can tell a clear narrative or story about their life (A. Antonovsky, 1988). Frankl (1946) gave the example of an elderly man who was suffering profoundly because his wife had died recently. Frankl asked him what would have happened if he had died first. The man responded that his wife would have suffered terribly. Frankl suggested that the man could feel good because he had prevented his wife from suffering. The man then felt better because his suffering now had some meaning (i.e., was comprehensible and made sense).

Many people go to therapy to make sense or meaning out of their lives and to develop a new and better framework (i.e., perspective, narrative) about themselves. Understanding where one comes from and how one got to be the way one is provides a sense of understanding and acceptance that life is predictable and coherent (Castonguay & Hill, 2007). Psychotherapists thus help clients make sense out of their lives in terms of understanding where they came from, who they are presently, and what they want their future to be. Such insight provides self-knowledge that allows clients to accept and understand themselves and thus to make better choices. In therapy, many clients also work to make sense out of their waking events and nighttime dreams (Hill, 2004). The feelings that events and dreams are random and meaningless is difficult for most people to accept. By making sense of events and dreams, one has a sense of coherence that life makes sense and follows some pattern.

Efforts to understand one's culture and to make sense of how one reacts because of this cultural background also fall into this idea of coherence. Relatedly, one can see this drive to coherence with the interest in genealogy and tracing roots as a way of finding out who one is and where one fits in the world.

Another example of coherence is making order out of the chaos of life. For example, when a person organizes their belongings, living in an uncluttered environment can create a sense of serenity and meaning. Or, when people decorate their home for the holidays, carrying out traditions can give them a sense of the continuity of life across generations and provide a sense of meaning. Similarly, a Japanese colleague described how the traditional tea ceremony with its art and beauty brings a sense of calmness and coherence.

Importantly, it is easier to make a coherent narrative out of a privileged life than a life that is fraught with suffering (e.g., from war, disability, poverty, trauma). It is easy, however, to fall into the trap of taking credit for the good fortune in our lives but displacing blame or feeling that it is not fair when bad things happen. The notion that such traumatic events do not seem fair requires each person to try to alter their cognitive schema to develop a new understanding of why such things happen.

Several theories have been developed that shed light on coherence as a component of MIL. For example, the meaning maintenance model (Heine, Proulx, & Vohs, 2006) suggests that people have an inherent need to make sense of their environment and that we feel distress when meaning is disrupted. Indeed, there is probably a survival advantage to being able to make sense, find patterns, and establish predictability because these abilities help people plan for the future (Martela & Steger, 2016).

Another perspective on coherence comes from McGregor and Little (1998), who contended that meaning derives from consistency among elements of the self (e.g., defining memories, relationships, personal projects, values, and possible selves). They suggested that people experience meaning to the extent that these elements fit together. McGregor and Little referred to this construct as *integrity*, the extent to which people appraise their personal projects as consistent with their values, commitments, and self-identity.

Similarly, Routledge, Sedikides, Wildschut, and Juhl (2013) postulated and provided empirical evidence that nostalgia (i.e., "reflecting nostalgically on the past"; p. 297) is a method by which we make use of specific sources (e.g., family, friends, religion, personal accomplishments) to derive meaning. They noted,

> When people are pressed to find meaning, they reflect nostalgically on treasured past experiences (e.g., family functions, personal accomplishments). . . . Narrative episodes could thus be characterized as snapshots of the personally treasured life experiences that infuse life with a sense of meaning. (p. 303)

George and Park (2016) provided some empirical evidence to justify their conclusion that comprehension is an aspect of MIL. They cited research on self-verification theory (Swann, 1987, 2012; Swan & Buhrmester, 2012), which posits that individuals' desire to understand the world around them leads to the development of self-views to organize their experiences and make sense of life. Research on this theory has shown that people create environments and engage in biased informational processing so that they can verify and maintain existing self-views. George and Park also cited research from the narrative identity literature (McAdams, 2008; McLean, 2008), which views the self as composed of stories that provide a sense of understanding. This body of research has shown that narratives bring together disparate aspects of experiences into a coherent understanding and help individuals interpret and predict future experiences.

REFLECTIVITY ABOUT MEANING

Reflectivity involves valuing and enjoying thinking about meaning ("Why are we here?" "What is my purpose in life?") and an interest in the existential pondering about the unknowable. Some people enjoy thinking about existential issues such as MIL (Yalom, 1980, identified death anxiety, isolation, and freedom as other existential issues). For some, this reflectivity leads to existential despair, with feelings of hopelessness and worthlessness and feeling inconsequential. For others, it is a life review and check-in, with time spent pondering goals, accomplishments, legacy, future, existence, and the unknowable.

Anyone can reflect on meaning. Young children frequently ask "Why?" in an effort to figure out their world. Adolescents reflect about meaning to determine what is important to them and to use the deliberations to make choices about life goals. People who have experienced major transitions reflect to make changes in their lives. People who lead meaningful lives can still find value in reflecting on meaning and their place in the universe.

It is important to reiterate that one does not have to be a brilliant philosopher to enjoy thinking about MIL, given that the construct is central and close to everyday life. In addition, it seems to me that someone could have a felt sense of meaning (e.g., "I have meaning because I work hard to support my family") and know that one matters ("I am worthy") without spending much time searching for, reflecting on, or prioritizing meaning. The person who thinks deeply about MIL may have a richer, more articulated, better developed sense of meaning, but that does not mean that the person is "better" or happier or more content as a result; indeed, they could well have more existential anxiety. An interesting question thus arises as to the optimal level of reflectivity. One could well imagine that a person who does not reflect at all would lack awareness but that a person who reflects obsessively or ruminatively would be quite distressed. It makes sense that a moderate level would be healthy.

I argue, as did Martela and Steger (2016), that reflectivity is necessary for the awareness of all the other components of MIL. Thus, one needs to reflect to feel that one's life is meaningful, to have a sense of coherence or to comprehend life, to develop and evaluate goals, and to feel that one matters and has significance. Reflectivity thus sets the tone for and valuing of thinking of existential issues, seems to set humans apart from other animals, and thus seems to be an important component of MIL.

INTERRELATIONSHIP OF THE FIVE COMPONENTS

MIL does not seem to be one single clear, distinct construct but a cluster of several highly interrelated ones (again, see Figure 1.2). Therefore, perhaps it would help to explore the connections among the components.

Martela and Steger (2016) argued for three connections between the components of their tripartite model (coherence, purpose, and significance). First, they suggested that coherence can be a source of significance, such that when life feels comprehensible, it is more likely for a person to feel that life has value. Second, they suggested that purpose and significance are entangled, such that purpose can be a source of significance (e.g., present life can feel more worthwhile when we have a valued future goal) and significance can be a source of purpose (e.g., if we feel good about ourselves, we are more likely to pursue goals). Third, they suggested that coherence and purpose are entangled, given that it is hard to imagine having goals without a sense of coherence (e.g., have to have a coherent basis from which to choose goals), and it is hard to have coherence without purpose (e.g., purpose provides structure).

Similarly, George and Park (2016) suggested that comprehension, purpose, and mattering mutually influence one another, such that low levels of one of the components might make it difficult to have anything other than low levels of the other two components. Thus, a lack of coherence would make it difficult to feel a sense of direction, a lack of direction would make it difficult to feel a sense of significance, and a lack of significance could make it difficult to feel a sense of significance. In contrast, high levels of any one of the components would make it easy to feel high levels of the other components. Thus, feeling that life is significant would make it easier to feel that life is coherent and that one has direction. In fact, experiencing high or low levels of one component might reinforce and intensify the experience of the other components.

Furthermore, although Martela and Steger (2016) and George and Park (2016) did not include reflectivity as a separate but related component, both sets of authors argued that reflective, linguistic thinking might unite the other components. Thus, reflection and a meaning framework could link coherence, purpose, and significance given that these all involve an interpretation and a reflective approach (i.e., one cannot interpret the world as comprehensible without reflection). In addition, although an affective component was not included in the tripartite model of coherence, mattering, and purpose, Martela and Steger indicated that they remained open to the idea of including an affective component that is not heavily laden with feelings of happiness, satisfaction, and fulfillment, but rather is unique to MIL (and I suggest that felt sense fits this criterion). We could thus say that reflectivity and felt sense unite the other three constructs, tying them all together more completely.

Thus, we can make a case that these components are highly related, such that each is a source for the other (e.g., reflectivity leads to all components, coherence leads to purpose/goals and mattering/significance, purpose/goals leads to significance and mattering, all other components lead to a felt sense of meaning and a felt sense leads to all the other components). So, even though these seem like somewhat separate dimensions, it is hard to separate them conceptually and statistically (see also Chapter 11).

We can also, however, make some distinctions among the components. According to Martela and Steger (2016), coherence involves a value-neutral process whereby we make sense of something, whereas significance and purpose refer to evaluating something to determine whether it has positive or negative value. They argued that coherence involves describing the world to create accurate mental models and facilitate prediction, whereas mattering/significance and purpose involve an aim to find value in the world and justify one's actions. Similarly, they differentiated meaning (as related to coherence) and meaningfulness (as related to the amount of significance). Thus, for Martela and Steger, mattering/significance and purpose/goals are more highly related to each other than either is to coherence/comprehension.

Martela and Steger (2016) further stated that although significance and purpose are both value-laden constructs, they are distinct. They argued that significance involves finding value and thus involves evaluation of one's life as a whole. In contrast, purpose is about finding valuable goals and thus involves motivation and is future oriented. Furthermore, George and Park (2013) considered purpose as a source of significance, in that if one is committed and has purpose, it generates significance and value. Martela and Steger, however, noted that significance could have other sources (e.g., positive affect, relationships, being treated fairly) in addition to goals.

In fact, even though the five components appear conceptually to be distinct, we found it difficult in our research (see Chapter 11) to distinguish them. Indeed, our analyses yielded a two-factor solution, such that felt sense, mattering/significance, purpose/goals, and coherence fit into a factor we called Experience, and reflectivity fell into a separate but moderately related factor (see Figure 1.3). Our factor structure is different from those posed in other literature (see George & Park, 2016; Martela & Steger, 2016), so further research is needed to clarify the structure of MIL and determine its components.

Relatedly, I suggest that not all these components have to be present for a person to have a sense of meaning. Thus, felt sense or mattering might be most central for one person, whereas purpose/goals or coherence might be more relevant for another. Some people might feel that their lives matter and make sense, but they do not necessarily have a strong sense of purpose or goals they are trying to accomplish. Others, in contrast, might base their sense of meaning on what they are accomplishing.

OTHER POSSIBLE COMPONENTS OF MEANING IN LIFE

As noted earlier, MIL seems to be a fuzzy set of closely interrelated constructs rather than one clear highly identifiable unidimensional construct. Thus, there is considerable controversy over what is and is not included in the construct of MIL. Some

FIGURE 1.3

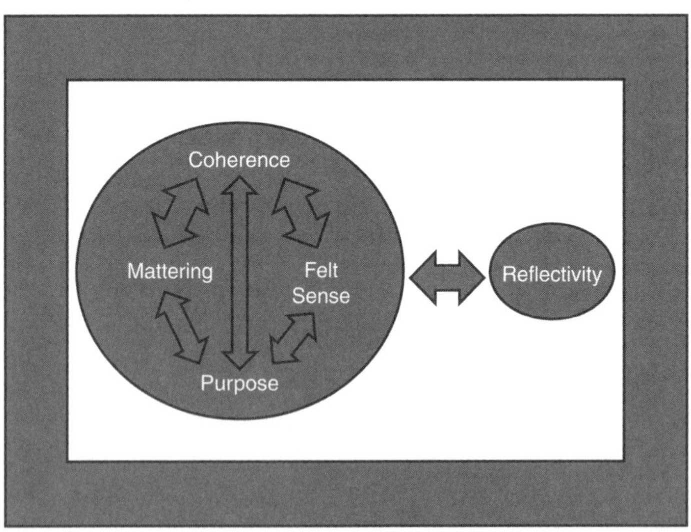

Components of a two-factor model of meaning in life.

constructs that have been considered (e.g., happiness, MOL, search for meaning, identity, subjective well-being) can be clearly distinguished (see the next section). Other constructs are more difficult to judge as to whether they should be included. Martela and Steger (2016) considered but rejected several components (e.g., leading an exciting life; leading an accomplished life; experiencing involvement, belonging, searching) as being antecedents or sources of meaning rather than meaning itself. Of these constructs, I struggle most with belonging because it is hard to distinguish from mattering. I suspect that the resolution of this controversy lies in better definitions and measures of the individual constructs and then clear criteria for what should be included. Given that MIL is an unobservable construct, we will never have a perfect answer to this question.

Distinguishing Meaning in Life From Related Constructs

To make sense out of MIL, we have to distinguish it from closely related constructs. Specifically, we can differentiate MIL from meaning *of* life, search for meaning, happiness, and identity (see Figure 1.4). We can also distinguish the experience or presence of MIL from sources of MIL (e.g., relationships, career), which we address in Chapter 3.

FIGURE 1.4

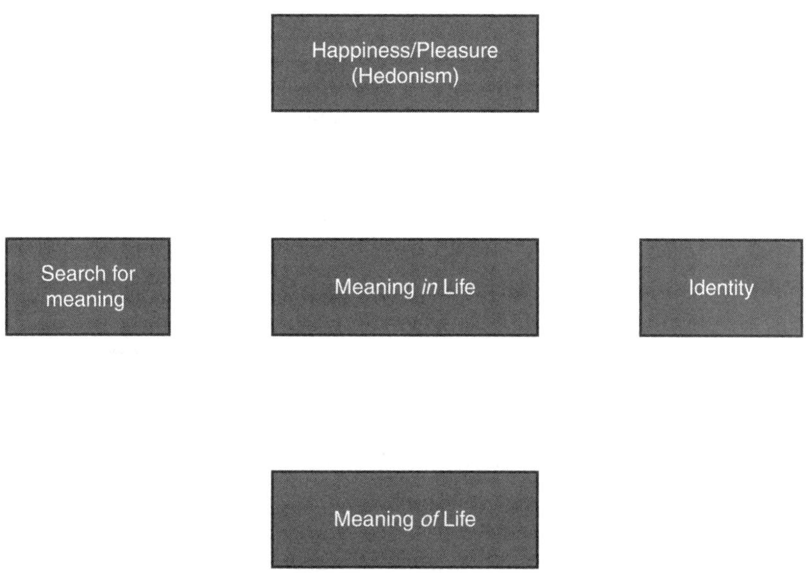

Constructs related to meaning in life.

MEANING IN LIFE VERSUS MEANING OF LIFE

MIL versus MOL are easily confused. In fact, in our first study (Hill, Bowers, et al., 2013), we naively called the construct we were interested in MOL. After further reading and thinking, we realized the appropriate term was MIL because we were studying the personal felt meaning rather than the universal meaning.

Yalom (1980) referred to MOL as cosmic, whereas he considered MIL to be terrestrial. Similarly, Metz (2013) described MOL as a "feature of the human species as such or of the universe in toto" (p. 406), whereas MIL is a "desirable, higher property that a person's life can exhibit to a certain degree" (p. 406). Perhaps more easily understood terms are universal versus personal, where MOL is the universal (as in "the" MOL or "the truth" for everyone; "Why do humans exist?") and MIL is the personal truth ("What is my meaning?" "How do I translate my beliefs about MOL into my personal MIL?").

DISTINGUISHING REFLECTIVITY ABOUT MEANING FROM SEARCH FOR MEANING

Reflectivity refers to thinking about meaning and valuing thinking about meaning, whereas *search* refers to looking for meaning. I view search as a related construct to the presence or experience of meaning, but I do not view it as the same as meaning.

First, let me talk about the distinction between presence and search, which comes primarily from Steger et al. (2006). In Steger et al.'s widely used Meaning in Life Questionnaire (MLQ; see also Chapter 11, this volume), there are subscales of Presence (an example item is "My life has a clear sense of purpose") and Search (an example item is "I am always searching for something that makes my life feel significant"). Thus, Presence involves experiencing meaning, whereas Search involves actively looking for meaning. The correlation between the two subscales was not significant ($r = -.19$). In addition, Presence was positively correlated with many measures of positive functioning, whereas Search was associated with neuroticism, depression, and negative emotions. These findings suggest that in fact presence and search reflect independent constructs, and I would argue that search for meaning is not so much meaning but rather is sometimes an antecedent to the experience of having meaning.

Steger et al. (2006) stated that Frankl (1963) should be given credit for the emergence of the construct of searching for meaning. They also cited Maddi (1970), who argued that the search for meaning is a fundamental motivation for people. They discussed the interplay between presence and search as somewhat paradoxical. They noted that someone high in presence could either be uninterested in further searching because of having attained meaning or could still be searching because the search itself is rewarding. They used Mahatma Gandhi and Malcolm X as examples of people who had lives with great meaning and purpose and yet who seemed to be still actively searching for greater understanding of meaning and purpose. Likewise, some people who score low on presence could be interested in searching for meaning (perhaps out of existential despair), but other such people might not be interested in searching for meaning because they are satisfied with their lives or feel that MIL is not relevant to them. Some people search compulsively for meaning but do not attain meaningful results. Some are "dreamers" whose search for meaning is a defensive avoidance of earthly demands. Some people who already lead meaningful lives seek meaning because they are searchers and always looking for what else there is. Thus, search can have many functions.

A construct that might resolve Steger et al.'s (2006) paradox between presence and search is reflectivity, described earlier as a component of MIL. Whereas search implies that one is looking for meaning, reflectivity reflects more interest in the existential pondering about the unknowable. I suggest that people like Mahatma Gandhi and Malcolm X probably had both high presence and reflectivity but low search. In other words, they probably valued reflecting about MIL even though they had no particular need to search for MIL later in life. In support of this idea, note that the experienced therapists in Hill, Kanazawa, et al. (2017; see also Chapter 11, this volume) who completed the MLQ were higher on presence but average on search compared with younger participants in other studies, presumably because they were leading fulfilling lives and were not actively searching for more meaning. Likewise, in our Meaning in Life Measure, we found that our Experience Scale (which was highly related to presence, indicating that they measure the same construct) was moderately related to the Reflectivity Scale, but both were less highly related to the Search Scale (Hill, Kline, Miller, et al., 2017).

MEANING IN LIFE VERSUS HAPPINESS

McGregor and Little (1998) suggested that happiness and meaning are separate but related constructs. They found that "doing well" was more associated with happiness, whereas "being yourself" was more associated with meaning. Similarly, Ryan and Deci (2001) distinguished between hedonic well-being (focusing on happiness, pleasure attainment, and pain avoidance) and eudaimonic well-being (focusing on meaning, self-realization, and functioning).

Baumeister (1991) gave two examples that illustrate the differences between happiness and meaning. First, in the "parent paradox," he noted that while parents have children living at home, they usually score low on happiness indicators, whereas once the children have left home, parents report that they are glad they had children because of the meaning they provide. Second, he gave the example that even though guerrilla revolutionaries are fighting for a cause that provides considerable meaning, they might still feel miserable living in bad conditions. They put up with the squalid living conditions because of the meaning they obtain from their revolutionary activities.

Baumeister et al. (2013) suggested that *happiness* can be conceptualized and defined as either affect balance (having more pleasant than unpleasant feelings) or life satisfaction (an integrative assessment of one's whole life). Furthermore, they noted that the integration of affect balance and life satisfaction provides an index of subjective well-being. Thus, happiness involves feeling good in the present moment and having one's needs met. They measured happiness with three general items (e.g., "In general, I consider myself happy").

In contrast, Baumeister et al. (2013) considered *meaning* to be a cognitive and emotional assessment of whether one has purpose and value in one's life. They suggested that meaning involves language, cognition, and culture, all of which help people figure out their place in the world. Thus, constructing meaning involves thinking about the past, present, and future; working toward some goal; and understanding one's life beyond the present. Furthermore, they suggested that meaning imposes stability on the ups and downs of life, giving the example of how marriage defines a relationship as constant and stable even though feelings fluctuate considerably on a situational basis. They also suggested that living a meaningful life involves doing things that express who one is, reflecting the symbolic self, such as taking care of others because that reflects one's values. They measured meaningfulness with three global items parallel to those about happiness (e.g., "In general, I consider my life to be meaningful").

Baumeister et al. (2013) set out to investigate how the constructs of meaning and happiness differed empirically. As they suspected, they found considerable statistical overlap between their parallel measures of happiness and meaning (with correlations of .63–.70). But they also found major, theoretically consistent differences between the two constructs in terms of relationships with other variables when they statistically removed the overlap between the measures of meaning and happiness (i.e., by removing the statistical overlap between the two measures they could determine the unique correlations of each construct with other variables). They found that happiness was uniquely positively related to satisfying one's needs and wants, being present oriented, and being a taker rather than a giver, and it was uniquely negatively related to anxiety. In contrast, meaning was uniquely positively related to integrating past, present, and future; being a giver rather than a taker (e.g., caring for children, buying gifts for others); having higher levels of worry, stress, and anxiety; and having concerns with personal identity and self.

On the basis of their findings, they suggested that one can have a meaningful but not happy life, giving examples of being a missionary or a political activist, sacrificing personal pleasure to make a difference in the world. In contrast, a person with a happy but meaningless life might be seen as relatively shallow, self-absorbed, and selfish. Of course, a person could lack both meaning and happiness (e.g., be depressed) or could have both meaning and happiness (e.g., be involved in a gratifying job such as researching meaning).

A related research program involves the relationship between meaning and positive affect. Halusic and King (2013) summarized this body of research, suggesting that positive affect precedes a sense of meaning. Specifically, when participants were primed in the lab for positive affect, they reported having meaning. Positive affect was more predictive of judgments of MIL than were religious faith, social relationships, and psychological need satisfaction. King and Hicks (2012) suggested that the association between positive affect and MIL is real and not just an artifact of measurement. They noted that individuals are more likely to recognize the meaning in their lives when they feel good, whereas meaning goes unnoticed when individuals feel bad. Thus, simple pleasures enhance the perception and experience of meaning whereas bad experiences inhibit the experience of meaning (although again, affect is not the same as meaning but a precursor or mediator of meaning).

MEANING IN LIFE VERSUS IDENTITY

Identity refers to self-construal, self-image, self-esteem, individuality, or sense of self (Weinreich, 1986). The concept of identity was articulated by Erikson (1950), who theorized that people begin during adolescence to feel both a sense of uniqueness as a human being and a part of society. For Erikson, this stage of identity versus identity confusion was a stage of psychosocial development following the initial stages of basic trust versus basic mistrust, autonomy versus shame and doubt, initiative versus guilt, and industry versus inferiority. Thus, as part of their development and in interaction with others in their lives, adolescents begin to figure out who they are in terms of their talents, skills, aptitudes, and likes and dislikes. Individuals begin to define who they are in relation to self and others to determine what they want to be or do in the future. It is during this time that the individual begins to ponder and think deeply about meaning, with this process continuing throughout the lifespan.

Thus, we can think of meaning as something a person incorporates into a sense of identity. Meaning can, therefore, be viewed as a part of self, just as talents and skills are part of the self but not the totality of the self. We would thus expect that a sense of meaning would develop in parallel or perhaps slightly behind the development of identity (see also Chapter 2).

Conclusion

MIL seems to be a fundamental concern for humans (although it is probably not unique to human beings). We all need to have meaning in our lives and some reason for living. I do not believe that there is "a" or "the" meaning of life that holds for all people and is given by some higher power that created the world. Rather, I believe that the world is essentially random, having developed through evolution over many millennia (see also E. O. Wilson, 2014). Each of us must make sense of the inherent randomness and construct our own meaning in life to figure out where and how we choose to fit into the world (although this can take the form of accepting that the given MOL is also one's personal MIL). Of course, some of us have more resources and privileges to figure out these issues, whereas others are limited by a lack of resources and privileges and thus have greater difficulty understanding and constructing a place in the world.

Recent reviews of definitions of MIL have converged on a tripartite model of MIL, including coherence, purpose, and significance. Although I agree with these three components, I expand the conceptualization by adding a felt sense of meaning and reflectivity about meaning. Thus, my definition is as follows: MIL involves a felt or intuitive sense of meaning, a sense that one matters and is significant, a sense that one has purpose and goals and is engaged in life, a sense of coherence or comprehensibility, and a sense of enjoyment of reflecting about meaning.

These components seem to be highly related and interconnected, as shown in Figures 1.1, 1.2, and 1.3, such that a felt sense is probably composed of some combination of mattering/significance, goals/purpose, and coherence; reflectivity unites the other four components given that all rely on an interpretative approach to life; mattering/significance and purpose/goals are entangled; and low or high levels of any component influence perceptions of the others. This overlap between the domains is shown clearly when, in Chapter 3 about sources of meaning, it appears that some sources can potentially provide meaning for several of the components.

Finally, MIL can be distinguished from MOL, search, happiness, and identity. Making such distinctions is important so that we have a clearer idea of what MIL is and is not. Thus, MIL is composed of at least five highly interrelated components and related to several components at a more moderate level. MIL is thus not a distinct phenomenon.

2 Development and Nature of Meaning in Life

> The mystery of human existence lies not in just staying alive, but in finding something to live for.
>
> —Fyodor Dostoevsky, *The Brothers Karamazov*

Given the definition of meaning in life (MIL) as involving the interrelated components of felt sense, mattering/significance, purpose/goals/engagement, coherence/comprehensibility, and reflectivity (see Chapter 1), this chapter examines how MIL develops and the nature of MIL. First, I review theories about the development of MIL and influences on the development of meaning. Second, I tackle questions about the nature of MIL (e.g., is it positive or negative, constructed or given, big or trivial?).

Although considerable empirical research exists for many sections in this chapter, I do not extensively review that research here. My focus is more on a broad overview of MIL rather than on basic research on MIL.

Theories About the Development of Meaning in Life

A number of theories have been proposed for how MIL develops. I review a few of these to give a flavor of how different theorists and researchers have conceptualized its development.

http://dx.doi.org/10.1037/0000083-004
Meaning in Life: A Therapist's Guide, by C. E. Hill

MASLOW'S SELF-ACTUALIZATION THEORY

In Maslow's (1970) influential theory of self-actualization, there is a hierarchy of needs. Needs at the lower levels must be satisfied before a person can move on to other needs, although Maslow believed that everyone has the need for self-actualization (the top need) and that there is some fluidity across levels (i.e., people can go back and forth among the levels and be working on needs at different levels).

The first four levels involve deficit needs (*D-needs*), which according to Maslow (1970), can only be fulfilled if certain conditions (e.g., freedom of speech, freedom to express oneself, freedom to seek new information) are present. Blockages of these freedoms would inhibit the person from satisfying these basic needs.

At the first level of D-needs, people have to fulfill basic physiological needs, such as breathing, food, water, sex, and sleep. The second level involves the need for safety in terms of body, employment, resources, morality, the family, health, and property. The third level is love and belonging, which are psychological needs met through friends, family, and sexual intimacy. The fourth level of esteem issues is met when a person feels comfortable with self (e.g., self-efficacy, self-esteem, confidence, achievement, respecting others, and being respected by others).

The higher levels of needs involve being values (*B-values*), which are not automatically fulfilled after D-needs are met but rather require additional striving. Although these are less well-known than the other levels, Maslow (1970) described a cognitive level, at which people enjoy intellectual stimulation, and an aesthetic level, at which there is a need for harmony, order, and beauty. The final level is self-actualization, which Maslow defined as achieving the fullest use of one's talents and interests or becoming all that one is capable of becoming. Self-actualization involves morality, creativity, spontaneity, problem solving, lack of prejudice, and acceptance of facts. It is by its nature different for every individual, and thus the manifestation of self-actualization reflects individuals' tastes, opinions, and values. Although Maslow did not explicitly include MIL in this hierarchy of needs, it fits into the self-actualization level because it is similar to the other being values.

WEINSTEIN, RYAN, AND DECI'S SELF-DETERMINATION THEORY

Self-determination theory seems to be a somewhat updated version of Maslow's (1970) theory, in that the underlying assumption of both is that human beings have a deep-rooted tendency toward growth and psychological integration. Weinstein, Ryan, and Deci (2012) proposed that when inherent needs are met, people can turn to developing and internalizing intrinsic life goals, which in turn fosters wellness and meaning. When needs are empty or thwarted, people adopt compensatory goals and purposes, which are less likely to provide a sense of having meaning. The authors noted,

> To feel whole and healthy we need to have a sense of purpose and to experience our lives as significant and valuable. Constructing and internalizing a sense of meaning is thus a formidable developmental project. It is likely to succeed only when one's family, community and culture provide the requisite

> nutriments for personal growth and integrity, namely supports for autonomy, competence, and relatedness. These needs underlie the central human quest and provide the signposts on how we can promote and maintain meaning in a universe pervaded by questions and uncertainties. (Weinstein et al., 2012, pp. 100–101)

Interestingly, Weinstein et al. (2012) disputed the notion that meaning is a basic human need or even the most important psychological need, as Frankl (1978), Andersen, Chen, and Carter (2000), and others have expressed. If the assumption is that MIL is a basic need, people would have to live deeply fulfilling lives to satisfy this basic need. Thus, when they have satisfied the need for meaning, people have a sense of psychological well-being and feel self-actualized. In contrast, Weinstein et al. suggested that meaning is the outcome of a life well-lived and results from the satisfaction of the basic needs for autonomy, competence, and relatedness. Thus, for Weinstein et al., meaning is not a basic need but a result of the satisfaction of other basic needs. It is important to emphasize that Weinstein et al. stated that support from one's family and community greatly facilitates the process of moving toward meaning.

COGNITIVE THEORIES

Theories about the cognitive development of MIL suggest that as a species, human beings could not and did not start thinking about meaning until they reached a certain level of cognitive maturity. The human species has been able to progress and do both wonderful and dreadful things on this earth because of our amazing intellectual capability. Likewise, having the cognitive capacity to reflect about meaning has been both a blessing (helping people have a sense of contributing to the world) and a curse (causing existential anxiety). It makes sense that many religions were developed to stave off such death-related anxieties. Humans seem to feel the need to understand their environment and their place in it.

Individuals' MIL is thought to develop in tandem with their cognitive capacity. A good exemplar of this theory was developed by McAdams (2012). In his theory of personality and development, McAdams postulated that humans are endowed from birth with temperaments that interact with the environment to develop into dispositional traits, such as extraversion (vs. introversion), neuroticism (vs. emotional stability), conscientiousness, agreeableness, and openness to experience. He noted that from middle childhood onward, people develop a second layer of characteristics (e.g., motives, values, defense mechanisms) that involve an assortment of motivational, social–cognitive, and developmental constructs contextualized in time, place, social role, and culture. Later, in emerging adolescence and early adulthood, people continue to develop a narrative identity, during which time they formulate "an internalized and evolving story of the reconstructed past and imagined future that aims to provide life with unity, coherence, and purpose" (McAdams, 2012, p. 114). Furthermore, he suggested that this story is influenced by the culture given that people can only choose from among the options to which they are exposed. Thus, according to McAdams, MIL is part of the narrative we tell ourselves about our lives.

McAdams (2012) noted that high levels of extraversion, conscientiousness, and openness to experience, along with low levels of neuroticism, tend to be associated with the overall feeling that life has purpose and value, that one is meaningfully connected to others, and that obstacles in life can be overcome. These dispositional traits provide psychological resources that people can draw on in their quest for meaning.

Furthermore, McAdams (2013) talked about how meaning depends on the particular position or standpoint from which meaning makers evaluate their life. As *social actors*, individuals are performing on the life stage and feel good if they give good performances. McAdams postulated that this position is inherent from birth and depends to some degree on temperament, traits, and skill. As *motivated agents*, a position that develops in mid to late childhood, people strive to attain personal goals and gain self-efficacy through fulfilling projects. As *autobiographical authors*, a position that develops during emerging adulthood, meaning comes from the life stories that tell who we were in the past, who we are today, and who we hope to be in the future.

Although most cognitive theorists suggest, as noted here, that the ability to think about meaning develops primarily during adolescence, other opinions have been offered. A colleague I met at the 2016 International Network of Personal Meaning conference noted that in her research she asks young children about meaning using questions similar to those reflected in our four components (felt sense, mattering, goals, coherence); these children can easily answer such questions when they are posed using language at the children's level. I think here of my 3-year-old grandson asking "Why?" and wanting to make sense out of his world. It makes sense that the cognitive complexity of thinking about MIL increases as children grow older, but it also makes sense that young children think about such issues at a rudimentary level.

YALOM'S THEORY ABOUT DEATH ANXIETY

Theories about the influence of death anxiety on the need to construct meaning have abounded in existential philosophy and psychology. Yalom (1980), for instance, talked about death anxiety, isolation, and loneliness as concerns that often have to be dealt with before people can deal with concerns about MIL. Yalom suggested that given we all are going to die, we must create a reason for living; even if we lived forever, we would need to find purpose in living. Yalom postulated that people deal with death anxiety by developing defenses about being special or by connecting themselves with powerful people.

TERROR MANAGEMENT THEORY

Similarly, terror management theory (TMT; e.g., Arndt, Landau, Vail, & Vess, 2013; J. Greenberg, 2012), a social psychology theory that has been supported by over 400 empirical studies, provides some explanation for how meaning develops. According to this theory, we develop meaning as a defense against death anxiety. In other words, because we are terrified by the thought of death and nonexistence, we develop the defense of thinking that we are special and significant enduring people in a meaningful world. We survive the existential threat and related perpetual anxiety from knowing that we could die at any moment by viewing ourselves as

> enduring beings in a permanent, meaningful world full of symbols instead of as mere material animals in an indifferent universe fated only to cease existing on death. From birth on, we are socialized into a worldview that tells us that we are significant beings in a meaningful world. We have souls and possible afterlives, and we are part of lasting entities such as nations and family lines. We have identities that will live on past our physical deaths in the seemingly permanent marks we have made on the world: children, memorials, artistic creations, accomplishments in business and science, and so forth. Thus, we function with our deepest anxiety under wraps as long as we believe we are enduring, significant contributors to a meaningful, permanent world. When we are not simply seeking survival or pleasurable experiences, we spend much of our time buttressing our claims of legacy within the symbolic reality we psychologically inhabit. When this view of ourselves and the world is threatened, we experience anxiety and defend against such threats by reasserting our own value and that of our groups, and strengthening our faith in the meaningful world in which we believe. (J. Greenberg, 2012, p. 19)

THE INFLUENCE OF TRAUMATIC LIFE EXPERIENCES AND VIOLATION OF EXPECTATIONS ON THE DEVELOPMENT OF MEANING

A big influence on the development of MIL is life experiences. Going through a traumatic event such as a major medical illness or disability often compels people to think of their fate and the fairness of events. Our subjective sense of justice in life is a huge component of both happiness and resilience. People vary in their need for the world to be a just meritocracy. Those who are highly idealistic may be less resilient, more rigid, and more bitter than those who find meaning in the inherent unfairness we all face. In contrast, a child who lives in a world of privilege might feel shock at seeing others living in abject poverty.

The trigger for thinking about meaning often comes at times of transition. When things are going along in a routine, there is little impetus to think about meaning. People are often forced to think about life and meaning, however, when something unexpected (e.g., a tsunami, war, rape, death of a loved one) occurs or even when an expected and desired transition (e.g., weight loss, marriage) occurs. During times of distress, people need to change old narratives and construct a coherent new narrative to make sense of the events. Often there is just a narrow window of time before things go back to "normal" and the person goes back to routine things. But at other times the transition is life changing (e.g., after the death of a tyrannical father, a young man decided not to pursue law but rather art, which changed his life).

Across the course of a "typical" lifespan, different events occur that challenge one's sense of meaning. Adolescents and young adults tend to find meaning in terms of relationships and careers and often get stuck because they think they have to find the one "right" romantic partner or career path when in reality there are typically multiple options depending on location and serendipity. During adulthood, events such as marriage, having children, unemployment, unhappiness in relationships and career, and physical health concerns challenge people to think about who they are and what they want out of life. Retirement then sends many people into a search for what their lives thus far have meant and what they want to do in the next chapter. Finally, deaths of partners and one's own looming death force one to make a final reckoning about meaning. Of course, all lives are not typical, and when things happen out of sequence (e.g., a child dying, a major accident, being fired from a job), even more thoughts about meaning can be triggered (see also Anderson, Goodman, & Schlossberg, 2012).

Janoff-Bulman (2013) provided a theory about the impact of traumatic life experiences. She noted that for the trauma victim, the world often appears to be meaningless, uncaring, indifferent, and even malevolent. Being victimized forces the awareness that one is not immortal and that awareness can be psychologically devastating. Even extreme negative events not involving a perpetrator (e.g., natural disasters) are also often felt as a moral inversion given that the victim has experienced unjustified harm and undeserved suffering. After the trauma, victims are confronted with an unfamiliar, immoral world that does not make sense; their notions of a just world are turned upside down, and they feel discombobulated. To recover, they have to rebuild their assumptive worlds and shift their meaning-related concerns. Thus, the trauma serves as a catalyst for the construction of meaning (coherence).

According to Janoff-Bulman and Yopyk (2004), "It is through a terrifying realization of fragility, mortality, and loss as ever-present possibilities that survivors recognize their own power to create lives of value and commitment" (p. 131). Janoff-Bulman (2013) noted that survivors of trauma often choose altruistic, prosocial activities to become involved in after the trauma (e.g., rape survivors volunteer at rape crisis centers). Caring and kindness of family and close friends also become more important to these trauma survivors.

Other theorists have noted that violation of expectations is a big impetus for thinking about meaning, suggesting that states of arousal motivate us to make sense of things and restore a sense of meaning when our sense-making efforts fail (Proulx, Markman, & Lindberg, 2013). Violation of expectations produces a physiological threat that motivates efforts to restore meaning and reduce anxiety (T. D. Wilson, Ndiaye, Hahn, & Gilbert, 2013).

ATTACHMENT THEORY

Feeling securely attached seems important for allowing one to have a sense of meaning. Mikulincer and Shaver (2013) suggested that

> attachment security encourages beliefs and feelings that contribute to life's meaning, such as feeling that one's life has a purpose and direction; that one has a stable, coherent identity; and that one's life is anchored in a philosophically or spiritually coherent framework. (p. 287)

Furthermore, they cited research showing that when a person feels threatened by the possibility that life has no meaning, this fear activates the attachment system, which propels the person to seek the proximity of a trusted attachment figure as a way of reestablishing a sense of security and safety. They also cited research showing that having a loving attachment figure and the resulting feelings of security helps one to sustain a sense that life has meaning.

According to Bowlby (1969, 1988), the ability to form attachment bonds is innate. The infant seeks protection from and proximity to the attachment figure when under threat. Optimally, the caregiver provides a safe haven that reduces anxiety and allows the child to explore the environment and engage with people. If the caregiver is not available, responsive, or effective in soothing, an insecure attachment develops and the child worries about whether it is possible to rely on others and about being worthy of love and caring. For example, a 50-year-old client with Stage 4 cancer said she felt she had not mattered to her parents and was an annoyance to them, and she did not feel loved. As a teenager, she described how she felt she could not leave home because she had such a fragile sense of self. In some sense, she had never grown beyond that insecure attachment and was almost willing to die from cancer rather than figure out her sense of meaning. Bowlby (1988) noted that the attachment style or pattern developed in childhood carries over into adulthood. Thus, a sense of mattering would flow from a secure attachment; it is hard to imagine how someone with an insecure attachment style could have a healthy sense of mattering.

Fortunately, changes are possible in attachment. Healthy relationships and psychotherapy can both help to build a sense of mattering and a more secure attachment. Thus, through psychotherapy and a caring relationship, the client with Stage 4 cancer learned to care for herself and build a more secure attachment to her husband and therapist.

The Nature of Meaning in Life

In this section, I consider issues related to the nature of the construct of MIL. Is MIL given or constructed? How big is MIL? Is MIL positive by definition? How much does it vary over time? Is MIL a uniquely human experience? Is reflecting about MIL solely the province of brilliant or philosophically minded people?

IS MEANING IN LIFE GIVEN OR CONSTRUCTED?

People who believe in God or some higher power believe that we were put in the world for a reason and that the meaning *of* life (MOL) is to serve God or that higher power. The argument goes that God or a higher power created the world and gives us our meaning, and therefore we must listen for our "calling" and follow His will. The world is thus an orderly place with a benevolent or harsh (depending on your beliefs) deity who watches over you, keeps track of whatever you do, and rewards you with everlasting life or nirvana (or whatever construct fits one's belief system) for following "the" way.

However, if one does not believe in God or a higher power who created the world and looks over us all, then "the meaning of life" makes less sense. Many people on this side of the argument believe that the universe started with the big bang and had nothing to do with a higher power. Following this logic, human beings developed through evolution and when they got to a certain level of cognitive functioning began to worry about meaning. If life is random, human beings have to construct their own meaning. This meaning is personal and something people have to struggle to determine. Some are blessed with clear talents (e.g., music, brilliance) and privileged environments (safety, security, wealth), and so it is relatively easy for them to figure out their MIL (although their MIL undoubtedly varies over time). Others have fewer talents (e.g., are not artistic or intelligent) and grow up in impoverished environments (e.g., due to war, poverty, abuse, neglect, trauma, health problems) and may thus have more difficulty constructing an MIL.

E. O. Wilson (2014) took on this argument in his book *The Meaning of Human Existence*. He noted that the heart of the religious argument is the creation story, which assumes that humanity exists for a purpose and that individuals have a purpose for being on Earth. Thus, we were created for a purpose by an intelligent designer. In contrast, he argued from the perspective of science that there is no advanced design but rather that the unfolding of the universe followed a random evolution in which each evolutionary change affected the future course of changes. From this perspective, he argued that we are not "predestined to reach any goal, nor are we answerable to any power but our own. Only wisdom based on self-understanding, not piety will save us" (pp. 15–16). He further stated,

> I believe the evidence is massive enough and clear enough to tell us this much: We were created not by a supernatural intelligence but by chance and necessity as one species out of millions of species in Earth's biosphere. Hope and wish for otherwise as we will, there is no evidence of an eternal grace shining down on us, no demonstrable destiny or purpose assigned us, no second life vouchsafed us for the end of the present one. We are, it seems, completely alone. And that in my opinion is a very good thing. It means we are completely free. (p. 173)

IS MEANING IN LIFE GRAND OR TRIVIAL?

Meaning can range from big things such as overall life purpose to small trivial things that give meaning in the moment (R. A. Neimeyer, personal communication, July 29, 2016). Similarly, we can distinguish capital-M meaning (i.e., involving matters of significance and worth and how things fit into larger values and meaning systems) from small-m meaning (i.e., involving comprehensibility or detecting and expecting patterns or associations; Chao & Kesebir, 2013). This distinction between the grand and trivial is important because it illustrates the complexity of what we mean when we talk about MIL. For example, one's overall meaning could be to save the children of the world, but a more modest short-term goal could be organizing up a meeting and printing pamphlets for that meeting.

For some people, there could also be a distinction between MOL as the grand level and MIL as the more trivial level. Thus, a person could believe that MOL is from God, but they could also think that they have to translate that larger universal meaning into their MIL. The implication here is that we have to know the level of meaning we are referring to when we talk about MIL.

IS MEANING IN LIFE POSITIVE BY DEFINITION?

Metz (2013) described MIL as "something other than base pleasure that makes an individual's life more worth living or in those facets of a person's existence that merit substantial pride or admiration" (p. 406). Similarly, McAdams (2013) noted that things that provide meaning are almost always assumed to be good, whereas those that strip meaning away are considered bad. McAdams said,

> Your friend may report that she finds meaning in her family, or in helping others, or in a new career, or in her religious faith. Family, career, faith, helping others—these are all good things, right? Of course they are, at least usually. If your friend told you, instead, that she feels her deep meaning stems from a lifelong desire to watch more television or from her latest plan to cheat her sister out of the family inheritance, you would probably be surprised. Watching television does not seem good enough, lofty enough, to support life meaning. And cheating your sister—well, that sounds really bad. In principle, a person should be able to find meaning in doing something crass, mindless, ignoble, or even evil. But we do not expect it—perhaps even resist it—so positively valenced is the concept of meaning in our lives. (pp. 171–172)

I agree with Metz (2013) and McAdams (2013) that meaning is by definition positive. Things that are inherently selfish, cruel, and evil are not typically included as sources of meaning. The difficulty arises, however, in determining who gets to decide what is positive or negative. We could define meaning as positive if it does not cause harm to another, but some situations that provide meaning do cause harm. For example, people might get meaning from fighting in what has been called a "just war" or killing out of self-defense or defense of others. Perhaps it is best not to judge what gives another person a sense of meaning. In other words, people could be on a mission to eradicate individuals of another religion because that has been part of their teaching; although we may not approve of that, coming from a different religious tradition, it is important to realize that for that person it might be a positive goal.

Furthermore and relatedly, I think MIL can be healthy or unhealthy. Pursuing good, true, and beautiful things is healthy, whereas pursuing pure pleasure is relatively neutral, and pursuing selfish, greedy, and evil things is unhealthy. As with defense mechanisms, there can be more or less mature forms of making meaning.

VARIATIONS OVER TIME IN MEANING IN LIFE

Frankl (1959) suggested that MIL differs from person to person, from day to day, and from hour to hour. Similarly, a person could feel that their life is meaningful, but that person could be discouraged one day and feel that it is not worth it to keep trying. In this sense, meaning is not a stable trait but something that fluctuates, perhaps depending on life circumstances and affect.

For the most part, meaning is in the background of awareness. It only comes into the foreground at specific times, as mentioned earlier, with life experience (e.g., funerals) or transitions (e.g., retirement). In other words, few people ponder meaning constantly. Rather, it is something that captures our attention in particular moments.

Yalom (1980) said that when we are engaged in life, we are busy doing things that matter. When those things end, we might pause to think about what to do next. If activities are interrupted or we are away from our regular routine, we might pause to think about whether we are living life as we want.

IS MEANING A UNIQUELY HUMAN EXPERIENCE?

One thing I have heard frequently is that MIL is a uniquely human endeavor because humans are at a different cognitive level than are other animals, as if we are qualitatively distinct from the animal world. The notion is that humans can try to find meaning and purpose in life but other animals cannot or do not do this.

When I was presenting my ideas about MIL at a local Society for the Exploration of Psychotherapy Integration (SEPI) meeting, the hostess had a lovely dog who made the rounds of everyone there, allowing them to pet him. Everyone's obvious affection for this dog and his seeming intent to put everyone at ease led us to a wonderful discussion of whether dogs can have meaning or whether it is exclusively a human thing.

Several people adamantly noted that some dogs and horses particularly like to have a purpose. There are certainly stories of working breed dogs, such as border collies and Australian shepherds, who get depressed and destructive if they have no jobs. Keepers sometimes pay to take their working breed dogs to ranches where they can herd sheep. Many organizations now train dogs to support people with many types of disabilities, and some train dogs to sniff for bombs and drugs. Perhaps dogs cannot articulate their thoughts about meaning to us, but it seems that a need for a sense of purpose exists for at least some animals other than human beings. The movie *A Dog's Purpose* (Polone & Hallström, 2017) illustrates this idea. E. O. Wilson (2014) similarly presented evidence about other species (e.g., ants, bees) that work together collectively for the common good.

Perhaps the answer here is that animals do not have the capacity to articulate their thoughts about meaning in a way that we humans can understand (thus lacking coherence and reflectivity), but some at least seem to feel a sense of purpose and mattering. Furthermore, this argument suggests that humans are qualitatively different from other animals and suggests that MIL is something one does or achieves (through goals and purposes) rather than something one just has by being in the world (having a felt sense of meaning). My perspective is that we evolved from other species and share much in common. I believe that many species need a sense of purpose and a feeling of belonging.

IS MEANING IN LIFE RESERVED FOR BRILLIANT PHILOSOPHICALLY MINDED AND PSYCHOLOGICALLY MINDED PEOPLE?

At this same local meeting of SEPI at which I presented my ideas about defining MIL, attendees brought up an interesting point related to purpose. Several people were therapists working with adolescent clients who had developmental disabilities. These therapists noted that these clients often despair of finding a purpose in life because of their severe limitations, and their parents were concerned with how their children could find meaning. Clearly, these therapists felt that their clients, even though challenged, wanted to find meaning and a reason for living. This point is important because it suggests that everyone can find meaning; meaning is not reserved for people with privilege. Although philosophers' jargon makes them sound more intelligent, meaning is a universal concern to all.

Conclusion

The evidence suggests that the development of MIL follows the course of cognitive and psychosocial development. Thus, early in life we are more concerned with growth and learning about the world and satisfying attachment needs, and although we may try to make sense of the world, we do not think about MIL in complex ways. As we enter adolescence, we begin to differentiate from our parents, which continues through adulthood. As part of developing an identity, we reflect or think about who we are and search for what we want out of life, although this search is limited by the prevailing worldview, religion, and culture. We ponder our future in terms of careers and relationships, which are cornerstones of meaning. We also tend to think about MIL when there are pauses in life (e.g., deaths of loved ones), discrepancies that force our attention to meaning (e.g., others with less advantages), violations of expectations (e.g., trauma, war), or death anxiety (e.g., awareness of the finiteness of life and of oneself getting older and inevitably dying). Thus, healthy development leads to a strong sense of identity and presence of MIL, whereas psychopathology is related to a diffuse identity, sense of self, and a lack of MIL.

For some, MIL is given by external sources, and therefore they need to discover it. They listen for a calling or try to discover "God's will" for their lives. For others (including me), MIL is constructed. Given the belief that the universe has evolved and is random, I believe that each of us needs to create a coherent narrative about our existence and find meaning within that narrative. It is not possible to "prove" whether MIL is given or constructed, but certainly, one's belief influences how one approaches this topic.

There is no commonly accepted theory at this point about the development of meaning. Meaning appears to be more highly developed in adults than in children of the human species. Thus, some cognitive development is undoubtedly necessary for the development of MIL and for the ability to reflect and articulate one's thoughts about MIL. In addition, not having to think about basic or deficit needs also undoubtedly aids in the development of MIL, as does cultural support and encouragement. Death anxiety and terror management also are compelling theories that address our fundamental anxiety about the shortness of life and how little control we have over our destiny and death.

In terms of the nature of MIL, I assert that MIL is ideally constructed by each individual, is essentially a positive phenomenon that serves socially sanctioned functions, exists on many different levels ranging from the grand and lofty long-term level to the immediate short-term level, and can vary over time. Thus, one does not possess MIL as a stable characteristic but rather as a transient experience. I also conclude that MIL is not necessarily restricted to human beings or highly intelligent philosophically minded humans. Rather, meaning is something that is pervasive and applicable to all human beings and some other animals (King, Heintzelman, & Ward, 2016).

The takeaway message from this chapter is that MIL varies considerably over the lifespan and over specific situations even within any given age period. Thus, we cannot assume to know what a person's MIL is, but instead we have to be open to exploring various influences on MIL.

Sources of Meaning 3

He who has a Why to live for can bear almost any How.
—Friedrich Nietzsche, *Twilight of the Idols*

What gives you meaning? What makes you get up in the morning? These questions reflect not whether you have meaning but where you get your meaning. Interestingly, when talking about meaning, I have noticed that more people talk about what gives them meaning (e.g., love, work) than what kind of meaning they have (e.g., felt sense, mattering/significance, purpose/goals/engagement, coherence/comprehensibility, reflectivity).

Metz (2013) suggested that philosophers have been attempting to come up with a formula for what makes life meaningful. He indicated that it is relatively uncontested that one's life is meaningful "the more one reared children to become healthy adults, engaged in loving relationships, undertook aesthetic pursuits such as gardening or painting, worked for charities that helped other human beings, and discovered knowledge that would satisfy human curiosity" (pp. 406–407). Thus, he suggested that meaning typically comes from having a positive attitude toward undertaking activities that are good or beneficent (e.g., rearing children to become healthy adults, engaging in loving relationships, working for charity, discovering knowledge), true (e.g., reflecting in an informed manner about society or nature, perhaps through formal education), and beautiful (e.g., by making art objects, decorating a room, or expressing humor) that make for a compelling or interesting life

http://dx.doi.org/10.1037/0000083-005
Meaning in Life: A Therapist's Guide, by C. E. Hill

story (e.g., progressing through life in a healthy way that one can be proud of, even when that requires redemption).

Furthermore, it is important to note that what gives meaning is highly personal. What provides meaning in life (MIL) for one person might not for another person, and what is positive for one person might not be positive for another. Theorists have supported the idea that not everyone must have the same sources of meaning (Baumeister, 1991; Frankl, 1963; Halusic & King, 2013). Thus, one person may gain meaning from mattering, whereas another person gains meaning from achievement.

It is thus important not to judge arbitrarily what gives meaning. I should mention, however, that some sources are probably healthier (i.e., more adaptive), whereas others are based more on defenses and are thus probably less healthy or less desirable for a given person. For example, helping others might be a terrific source of meaning for a person because one has been given to and has much left over to give to others. Helping others can be less healthy, however, when engaged in as a defense against bitterness of deprivation, when one then acts condescending or angry to those whom one is supposed to be helping. Another example is striving for something that is out of reach, which could be unhealthy if the person's self-worth is on the line (e.g., having a goal of wanting to be a medical doctor even though one's grades are low). Although labeling something as healthy or unhealthy involves a value judgment, I believe that MIL involves a value judgment, and thus it is best to be up-front about that. We could thus think of sources of meaning as existing on a continuum from healthy to unhealthy (see Figure 3.1).

We can also distinguish sources that provide meaning from things we do to keep busy and occupied (e.g., obsessive cleaning). As Yalom (1980) noted, people often rush around doing tasks as a way of avoiding thinking about what is important to them or what they want out of life or engaging in life. Similarly, we have to distinguish sources that provide meaning from "vegetative activities" (ruminating, watching excessive television). One might simply be filling time or "killing" time rather than feeling a sense of meaning.

Some situations, however, are complicated. For example, a landlord who has plenty of money might evict an elderly, disabled tenant because he can charge much more for that apartment. The landlord may appear selfish, but he might find earning

FIGURE 3.1

Negative or unhealthy sources of meaning (e.g., purpose at the expense of others, obsessive busyness, cruelty, being a shopaholic, using defense mechanisms)	Neutral sources of meaning (e.g., being a sports fan, experiencing pleasure)	Positive or healthy sources of meaning (e.g., contributing to social good, leading to personal growth)

Valence of sources of meaning.

money meaningful due to having grown up poor and watching his mother skip meals so she could feed her children. Some of that additional income might go to his mother.

Sources of Meaning Described in the Literature

Exhibit 3.1 shows the variety of sources that have been described in the literature. Note that some of the entries are based on theory (e.g., Frankl, 1959; Yalom, 1980), some are based on a review of the empirical literature (e.g., King, Heintzelman, & Ward, 2016; Martela & Steger, 2016), and some are based on items from measures that were developed to assess sources of meaning in life (e.g., Sources of Meaning Profile; Prager, 1996).

In my opinion, these lists are problematic because they consider almost all human activities as providing meaning without distinguishing between sources that provide meaning from sources that provide other human needs (e.g., basic needs/survival, pleasure/happiness, belonging, self-esteem). Having a clear sense of the definition of MIL helps us separate out what provides meaning from what fulfills other needs. Thus, I would assert that hedonism, leisure, and pleasure; satisfaction of basic psychological needs; positive affect, financial security; and material possessions are all things we might want or need or that give us happiness or security, but I argue they do not provide a sense of meaning.

My List of Sources of Meaning

I propose that the sources can be clustered under the five components of MIL described in Chapter 1 (see Exhibit 3.2). Thus, some of the sources are more likely to provide a felt sense (e.g., self-acceptance), others provide mattering/significance (e.g., intimacy), others are more relevant for purpose/goals/engagement (e.g., having a passion for one's work), others serve a sense of coherence/comprehensiveness (e.g., religion), and yet others provide a sense of reflectivity (e.g., introspection). Note that there is some overlap in that some sources can provide meaning for more than one component (e.g., work and helping others can both provide a sense of mattering and purposes/goals), which makes sense given that the components are highly interrelated. It is also important to note that I did this clustering conceptually rather than through research and it needs to be studied empirically to determine whether these sources do fit under these components.

SOURCES FOR FELT SENSE

As noted in Chapter 1, *felt sense* is a vague, abstract sense of meaning. Thus, I suggest that sources for a felt sense of meaning are self-acceptance, self-transcendence, self-worth, and personal growth. If a person feels good about where he or she is in life and has a sense of self-efficacy, autonomy, and competence, that person is likely to

EXHIBIT 3.1

Sources of Meaning Cited in the Literature

Big four taxonomy of personal meaning (Emmons, 2005)
- Achievement/work
- Relationships/intimacy
- Religion/spirituality
- Self-transcendence/generativity

Contemporary science of the experience of meaning in life (MIL; King, Heintzelman, & Ward, 2016)
- Social relationships
- Religious faith
- Socioeconomic status
- Good mood or positive affect
- A world that makes sense
- Satisfaction of chronic organismic needs (e.g., autonomy, competence)

Halusic and King (2013)
- Religious faith
- Social relationships
- Satisfaction of basic psychological needs
- Positive affect (i.e., a person's experience of positively valenced mood states, including happy, cheerful, enjoyment, and pleased)

Logotherapy (Frankl, 1959)
- Creating a work or doing a deed
- Experiencing something important or encountering or loving someone
- Attitude toward inevitable suffering

McAdams (2013)
- External sources (e.g., good friends, good food, good jobs, religion, and cultural traditions)
- Internal sources (e.g., purpose, value, efficacy, and self-worth)

Neimeyer (2001)
- Working through suffering or loss

Personal Meaning Profile Brief (McDonald, Wong, & Gingras, 2012)
- Achievement
- Religion
- Relationship
- Self-transcendence
- Intimacy
- Self-acceptance
- Fair treatment

Sources of Meaning Profile (Prager, 1996)
- Participation in leisure activities
- Meeting basic, everyday needs
- Taking part in creative activities
- Engaging in personal relationships with family and/or friends
- Being acknowledged for personal achievements
- Experiencing personal growth
- Taking part in religious activities
- Interest in social causes

EXHIBIT 3.1 *(Continued)*

Sources of Meaning Cited in the Literature

- Being of service to others
- Preserving human values and ideals
- Preservation of culture and tradition
- Leaving a legacy for the next generation
- Feeling financially secure
- Interest in human rights (humanistic concerns)
- Participation in "hedonistic" activities (e.g., gambling, parties)
- Acquiring material possessions to enjoy the good life

Schedule for Meaning in Life Evaluation (Fegg, Kramer, L'hoste, & Borasio, 2008)
- Family
- Partnership
- Friends
- Work
- Leisure
- Home/garden
- Finances
- Spirituality
- Health
- Satisfaction
- Nature/animals
- Altruism
- Hedonism

Terror management theory (e.g., Arndt, Landau, Vail, & Vess, 2013; J. Greenberg, 2012)
- Managing the terror of death

Yalom (1980)
- Altruism (i.e., giving selflessly to others)
- Dedication to a cause (i.e., contributing to something greater than ourselves)
- Creativity (i.e., creating something new or beautiful)
- Hedonism (i.e., living life fully and prioritizing pleasure)
- Self-actualization (i.e., realizing our inner potential)
- Self-transcendence (i.e., going beyond oneself to immerse oneself in higher causes)

Martela and Steger (2016)
- Happiness, satisfaction, fulfillment
- Leading an exciting life
- Having an accomplished life
- Involvement in life
- Authenticity
- Autonomy
- Belonging
- Search for meaning

Martela, Ryan, and Steger (2017)
- Satisfaction of autonomy
- Satisfaction of competence
- Satisfaction of relatedness
- Satisfaction of benevolence

EXHIBIT 3.2

A Clustering of Sources for Five Components of Meaning in Life

Sources for Felt Sense
- Coherence
- Having purpose/goals
- Having a sense of mattering/significance
- Reflecting on MIL
- Self-acceptance
- Self-transcendence
- Self-worth
- Personal growth

Sources for Mattering/Significance
- Relationships (partners, family, friends)
- Belonging
- Intimacy
- Purpose/goals
- Coherence
- Reflecting on meaning in life (MIL)
- Career/work
- Vocation
- Helping others
- Leaving a legacy

Sources for Goals/Purpose/Engagement
- Having a sense of mattering/significance
- Reflecting on MIL
- Coherence
- Achievement
- Career/work
- Vocation
- Dedication to a cause
- Altruism or helping others
- Doing important or valuable work
- Having a passion for one's work
- Creativity

Sources for Coherence/Comprehensibility
- Religion or spirituality
- Preserving human values, culture, traditions, ideals
- Introspection about past, present, and future
- Reflection about existential issues (meaning, death, isolation, freedom)
- Purpose/goals
- Mattering/significance
- Belonging
- Attitude toward suffering (working through suffering or loss)
- Managing death anxiety
- A world that makes sense

Sources for Reflectivity
- Education about the benefits of reflection
- Encouragement to reflect
- Curiosity about the unknown
- Introspection

have a felt sense of MIL. Hence, these are characteristics that come from an internal valuing and working to improve oneself, although of course, external reinforcements can certainly help the person value him- or herself.

SOURCES FOR MATTERING/SIGNIFICANCE

People typically cite the most important source of meaning as social relationships (Hicks & King, 2009; Hill, Bowers, et al., 2013; C. E. Hill et al., 2015; Lambert et al., 2010). Indeed, a substantial body of research indicates that social relationships are a central aspect of experience that makes life feel meaningful (King et al., 2016). For example, MIL was positively related to how much one's need for relatedness is met (Hicks & King, 2009), how much one feels a sense of belonging (Lambert et al., 2013), and how much one feels close to and supported by family (Lambert et al., 2010). On the negative side, MIL is lower when one feels excluded or ignored (Stillman et al., 2009; Zadro, Williams, & Richardson, 2004).

Belonging needs are important for all of us (see Bowlby, 1969, 1988) and certainly are related to mattering/significance, but I argue that belonging is not the same as mattering but is rather a precursor of mattering. If one feels that one belongs, is included, and is important, one feels a sense of significance and mattering. Furthermore, being nurtured (e.g., being fed, taken care of) probably leads more to a sense of mattering (i.e., someone cares about me enough to take care of me) than does taking care of others, which might provide more of a sense of purpose (i.e., being needed). Having people care about you and caring about others probably also provides a sense of coherence to the world given that we then feel we have a web or network of relationships.

One can also feel that one matters and is significant because of the work one does, the contribution one makes to society, and the legacy one leaves behind. The Sagrada Familia cathedral in Barcelona is a good example of a legacy that Gaudi left behind. Helping others is a particularly gratifying source of mattering for some people because it gives them a sense of making a difference in people's lives (see C. E. Hill et al., 2015).

SOURCES FOR GOALS/PURPOSE/ENGAGEMENT

We immediately think of achievement in the work arena as a source of goals and purpose. The doctor wanting to find the cure for cancer, the astronaut striving to get to Mars, the writer who has a goal of finishing a book, the student who gives up sleep to get through exams, the child who gives up one marshmallow to get two later all have goals they want to accomplish. Such goals often help people put off immediate gratification for greater later reward.

SOURCES FOR COHERENCE/COMPREHENSIBILITY

Things that help us make sense of our world provide us with meaning. Thus, a worldview, a good legal argument, rationality, a new perspective, and insight all help us understand our world and our role or place in the world. Especially salient is the understanding that helps us comprehend existential realities (e.g., death, isolation, meaning) and helps us develop a positive attitude toward inevitable suffering and the slings and arrows of life.

Religion is particularly salient in terms of giving people a sense of meaning (Emmons, 2005; Hicks & King, 2008; Park, 2005; Steger & Frazier, 2005). Religion provides a framework or way of understanding the world, which makes life seem coherent. Religion also helps people establish goals (e.g., helping others) to foster meaning. However, if one does not believe in God or a higher power, one has to construct one's own meaning, and it is often harder to construct some narrative for what life is all about. Is it just random? If you can be or do anything, you might make bad choices, and it is sometimes hard to derive meaning from a life that has not been well-lived.

The issue of the origins of meaning comes up here too. If one believes in God or a higher power, one's life necessarily has meaning, typically that of serving or glorifying God or the higher power. Indeed, religious faith has been found to be strongly related to having a sense of meaning (Emmons, 2005; Fry, 2000; Park, 2005; Steger & Frazier,

2005; Steger et al., 2010), so it seems that religious faith can serve a meaning-making function. Halusic and King (2013) suggested,

> Religious views may constitute a cognitive structure, or schema, which acts as a lens through which people weave all manner of information, such as daily experience, into a consistent structure . . . as long as one's meaning system remains unchallenged by the environment, a sense of MIL ensues. (p. 448)

Organized religion is often not about individuals creating meaning; rather, it is often about being provided with guidelines for decisions that will lead to a life well-lived. For people who have not thought for themselves about their beliefs, religion can be a paint-by-numbers version of coherence. Others, however, think through what they believe and come to their own internalized beliefs that provide them with meaning.

Although more typically written about as a source of meaning, it makes sense that religion can also serve a role in the development of meaning. Those who grow up with a strong religious tradition probably start to believe that meaning is tied up with religion. If one believes that the meaning of life (MOL) is given by God, Allah, or some such higher power, one's task is to accept and work to understand the meaning or calling (i.e., God's will) that one is given and then translate the MOL into one's own personal MIL. If, however, one does not believe in religion or some higher power, one has to construct one's own meaning and make sense out of the seemingly random nature of the universe.

Another source of coherence is living in a world that makes sense and is orderly. For example, people in one study who read about trees growing in a patterned versus chaotic fashion rated themselves as having a stronger sense of purpose (Kay, Laurin, Fitzsimons, & Landau, 2014). In another study, people who saw photographs of trees arranged according to season (winter, spring, summer, fall) versus a random order rated themselves as having more meaning (Heintzelman, Trent, & King, 2013).

SOURCES FOR REFLECTIVITY

Major sources for reflectivity include education and being taught that curiosity is a good thing and that it is good to seek one's own answers to life's dilemmas. Relatedly, being supported or encouraged to question and challenge can be a powerful stimulus for looking inward to find answers rather than being told just to follow what others say. There is probably a feedback loop such that when one challenges and experiences the delight of solving problems on one's own, it is reinforcing and encourages such behavior.

Sources Cited in the Literature but *NOT* Considered Here As Sources of Meaning in Life

Several sources have been cited in the literature that I do not include in my list. Specifically, I considered but reject hedonism, positive affect, socioeconomic status, gender, and age as sources of MIL.

HEDONISM IS NOT A SOURCE OF MEANING IN LIFE

Hedonistic activities, leisure, and pleasure have been cited as sources of meaning on several of the lists in Exhibit 3.1. Such activities, however, seem more likely to lead to happiness and only weakly to meaning. As an example, a friend brought up the idea that being a sports fan is a source of meaning for many people. I argue that being a sports fan can provide a sense of belonging, passion, and excitement, but it seems a stretch to say that it provides meaning in the sense of felt sense, mattering, goals/purpose, and coherence or in terms of the social good. Another example is a person who restores antique cars to their original condition with no goal other than to enjoy the process. Hedonism provides a clear example of how having a good definition of MIL allows us to distinguish between levels or types of MIL. The person is certainly engaged in life, but often he or she is passively engaged rather than actively doing something. I consider such activities weak sources of meaning at best.

POSITIVE AFFECT IS NOT A SOURCE OF MEANING IN LIFE

Positive affect has probably been the most frequently studied predictor of MIL. On the basis of their laboratory research, Halusic and King (2013) suggested that positive affect precedes a sense of meaning, being more predictive of judgments of MIL than were religious faith, social relationships, and psychological need satisfaction. King and Hicks (2012) argued that when people feel good, they recognize the meaning in their lives, whereas when they feel bad, they do not recognize the same things that give them meaning.

King et al. (2016) thus suggested that good mood or positive affect is a source for meaning. They cited considerable evidence that people who say that they are happy, cheerful, enjoying life, and in a positive mood rate their lives as meaningful (King et al., 2016; King, Hicks, Krull, & Del Gaiso, 2006) and that experimentally inducing positive affect results in higher ratings of MIL (King et al., 2006; Ward & King, 2016). In fact, they noted that even if individuals lack social relatedness and religious faith and have a low socioeconomic status, they rate their lives as meaningful if they are in a good mood (Hicks & King, 2008; Hicks, Schlegel, & King, 2010; Ward & King, 2016). Despite the evidence that good mood and positive affect are associated with and even causally related to ratings of MIL, I do not believe they are sources MIL.

Martela, Ryan, and Steger (2017) argued that it is not positive affect that is the source of meaning but rather it the satisfaction of needs of autonomy (i.e., volition and responsibility for one's actions), competence (i.e., efficacy and mastery), relatedness (i.e., belongingness), and beneficence (i.e., prosocial impact). Indeed, they showed empirically that the association of positive affect dropped out or was minimal once these other variables were included in analyses. Thus, it may not be positive affect per se, but rather what positive affect is related to, such that if people feel autonomous, competent, related, and benevolent, they are more likely to feel positive affect and thus would be more likely to judge themselves as having MIL. These results show that the pathways to MIL could be quite complicated and multidetermined.

I thus agree with Martela et al. (2017) that positive affect per se is not a source of meaning but rather a by-product of engaging in activities that provide a source of meaning. It is the engagement in meaningful activities that provides the meaning. But I also agree with King and Hicks (2012) that having positive affect makes it easier to recognize the sources of meaning in one's life. It makes sense that people are able to view sources as meaningful when they are in a good mood, whereas they do not see the same sources as meaningful when they are depressed. But that does not suggest that the mood is the source of the meaning, but rather that the mood allows them to perceive the source as meaningful. For example, family might be ignored as a source of meaning when a person is depressed but recognized when the person is in a good mood. Thus, the mood facilitates or hinders (or in statistical terms, mediates) the perceptions of a source as meaningful, but I think it is a mistake to consider the mood itself as the source. To take it a step further, to suggest that mood is a source of meaning would be to suggest that a person should strive for a good mood, although such striving would not be based on substance, but rather would be more like the mad search for pleasure. Here I echo Yalom (1980), who said that people should seek to engage in life and find things that are meaningful to them and mood will follow (unless of course, the person has a mood disturbance that requires medication).

SOCIOECONOMIC STATUS IS NOT A SOURCE OF MEANING IN LIFE

Socioeconomic status has also been proposed as a source of MIL. King et al. (2016) cited considerable evidence that people who have more financial resources rated themselves as having more meaning than did people with fewer such resources (e.g., Pinquart, 2002; Ward & King, 2016). I suspect that socioeconomic status or financial stability is not the direct cause of people having MIL. Rather, people with higher social status and more money have more access to education, good jobs, good neighborhoods, and all the accompanying benefits that allow them to be able to do more things that contribute to a sense of having meaning. Financial stability itself is not the source of meaning but a vehicle for enabling people to engage in things that provide meaning. One need only think of people who have financial security but no meaning in their lives. In fact, having financial security hinders some people from finding meaning because too much is handed to them. Similarly, if we lived forever instead of knowing that our lives are finite, we might not be pressed to search for meaning now and make the most of what we have.

GENDER IS NOT A SOURCE OF MEANING IN LIFE

Gender has been found to be related to MIL in some studies (Hill, Kline, Miller, et al., 2017) but not in others (Steger, Frazier, Oishi, & Kaler, 2006), with women reporting more MIL and reflectivity about meaning than men. We could interpret these results as reflecting gender role expectations in our culture, such that women are allowed to be more empathic and to reflect about meaning than are men. But again it is not gender per se that is the source of meaning but rather that being a woman provides a greater likelihood of being allowed in our culture to seek meaning as an end in and of itself.

AGE IS NOT A SOURCE OF MEANING IN LIFE

Age has also been found to be related to the presence of meaning (Hill, Kline, Miller, et al., 2017; Steger et al., 2006). It makes sense that with increasing age come wisdom and the ability to attain meaning, much as Erikson (1950) theorized. For example, our experienced therapists reported more presence of meaning (Hill, Kanazawa, et al., 2017) than did undergraduate students (Hill, Bowers, et al., 2013) and doctoral students (C. E. Hill et al., 2015). But again, it is not age per se as much as the passage of years that allows one to find meaning.

Changes Across Time in Sources of Meaning

Sources of meaning change over time as things that once had meaning come to have less meaning and others take the forefront. Kristen Pinto-Coelho, a doctoral student at the time, gave the example of volunteering for hospice bereavement. She started volunteering prior to her doctoral program because she wanted to provide assistance to the bereaved. After her mother died, the volunteering continued to have meaning for Kristen, and she felt passionate about it. She became close to the social workers and the other bereavement volunteer working at the hospice. After a few years, however, the social workers both left the organization and were replaced by two new people, and the other volunteer went on a hiatus because her husband was terminally ill. Kristen found that some of the meaning she got from volunteering was actually related to the relationships she had developed with these three women and to her sense of belonging and contributing to a collective cause. She found herself considering giving up the volunteering because it no longer provided her with the same sense of meaning.

Conclusion

Many things can provide meaning. Some people have a passion to change the world, whereas other people are more content with simply being. The two sources of meaning that seem to have the most relevance are relationships (e.g., family, partners, friends) and finding something meaningful to do with one's time (e.g., a career, a hobby, a creative endeavor). Religion and spirituality is more varied across people, with some believing it to be the bedrock of their meaning and finding great solace in their beliefs and others constructing their own meaning in more secular pursuits.

The idea of sources existing on a continuum from destructive to neutral to healthy resolves some of the confusion inherent in discussions of sources. Not all sources are good for all people. In fact, some may be used for unhealthy, defensive reasons; others might be weak sources of meaning (i.e., provide a passive form of meaning); and others might be more positive, healthy, adaptive, and for the social good.

THERAPEUTIC APPLICATIONS FOR WORKING WITH MEANING IN LIFE

II

Existing Psychotherapy Theories About Meaning in Life

4

Life is never made unbearable by circumstances, but only by lack of meaning and purpose.

—Viktor Frankl, *Man's Search for Meaning*

How does a being who needs meaning find meaning in a universe that has no meaning?

—Irving Yalom, *Existential Psychotherapy*

Meaning in life (MIL) in psychotherapy has been addressed in three major theoretical approaches. First, Victor Frankl is widely credited with bringing attention to MIL in psychology with his development of logotherapy. Second, Irving Yalom is the best representative of the existential psychotherapists and their focus on MIL along with other existential concerns. Finally, acceptance and commitment therapy (Hayes & Lillis, 2012) is the best representative of how more recent behavioral approaches address MIL.

Frankl's Logotherapy

Frankl (1959, 1978, 1986) was a theoretician and a charismatic speaker. His book *Man's Search for Meaning* (1946, 1959, 1963) has been widely read and is one the most influential books in all of psychology. His story is particularly

http://dx.doi.org/10.1037/0000083-006
Meaning in Life: A Therapist's Guide, by C. E. Hill

compelling because he survived several concentration camps during World War II. He saw many people die in the camps because they gave up and felt they had nothing to live for. Frankl believed his passion for communicating to the world his ideas about meaning and logotherapy helped him survive.

THE GOAL OF LIFE

For Frankl, the goal of life is not the will toward pleasure (as advocated by Freud), or the will toward power or striving toward superiority (as promoted by Adler), but the will toward meaning. In fact, Frankl suggested that lack of meaning is the paramount existential crisis and primary motivational force in people. He assumed that life always has meaning and that people can find meaning if they accept the task of searching for it.

RESPONSIBILITY FOR DISCOVERING MEANING

According to Frankl, meaning is unique to each individual and varies at each given moment. He asserted that one should not search for an abstract meaning but rather should take responsibility for finding the specific purpose in life that one is uniquely qualified to fulfill. In addition, Frankl asserted that true meaning is to be found in the world rather than in the self; in other words, we are to transcend ourselves and give to a cause or serve others.

Frankl believed that people need to be confronted with the finiteness of life and the finality of what we make of ourselves and our lives and thus take responsibility for making the most of life. Thus, he asserted that each of us must take responsibility for discovering our meaning. Frankl (1959) noted that this responsibility is an awesome but terrifying concept because "no instinct tells [man] what he has to do, and no tradition tells him what he ought to do; sometimes he does not even know what he wishes to do" (p. 111).

SOURCES OF MEANING

Frankl emphasized that in discovering meaning, not all meanings are equal. Rather, meaning must have virtue or value to be considered adequate. Thus, even though Hitler had a mission and purpose in wanting to exterminate all the Jews, Frankl did not consider this to be a desirable or adequate meaning because Hitler was not oriented toward societal good.

Frankl suggested that people could discover meaning in three sources. The first involves creating a work or performing a deed. For example, one can achieve or accomplish something important (e.g., cure cancer, create a work of art). Second, one can experience something important (e.g., goodness, truth, beauty) or encounter and love someone. Third, one can attain meaning in one's attitude toward inevitable suffering. Frankl noted that it ceases to be suffering when one finds meaning in it. For Frankl, the goal is not to seek suffering, nor indeed is it to seek happiness, but rather to change one's attitude so that one can cope with suffering.

LOGOTHERAPY

Frankl developed *logotherapy*, or therapy related to meaning, to help the client who has meaning concerns to "become aware of what he actually longs for at the depth of his being" (p. 103). In logotherapy, Frankl recommended four major interventions as particularly useful for helping clients with anticipatory anxiety become less self-absorbed and more engaged in life.

His first intervention involved *dereflection*, helping to shift the focus of the client away from self-absorption and toward searching for meaning outside him- or herself (such as in developing empathy for others). He wanted to move clients away from thinking about their neuroses and into the intact parts of their personalities and the meanings available to them. In other words, Frankl's goal for clients was to transcend self rather than actualize self (the emphasis is on not being self-centered). As one example, Frankl described a young woman with schizophrenia whom he challenged to reconstruct her life and find goals. The client responded by agreeing with the importance of this task, but she wanted to know more about what was going on inside her. Frankl responded by telling her not to brood over herself and think about her troubles but to leave that to the doctors. Instead, he told her to search for something creative she could do. When she persisted with wanting to know what was wrong with her, Frankl again emphasized not to focus on what was wrong with her but rather to focus on what she could achieve creatively.

His recommended second intervention was *discernment of meaning*, through which therapists help clients find some coherent pattern to make sense of the random events of life. He often helped clients find meaning in the past in terms of creative accomplishments, experiences, and attitudes toward suffering. He gave the example of an 80-year-old woman near death from cancer who was deeply upset because she felt that she had not lived a worthwhile life. He helped her remember all the things she had experienced and enjoyed in life and reminded her that no one could blot those things out and that these experiences endured forever. He also helped her see that what matters in life is what one has achieved and accomplished, how one has dealt with suffering, and how one has provided a model to others of a life worth living. Following this session with Frankl, the woman was able to die in peace.

Third, Frankl recommended *Socratic dialogue*, an intervention also commonly used in cognitive behavioral therapy, in which therapists ask open-ended questions to guide the client in examining and discovering hopes and desires related to meaning. For example, a therapist might ask clients about creative accomplishments, experiences, and attitudes toward suffering (his important triad of meaning categories) to lead them to think about what brings meaning.

Finally, Frankl recommended the use of *paradoxical interventions* to help "take the sails" out of anticipatory anxiety (worrying about the future). With paradoxical interventions, therapists prescribe the symptom (e.g., he gave the example of telling a client worried about sweating in front of people to try to sweat more). Paradoxical interventions thus help clients detach from the symptom, view themselves more dispassionately, and learn to laugh at themselves.

In general, Frankl did not advocate endless discussions of philosophy related to the cosmic questions about meaning, nor in fact did he advocate talking directly about MIL concerns with clients. Rather, he suggested getting clients out of self-absorption and into engagement in life.

EXTENSIONS OF FRANKL'S LOGOTHERAPY

P. T. P. Wong (2010, 2012) expanded Frankl's logotherapy into meaning-centered therapy. Wong sought to affirm that life has meaning through an approach that integrates theories; incorporates spirituality; has a relational, healing, and wellness focus; is positive and hopeful; is multicultural in its orientation; emphasizes clients' narratives; and is narrative and psychoeducational. Wong developed a PURE model to help clients find Purpose, Understand situations, take Responsible actions, and Evaluate satisfaction. His extensive list of possible interventions includes Socratic dialogue, dereflection, perspective taking, and gratitude exercises.

Similarly, several manualized treatment programs based on logotherapy have been developed specifically for helping patients with advanced cancer find meaning. For example, Breitbart and Poppito (2014a, 2014b) developed an eight-session manualized logotherapy-based group and individual treatment program called individual meaning-centered psychotherapy (IMCP). IMCP uses structured exercises to help patients focus on the three ways Frankl talked about for discovering meaning: achievements, experiences, and attitudes toward suffering. In addition, they added a fourth component that stresses rewriting narratives to help clients make sense of their past. Breitbart and colleagues have found considerable evidence in randomized clinical trials for the efficacy of this approach for both individual and group treatment, particularly in terms of spiritual well-being (e.g., Breitbart et al., 2010, 2012, 2015).

Chochinov and colleagues (Chochinov, 2002; Chochinov et al., 2011) similarly developed a narrative treatment approach focused on preserving dignity, esteem, and respect with a focus on encouraging clients to have a positive self-reflection. Chochinov et al. (2011) found evidence that this approach helped clients sustain a sense of dignity and legacy, although there were no changes in depression, desire for death, or suicidality.

Lethborg, Schofield, and Kissane (2012) developed a four-session treatment aimed at reducing suffering and increasing meaning. In this approach, called meaning and purpose therapy (MaP), narrative, existential, and cognitive techniques are used to challenge clients to move beyond insight and toward action that will increase meaning. Some research has shown that MaP therapy facilitates a refocusing of life goals and an increase of meaning.

Existential Psychotherapy

Several existential theories for working with MIL in psychotherapy have been offered (e.g., Cooper, 2015; Hobbs, 1962; Maddi, 1967; Wolman, 1975). In their meta-analysis, Vos, Craig, and Cooper (2015) cited evidence for the effectiveness of these existential approaches. Of these existential theories, Yalom (1980) has written the most eloquent and detailed description of theory and practice. I should note that Yalom was clearly influenced by Frankl and devoted considerable space in his book reviewing Frankl's work.

THE EXISTENTIAL DILEMMA

The existential dilemma, as described by Yalom (1980) is, "How does a being who needs meaning find meaning in a universe that has no meaning?" (p. 423). Thus, Yalom believed that we as humans have a strong need to make sense of our world and find meaning, but he also believed that the universe is essentially random and does not provide meaning. He suggested that people must construct their own meanings rather than hoping to get them from some other source. Yalom thus differed from Frankl in asserting that meaning is to be constructed rather than discovered.

SOURCES OF MEANING

For Yalom (1980), there are several possible sources of meaning. First, altruism involves leaving the world a better place. Second, dedication to a cause is altruistic and transcends death in some ways. Third, he suggested that creativity is inherently meaningful. Fourth, the hedonistic solution involves the pursuit of pleasure as an end in itself. Fifth, self-actualization involves becoming oneself and reflects a blueprint toward growth that we all have at birth. Finally, self-transcendence involves getting away from self-absorption.

Yalom suggested that meaninglessness is intricately interwoven with too much leisure and disengagement with life. He also noted that with the decline in religion, agriculture, and living with nature from the time of our ancestors, people are increasingly at a loss for meaning and do not know how to live their lives in a meaningful way. He noted that people often fill the existential vacuum of boredom, apathy, and emptiness with conformity and submission to totalitarianism. They might get involved in crusaderism (connecting oneself to dramatic causes). Or they might sink into nihilism (discrediting all activities as having any meaning), vegetativeness (a severe state of aimlessness and apathy), or compulsive activity (being busy and rushing around just for the sake of keeping busy). Obviously, people often need assistance to help them learn to cope with their existential angst and seek better sources of meaning.

EXISTENTIAL PSYCHOTHERAPY IS A DYNAMIC PSYCHOTHERAPY

Yalom (1980) placed existential psychotherapy within the cluster of dynamic therapies, given that it has in common with other dynamic theories the assertion that people are governed by conflicting forces and have varying levels of awareness. In contrast to other psychodynamic theories, however, existential theory focuses on existential or ultimate concerns (death, isolation, freedom, and meaninglessness) rather than conflicts related to instincts and early experiences.

According to Yalom, in Freud's model, the innate drives (e.g., sex, aggression) lead to anxiety, which is suppressed and reduced by defense mechanisms. In contrast, in existential theory, the awareness of the ultimate concerns leads to anxiety, which in turn leads to the construction of defense mechanisms. In other words, the anxiety about knowing that one will ultimately die and that the world has no preordained purpose can be terrifying, such that people resort to erecting defense mechanisms to protect themselves from the void and anxiety. Yalom noted, however, that extreme and maladaptive defense mechanisms restrict growth and experience and lead to psychopathology. Not surprisingly then, Yalom noted that clients often become more rather than less anxious after reducing their defenses against existential anxiety in psychotherapy, which is interesting in that most of our outcome measures in psychotherapy research focus on reduced symptomatology. The goal of psychotherapy, for Yalom then, is to accept and live with existential anxiety rather than try to eliminate it.

YALOM'S APPROACH TO WORKING WITH MEANING IN LIFE

In preparation for working with clients who are concerned about existential concerns, Yalom (1980) strongly advocated the importance of therapist self-awareness. He suggested that if therapists have not struggled themselves with existential concerns and found some MIL, they will not know how to help clients and will thus avoid the topic because of anxiety.

Yalom provided a number of strategies for therapists to consider in working with MIL with clients in psychotherapy. First, he noted the importance of examining whether other concerns (death anxiety, isolation, groundlessness) are more important and thus need to be addressed before meaninglessness. He suggested that death anxiety is particularly important to deal with first because meaninglessness is often provoked by death anxiety. He noted, however, that even if we lived forever, we would still need to find something meaningful to do with our time.

Second, he said that therapists have to develop a mind-set of thinking about meaning. To develop this mind-set, he suggested therapists become attuned to the importance of MIL and listen differently to clients for hints about MIL concerns (e.g., talking about aging, wrinkles, less energy). He suggested that therapists can probe further to bring out meaning-related concerns by asking about belief systems, loving others, long-range hopes and goals, and creative interests and pursuits.

Third, similar to Frankl, Yalom (1980) suggested dereflection as a strategy for working with MIL. In other words, he suggested "diverting patients' gazes away from themselves, from their dysphoria, from the sources of their neuroses and toward the intact parts of their personalities and the meanings that are available to them in the world" (p. 472). Although he disagreed with Frankl's authoritarian methods for dereflection, he agreed with the need for the therapist to help the client develop curiosity and concern for others. Ways to do this, suggested by Yalom, are through therapy groups in which clients can hear about other people's concerns and empathy training during which clients can learn to identify with and experience other people's feelings.

Another strategy suggested by Yalom that had also been suggested by Frankl is the discernment of meaning. Yalom asserted that it is the therapist's task to help the client construct some meaning (i.e., understanding, coherence) around seemingly disparate and incoherent aspects of experiences. He suggested that gaining insight into the influence of one's past or history could help one cope better with the present and daily life. As with dereflection, however, Yalom was concerned that Frankl's approach was too authoritarian and removed some of the personal autonomy from the client; still, he stressed the need to help the client make sense out of the chaos of life.

Most importantly, Yalom advocated encouraging clients to become actively involved in life. He thought that when people are actively engaged, they inherently have meaning because they are doing what nurtures them ("When things matter, they don't need meaning to matter"; Yalom, 1980, p. 479). He implied that one cannot actively search for meaning, but rather must approach it obliquely as a by-product of engagement. Citing Tolstoy ("It is possible to live only as long as life intoxicates us"; Yalom, 1980, p. 481), Yalom advocated leaping into commitment and action, arguing against the mad search for pleasure or staying busy just to escape life. Rather, he encouraged meaningful engagement in life and doing things for which one has a passion.

In this regard, he strongly promoted staying away from the endless cosmic questions about meaning *of* life and the nature of the universe. Rather, he suggested encouraging engagement in life. Noting that the desire to engage in life is always there, Yalom advised that the therapist's job is to remove the obstacles that get in the way of engagement. Thus, the therapist can ask, "What prevents you from loving another person?" "Why do you have so little job satisfaction?" "Why are you neglecting religion or creativity?"

Yalom also suggested that therapists challenge the client's need to achieve and promote "being" instead. He asserted that in Western countries such as the United States and those in Europe we focus too much on achievement and could learn much from the Eastern cultures that cultivate an inward focus.

Finally, Yalom noted that the therapist's primary tool for existential therapy is self. By authentically and deeply relating to clients, therapists can provide an experience of engagement in life. They also can model active and passionate involvement in career and life. To this end, he also thought that therapists have to be aware of their own MIL issues before they can be fully and appropriately engaged with clients.

Acceptance and Commitment Therapy

Acceptance and commitment therapy (ACT), along with mindfulness-based cognitive behavioral therapy, explicitly targets MIL or purpose in life as a goal for therapy (Hayes & Lillis, 2012; Hayes, Stosahl, & Wilson, 1999; Kashdan & McKnight 2013; K. G. Wilson & Murrell, 2004). In these approaches, therapists help clients develop, clarify, and pursue their purposes to better organize their lives and ensure that their actions are deliberate and consistent with their purposes. The aim, as with existential–humanistic therapy, is to "help clients, through existential reflection, understand how they miss a fuller life by constricting their living" (Krug, 2017, p. 91).

More specifically, according to ACT, the key to living fully is constructing meaning, which we do through composing narratives about ourselves and the world (Zetzer, in press). Although we as humans have the ability to be conscious, we are also prone to intense anxiety as we become aware of the existential realities of freedom, death, isolation, and responsibility. We deal with this anxiety through the defensive mechanisms of cognitive fusion (i.e., my thoughts are facts) and experiential avoidance (i.e., "the attempt to change the form, frequency, or situational sensitivity of experiences even when doing so causes life harm"; Hayes & Lillis, 2012, p. 51). The desire to avoid pain and suffering thus causes us to restrict our awareness and become psychologically inflexible.

The goal of ACT is to help clients become mindful observers rather than reactors, to approach difficult situations with acceptance rather than avoidance, and to choose behaviors that are consistent with their values (Heffner & Eifert, 2004). Thus, the goal is to help clients "develop a rich, full, and meaningful life while accepting the pain that inevitably goes with it" (Harris, 2009, p. 7).

In terms of treatment, the ACT approach is not to fix problems directly because that would just maintain the struggle. Rather, the therapist tries to foster client change through core processes (Harris, 2009):

- teaching mindfulness to help the client stay in contact with the present moment,
- defusing thoughts by teaching the client to step back and watch their thinking,
- fostering acceptance by helping clients open up to their experience,
- expanding awareness by encouraging clients to observe themselves in light of the context,
- identifying values, and
- choosing actions that are consistent with values.

Conclusion

Frankl has had a major influence on psychology, particularly in his emphasis on the importance of meaning as a fundamental need and reinterpreting and coping with suffering. The logotherapy community is vibrant and active, and there have been many applications of the theory as well as modifications of the practice. There are active international logotherapy organizations open to both professional and lay people. Clearly, Frankl had a huge impact in turning attention to meaning.

As with Frankl, Yalom did not advise extensive discussions of MIL. Rather, he suggested methods of working with clients to help them become engaged in life and thereby find meaning. In fact, he agreed with Frankl that meaning cannot be actively pursued, but instead is a result of being engaged in meaningful pursuits. Yalom's (1980) book on existential psychotherapy is an important text for therapists who want to work with existential concerns including MIL.

Both Frank and Yalom have been influential in my thinking about MIL. I resonate more with Yalom's existential approach and keep coming back to his book and using it in my graduate class in theories of psychotherapy. I particularly value Yalom's thinking about the importance of therapist self-awareness, given that if therapists are not willing to probe deeply into their own feelings about MIL, they are unlikely to help clients explore their feelings. Although I find Frankl's approach too authoritarian, it is important to keep in mind the cultural context of his being born and raised during the mid-20th century in war-torn Europe and enduring unthinkable conditions in concentration camps. I think that Frankl's ideas about changing one's attitude toward suffering are particularly important given that we all suffer and thus can benefit from learning to make sense of (gain coherence or understanding about) and cope with suffering. I also particularly like that Frankl and Yalom offer a balance to the excessive current focus on symptomatology by focusing on existential concerns as a valid and important focus of psychotherapy.

Although I agree with Frankl and Yalom that engagement in life is crucial and that having a sense of the presence of MIL often follows engagement, I disagree with their advice to avoid directly approaching MIL in psychotherapy. I think it is possible to work directly with MIL in psychotherapy, and I think that labeling concerns as MIL gives clients more of an opportunity to process their feelings and think more deeply about MIL. They then have a handle on which to reflect about meaning, thereby possibly deepening their thinking about it. This approach is essentially collaborative; it is not the therapist determining what is best for the client but rather trusting that with the help of the therapist the client can think deeply about MIL and then make decisions about what to do in life.

The more recent ACT approach added to logotherapy and existential approaches by focusing on mindfulness, awareness, acceptance, and values. Like the other two approaches, ACT stresses the person's living fully and facing existential issues, though it offers a more direct approach for constructing meaning by identifying values and choosing behaviors that are consistent with these values.

Unfortunately, I know of no studies comparing different approaches to working with MIL in psychotherapy. I suspect, however, that just as with the finding that many sanctioned approaches are equally effective in psychotherapy (Wampold & Imel, 2015), there are undoubtedly many approaches that can be helpful for working with MIL in psychotherapy.

In the next chapters, I turn attention to working therapeutically with MIL. In Chapter 5, I present my theoretical approach, and in Chapter 6, I discuss working with MIL in specific client problems that have MIL as an underlying component. Chapter 7 includes case examples of therapists working with clients on MIL issues. In Chapters 8 and 9, I cover multicultural and ethical concerns about working with MIL. Chapter 10 presents a self-help guide for working with MIL.

A Model for Working With Meaning in Life

5

> When successful, psychotherapy helps the patient retell his life story, to provide a different frame and give a different moral to the story. Hence, it enables him to give a different meaning to events and experiences that had previously been a source of hopelessness and blockage and had contributed to a demeaning or depressing view of himself and his life.
>
> —Paul L. Wachtel, *Inside the Session: What Really Happens in Psychotherapy*

My approach to working with meaning in life (MIL) in psychotherapy has been informed by existing theories (especially Yalom, 1980; see Chapter 4). My approach has also been influenced by my research on helping skills and psychotherapy (see Hill, 2014), as well as my more specific research on MIL (see Chapters 10 and 11). Finally, my approach has been informed by my own reflectivity about meaning (see Prologue), my training (initially in client-centered therapy and then psychodynamic and interpersonal theories throughout my career but always with a regard for the role of behavioral therapy), my personal therapy for 30 some years with a psychodynamic therapist, and my work with students and clients who were struggling to find meaning in their lives. All of these experiences have provided a foundation that has helped me construct this approach to working with MIL in psychotherapy.

To set the foundation, I first provide some thoughts that have influenced the development of my approach. First, I believe that MIL is an important topic for psychotherapy, although it is only one of many important topics and is

http://dx.doi.org/10.1037/0000083-007
Meaning in Life: A Therapist's Guide, by C. E. Hill

probably rarely, if ever, the sole topic of therapy. That said, I think the focus on MIL, and on related topics such as subjective well-being and quality of life, are important antidotes or corrections to the excessive focus on symptomatology and the medical model in much of current psychotherapy. People are not just their neuroses and symptoms but are also a product of their behaviors, values, goals and ambitions, and relationships. Third, the topic of MIL is pantheoretical given that it a universal concern and thus relevant to all clients. Furthermore, I believe that all the major theories can make important contributions to an approach to working with MIL. There is not one "right" way to do MIL work; instead, we can learn from many different approaches about how to work with this topic.

Background Conditions for Working With Meaning in Life in Psychotherapy

In preparation for working with MIL in psychotherapy with any and all clients, I agree with Yalom (1980) that it is important for therapists to engage in self-examination and have some awareness of their issues related to MIL. A second important background variable is building and maintaining a therapeutic relationship.

THERAPIST SELF-EXAMINATION AND SELF-AWARENESS

It is wise for therapists to examine their own MIL concerns, anxieties, and beliefs. This self-examination is not a one-time event but rather an ongoing reflection about life and meaning given that meaning shifts over time.

If therapists expect clients to focus deeply on MIL, it is important for therapists to be aware of their understanding about MIL. By experiencing the depths and ambiguities of self-examination, therapists are more likely to be humble and compassionate and thus able to help and encourage clients in navigating their journey toward self-awareness (Hook, Davis, Owen, Worthington, & Utsey, 2013). If therapists do not think deeply about their MIL, they might miss opportunities to explore MIL more deeply with clients or minimize the importance or depth of this struggle, especially if clients are in a different life stage and the therapist is not familiar with the MIL issues at that stage (a 25-year-old therapist just starting her career and thinking that there are endless possibilities might have difficulty empathizing with a 70-year-old client who is struggling to find any meaning after retirement). Furthermore, if they have reflected deeply on meaning in their own lives, they are more likely to encourage clients to find meaning. Because they have also struggled with being broken and having suffered (and it is important to note that all of us have suffered and are broken, albeit to different degrees), therapists know what it feels like to reflect on and search for meaning.

I also agree with Yalom (1980) that when therapists have a solid sense of meaning, they can serve as a role model for clients. Therapists thus provide a model of a person who is passionately engaged in life, loves their work, is willing to face difficult concerns, and is willing to relate authentically with clients.

To start their self-examination, therapists can ask themselves about how much meaning they have in terms of felt sense, mattering/significance, purpose/goals/engagement, coherence, and reflectivity (perhaps taking the Meaning in Life Measure [Hill, Kline,

Miller, et al., 2017] as a stimulus). In addition, therapists can ponder whether and how they obtain meaning from doing therapy. And they can also ponder what meaning they get from sources other than providing psychotherapy because it is good to have some balance in life (for a list of sources, see Chapter 3).

Another thing for therapists to consider is their "hot buttons" related to MIL. Each of us has things that we focus on too much or too little for our own reasons or needs. If we think that each client must be engaged in creative pursuits or that each client must have spiritual beliefs, these hot buttons are likely to influence the way we approach the topic of MIL with clients. To become aware of their hot buttons, therapists might think about their values related to such things as relationships, work, culture, gender, death, and spirituality and religion. By engaging in values clarification and becoming aware of these issues, therapists can devise strategies to help them change or manage their biases so as not to unduly influence clients.

In addition, therapists can ponder how they are approaching the topic of MIL with each client. Are they pressuring a particular client to find meaning? Are they not concerned about broaching the topic of MIL with a client? Have they given up on a client finding meaning? Are they trying to impose their values for meaning on a client? What do their behaviors mean about them and their clients? If a therapist's values differ from a client's, which is inevitable, the therapist can reflect on the discrepancies and work hard to treat the client's values with respect and curiosity; only by having self-awareness can therapists begin to address these discrepancies (see also Chapter 8 on ethics; dealing with value differences is an ethical issue).

We can also learn from our clients about MIL. Hearing about their inspiring activities can spur us on to better things. Hearing about their despair can force us to examine our own despair. Thus, exploring MIL issues with clients can serve as an impetus for therapists to think more deeply and productively about these issues in their lives. The key is being open to learning and being willing to be moved by our clients' struggles.

Although it is good for therapists to examine their MIL and their values, I could imagine a therapist (as is also true for clients) thinking too much and getting bogged down and stuck into the quagmires of thinking about the meaning *of* life and despairing about not having all the answers. Emotional contagion is also always a danger as clients' anxieties and rumination affect us. A client who is despairing can cause us to rethink our circumstances and sometimes sink into despair ourselves. I strongly advocate seeking personal therapy, supervision, and consultation across the lifetime given that being a therapist stimulates much personal angst.

IMPORTANCE OF THE THERAPEUTIC RELATIONSHIP

Regardless of the topic being discussed in psychotherapy, the therapeutic relationship is crucial. Indeed, considerable empirical evidence indicates that the therapeutic relationship is the most robust predictor of therapy outcome (see Horvath, Del Re, Fluckiger, & Symonds, 2011). If clients feel their therapists accept them, are empathic and compassionate, and do not judge them, clients are more likely to open up, explore, and change in therapy. Knowing the therapist is on their side can encourage clients to venture out of their comfort zones and try new things. Having a good relationship with a therapist also provides a model for the client that it is possible to relate to others in a healthy way. In addition, because relationships are a key source of meaning, figuring out how to have a good relationship with a therapist can be helpful in and of itself as well as by perhaps encouraging clients to realize that it is possible to have satisfying relationships in their lives outside therapy.

An interesting question is whether a solid therapeutic relationship is needed before therapists approach the topic of MIL. I suggest that it depends on the client and the client's readiness to engage in the topic. If the client initially brings up MIL as the central concern and there are no other more pressing concerns, it could inhibit the building of the relationship if MIL were not focused on immediately, and in contrast, it could help to build the relationship if the discussion goes well. If the client brings up MIL as a presenting problem but other concerns are more pressing (e.g., imminent unemployment, marital crises), it might be better to help the client stabilize before focusing on MIL. Furthermore, if MIL is more of an unstated concern underlying other more pressing concerns (e.g., depression), it could hinder the building of the relationship if the therapist tries to force discussion of MIL rather than following the client's lead. In such a case, it would be wise to wait until the relationship is established, so the client feels safe to delve deeper into MIL concerns. It often helps if some resolution has been reached on other problems before focusing on MIL, as suggested by our research (Hill, 2016; Hill, Kline, Kivlighan, et al., in press).

Finally, as with all other topics, if the therapist initiates the discussion of MIL or puts an MIL label on an existing concern, he or she can attend to the client's reactions and think about possible ramifications for the relationship (see Hill, Kanazawa, et al., 2017). Observations of client reactions help therapists be responsive to client needs.

Conceptualizing the Role of Meaning in Life in Psychotherapy

Because MIL is such a basic human concern, therapists from all theoretical orientations have to be able to conceptualize the role of MIL for each individual. Even though a client does not explicitly express MIL concerns, the therapist can think about whether the client has MIL and where the client obtains meaning.

Most clients, especially those who are first-time therapy seekers, seek out psychotherapy because they are unhappy, do not feel good, sense that something is out of balance in their lives, are not thriving, or have exhausted other avenues for help (e.g., friends, ministers). They often are unaware of their underlying problems but are aware of feeling miserable and hurting. They rarely identify meaning as something they want to work on. Rather, they want symptom relief so they can feel better. They may have MIL concerns, but they may not label them as such or see the value in working on them.

There are at least four subsets of clients to consider when we think about MIL concerns. First are clients who explicitly ask to focus on MIL. Second are clients who do not explicitly ask for MIL work but for whom MIL is an underlying or implicit concern. Third are clients for whom MIL work is not a priority. Fourth are clients for whom MIL work is not appropriate and could perhaps be harmful. I briefly focus on these four subsets here, but specific client problems are discussed more fully in the next chapter.

EXPLICIT MEANING-IN-LIFE FOCUS

In a few cases, clients explicitly indicate that they want to work with MIL (e.g., they want to do a life review). In such cases, the therapist's first task is to determine whether this request is clinically appropriate. In cases in which the client is relatively healthy and is perhaps looking back over life, this focus can be beneficial. In contrast, if other problems are more immediate, the therapist might have to make a decision about the focus. For example, if the client is ruminating excessively over MIL and is in a nihilistic depression, the therapist might first have to focus on the depression and help the client engage in life. As both Frankl (1959) and Yalom (1980) stated, too much excessive rumination without engagement in the world can be devastating. Similarly, if a client is talking about MIL but has neglected physical health concerns or marital dysfunction, the therapist must determine whether it would be more clinically appropriate to focus on these other concerns first. Finally, some clients might indicate an interest in focusing on MIL but not really be interested in pursuing it. I think of a recent client who expressed at intake an interest in working on MIL, perhaps because my *Psychology Today* listing indicated that I work with MIL, but never again mentioned the topic of MIL nor seemed at all interested when I broached the topic.

IMPLICIT MEANING-IN-LIFE FOCUS

More typically, clients do not directly state that MIL is a concern, but it is an implicit concern embedded in what clients are discussing. For example, a client might be dissatisfied with his job as an investment banker but not be aware that one reason for the dissatisfaction is that the job does not enable him to help others and use his creative talents. Another client might be depressed but not be aware that she is trying to live up to her parents' expectations rather than finding her own MIL. Yet another client might be transitioning from being in the military and not be aware that part of his distress might be due to not feeling part of a community involved in a goal of keeping the country safe.

Importantly, MIL underlies many client problems. For example, a person who is depressed also often despairs about life having no meaning. A person who lacks interpersonal relationships might feel that she or he does not matter, is not significant, or is not worthy. A person who is chronically ill and fatigued might also have a lack of meaning from not being able to work and engage in life. Furthermore, many people have not developed the emotional capacity to construct or discover meaning. Because of family issues and attachment deficits, some clients may not have had the opportunity to develop a sense of self and a stable identity, and thus they function according to what others want for them rather than what they want out of life. They may have thus failed to find fulfilling relationships, satisfying careers, or comprehensive worldviews to help them make sense of the world.

Therefore, therapists can be attentive in listening for markers that indicate that MIL is implicated. By being aware of possible MIL concerns at these times, therapists can bring the MIL issues to the foreground when clinically appropriate (see also Chapter 6).

MEANING-IN-LIFE WORK IS NOT A PRIORITY

Some clients have other concerns that are more pressing than MIL. For example, they may have an impending divorce, child custody concerns, unemployment, financial stress, anger problems, or difficulties in dealing with medical issues. These issues may be so overwhelming that clients need help to experience immediate relief. Talking about MIL may seem irrelevant to them and not a way for them to cope with their immediate problems. Once other problems are at least somewhat resolved, these clients might (or might not) be interested in examining issues related to MIL.

Some clients simply have no interest in working on MIL in psychotherapy. The topic is not important to them, perhaps because it is too philosophical or distant or they just do not think in that way. They may respond hostilely, dismissively, or with disinterest to questions about meaning.

Therapists do better when they pay attention to what clients want in therapy. After all, therapy is for the clients rather than for fulfilling the therapist's needs. Therapists can, however, always conceptualize where MIL fits into the picture for a given client (see the next section in this chapter) and think about other ways of attaining a therapeutic goal if the client does not want to talk directly about meaning. For example, a client who has been unemployed for 9 years might not want to talk about how he finds meaning per se, but helping this client focus on emotion regulation and interviewing skills might help the client end up being able to get a job and become engaged in life. These changes might be more important for this particular client than talking explicitly about meaning.

MEANING-IN-LIFE WORK IS CONTRAINDICATED

Clients sometimes focus on meaning of life (MOL) and MIL as a defense against deeply reflecting on current problems. Frankl (1959) and Yalom (1980) both strongly advocated not engaging in discussion of MOL with clients who are into nihilism (despair over the lack of meaning), ruminating, and wanting to engage in philosophical discussion rather than becoming engaged in life. Thus, we could think about such rumination as a defense against engagement in life and become curious about why such a client is paralyzed and not able to engage in life.

Similarly, an important issue related to conceptualization and then potential intervention is determining the client's level of ego strength, resilience, or grit. If the client is fragile psychologically, the therapist might be cautious about even asking about meaning for fear that the client might crumble given weak defenses. The therapist might attempt trial interventions to see how the client responds in such cases rather than rushing in.

QUESTIONS TO THINK ABOUT IN FORMULATING A CONCEPTUALIZATION

After the first few sessions with a client, therapists will probably have enough information to begin to formulate a conceptualization. They can begin by asking themselves:

- Is the client engaged in life?
  - If so, in what ways is the client engaged?
  - If not, what might be the reasons?
- How does the client find meaning?
  - Relationships?
  - Career?
  - Religion or spirituality?
  - Creative pursuits?
- What does the client say regarding meaning?
  - Does the client bring up the topic spontaneously?
  - How does the client respond to queries about MIL?
- Does the client present concerns for which MIL might be an underlying construct?
  - Depression
  - Lack of career focus
  - Isolation
  - Physical illness
  - Aging
  - Death anxiety
- Are the concerns about MIL a defense against engagement in life?
- What are the client's talents, abilities, strengths, or weaknesses or limitations that might be related to finding meaning?

Therapists thus can conceptualize how MIL fits into the client's dynamics and psychopathology. Constructing a conceptualization of the client's dynamics, psychopathology, defenses, strengths, and weaknesses allows the therapist to know whether and how to approach the topic of MIL.

In addition, or alternatively, the therapist could ask the client to take the Meaning in Life Measure (MILM; see Chapter 1) or record up to five goals in life and rate each one on a 1-to-7 scale as to the importance of that goal (1 = *not at all important*; 7 = *extremely important*) and perhaps as to how engaged they are in seeking this goal (1 = *not at all engaged in seeking goal*; 7 = *extremely engaged in seeking goal*) and then discuss the results. Throughout the course of therapy on a periodic basis, the MILM can be readministered and the goals reexamined (and perhaps modified) and rated again to see how the client is doing.

Educating the Client About Meaning-in-Life Work

Expectations are a crucial part of psychotherapy (Constantino, Arnkoff, Glass, Ametrano, & Smith, 2011; Elliott, Westmacott, Hunsley, Rumstein-McKean, & Best, 2015), and it is often necessary to spend time at the beginning of psychotherapy educating clients about one's style of doing psychotherapy so that clients can make wise decisions about whether to engage in the therapy process and also know how to behave to get help. Also, given that, as noted earlier, clients often do not think about MIL as an appropriate focus of therapy, it can be useful for therapists to spend some time educating clients about why it would be appropriate to focus on MIL (and other topics).

I suggest that therapists post their interest in MIL on their website and in materials describing their approach to therapy. In initial sessions, therapists can also mention that MIL is an appropriate topic for therapy and provide some psychoeducation about it (e.g., MIL is a universal concern and often underlies other major concerns; struggling to cope with such existential concerns can help the person engage more in life and lead a more meaningful life). Furthermore, if therapists suspect during therapy that MIL is an underlying concern for clients, they can label the concern as involving MIL and ask clients about their reaction.

Three-Stage Model for Working With Meaning in Life

Once the therapist has some preliminary conceptualization of how MIL fits into the client's dynamics, it might be appropriate to begin to focus on MIL in psychotherapy. If so, therapists can use the three stages of exploration, insight, and action to work more specifically with MIL in therapy.

This three-stage model is similar to models I have constructed for psychotherapy (Hill, 2014) and working with dreams in psychotherapy (Hill, 2004), with some variations for the specific focus on MIL. How these stages are implemented depends, of course, on the individual therapist working with a specific client, but the use of the three-stage model provides a gentle structure for therapists when thinking about how to work with this topic in psychotherapy. In Chapter 6, I provide more explicit ideas for how to work with MIL underlying specific client problems (e.g., career concerns, transitions).

EXPLORATION STAGE: FACILITATING CLIENTS IN NARRATING AND EXPERIENCING MEANING

The goal of the exploration stage is to enable clients to tell their stories (i.e., narratives) related to MIL. With those clients who explicitly want to talk about MIL, the goal is to allow them to experience and express their concerns. Importantly, therapists do not ignore clients when they talk about MIL concerns unless there are other more pressing clinical concerns that must be addressed. A major factor here is the support the therapist provides for the client in terms of feeling safe enough to explore MIL.

For those clients for whom MIL is not explicitly stated as a concern, therapists can listen attentively to understand whether MIL concerns play an underlying role. They can listen for hints about MIL in clients talking about such topics as aging, concerns about retiring, difficulties with transition, and death. They can rely on their conceptualization for how MIL fits into the person's psychological dynamics, with a window toward thinking about when it might be appropriate to raise the topic.

If clients seem ready for MIL exploration, therapists might focus on three of the components of MIL covered in the definition of MIL in Chapter 1 (focusing on coherence is more appropriate in the insight stage; reflectivity is not as much of a direct focus).

- Therapists might ask broadly about a *felt sense* of having meaning.
  - Tell me about what meaning you have in your life.
  - Describe your sense of having meaning in your life.
- Therapists might ask about *mattering*.
  - Tell me about whether you feel significant to others.
  - Do you feel that you matter to others?
  - What are your relationships like?
  - What are you doing that makes a difference or is worthy?
  - What provides you with passion, pleasure, and meaning?
  - What do you do with your free time?
  - What things matter to you?
  - What things are important to you?
  - What would you like your legacy to be?
  - What do you want people to remember you for?
- Therapists might also ask about *goals, purpose*, and *aspirations*.
  - What are your goals and aspirations?
  - What were your goals and aspirations when you were younger?
  - Why have your goals and aspirations changed?
  - What gives you a sense of purpose?
  - What do you look forward to doing?
  - What do you do for fun?
  - When do you feel most engaged in life?
- Therapists might ask about *sources* of meaning
  - What are you most passionate about doing in your life?
  - What activities give you meaning?
  - Tell me about your relationships in terms of meaning.
  - Talk about whether religion or spirituality provides you with meaning.

Importantly, effective therapists do not just ask open questions and expect clients to answer. Rather, they also listen empathically and help clients explore the underlying thoughts and feelings. By restating thoughts and reflecting feelings, therapists allow clients to hear what they are saying and to reflect more deeply. Therapists can thus provide the space for deep exploration and reflection about MIL. However, therapists have to observe client reactions and attend to how clients respond to questions about MIL. If clients respond positively to discussing MIL, therapists can proceed. If clients have negative reactions, therapists should be more cautious.

Interventions relevant to the exploration stage are summarized in Exhibit 5.1. This exhibit summarizes interventions discussed in this chapter; those derived from Cooper (2015), Frankl (1959, 1978, 1986), P. T. P. Wong (1998, 2010, 2012), and Yalom (1980); as well as interventions identified in our research (Hill, 2016; Hill, Kanazawa, et al., 2017).

I provide here a hypothetical example (a compilation of a number of stories) of how a therapist might work with "Kay," a client who initially presents with depression concerns following her husband's death. I follow this example of Kay throughout the three stages. In this segment during a first session, MIL emerges as a result of general exploration.

Therapist: Tell me more about why you're wanting therapy at this time.

Client: My husband just recently died, and I'm having a hard time adjusting. The world just seems very different, and I feel out of tune with it. I feel like I'm in a time warp and just don't fit in any longer.

Therapist: Tell me more about what happened.

Client: To go way back, I took time off from a career to raise our four children. My husband was a lawyer, so we had enough money

EXHIBIT 5.1

Interventions for Working With Meaning in Life in the Exploration Stage

Intervention	Definition or method
Restatement	Paraphrase in a more concise and clear way to encourage clients to talk about the meaning in life (MIL) concern openly and deeply.
Reflection of feelings	Emphasize clients' feelings to facilitate deeper experiencing of emotions related to MIL concerns.
Model engagement	Relate authentically and deeply with clients, use self in the relationship to model active engagement.
Open questions and Socratic dialogue	Inquire about thoughts and feelings related to MIL. Pose questions in such a way that clients become aware of unconscious decisions, repressed hopes, and unadmitted self-knowledge.
Self-disclose personal struggles related to MIL	Describe how you have reflected about MIL to provide clients with sense that others also struggle with such concerns. Must be done cautiously so as not to turn focus onto self.
Support	Provide a setting so that clients feel safe talking about MIL, be nonjudgmental, do not ignore stated MIL concerns.

to be comfortable without my working. When the kids were all in school, I wanted to do something more meaningful, so I started volunteering at the local school so that I could make use of my master's degree in special education. After a year, they hired me full-time, and I really enjoyed working with the children. About 5 years ago, when my husband started getting dementia and needing constant supervision, I quit that position and became his caretaker. In the last 6 months of his life, it got to be too much for me, and so we hired people around the clock to come in and help me care for him. Just about 2 months ago, he contracted pneumonia and never really recovered. He passed away quietly in his sleep a month ago. I thought that it would be easier to accept the loss since he had been slowly deteriorating for so long, but, strangely, it wasn't at all easy. It was okay throughout the funeral with all the children and grandchildren here, but then now that all the hubbub has quieted down, I find myself at loose ends. I don't have anyone to talk to who has any patience for listening to me anymore, or maybe I just don't feel comfortable asking for their attention. I remembered a time years ago when my husband and I were in marital therapy, and it really helped, so I decided to seek out some therapy.

Therapist: So a lot of changes.

Client: A lot of changes. Nothing is the same. I was so busy and had so much caretaker stress. I felt resentful that I had no time to myself. Now, all of a sudden, I have nothing but time.

Therapist: Sounds like you're feeling pretty anxious at the loss of identity.

Client: Yes, I keep looking around for all the things I need to do, and then I remember that he's gone, and I can't quite get myself to do anything.

Therapist: Mm-hmm.

Client: [After a pause] And I know I shouldn't be, but I'm angry at my children for not being there for me. I mean, I know that they are all extremely busy with their own lives and children and problems, but I guess I just feel so lonely [starts to cry]. I haven't been in touch with friends much at all because I just didn't have time when my husband was sick, and they are all into other things now. There's just no one to call.

Therapist: You sound so sad.

Client: I am sad. It's been very hard being alone. I've never been alone in my life before. I was pretty dependent on my husband, and he was happy to be domineering and take charge of everything. I feel like I'm just not equipped for being alone.

Therapist: Beyond being sad, lonely, and anxious, I wonder if you're feeling a lack of meaning or purpose in your life.

Client: That's so true. For so long, I was raising children and I was a wife, then I was a special education teacher, and then I was caring for my husband. Now what? I don't have any role in life. I have nothing to get out of bed for in the morning. No one cares. No one notices. I feel very alone.

Therapist: That must be very hard to not have something that you're needed for or a way that you can contribute.

Client: Yes [quietly sobbing].

Therapist: [After a pause] What's it like for you to talk about this with me here today?

Client: I worried that you would judge me, but it feels surprisingly easy to talk with you. It really helps to talk. I feel like you understand what I'm talking about.

Therapist: I'm glad. Any other feelings?

Client: I do have a bit of a panic about what now. Will we just talk or how does this work?

Therapist: We'll try to understand a bit more about what is going on, try to understand how all that fits into your past, and then we'll try to help you make some changes in your life to perhaps gain some more meaning.

Client: Whew! That sounds good. Thank you.

Therapist: Meantime, I wonder if you would complete this measure about meaning [the MILM] and tell me about your reactions next week.

Client: Sure. I'd love to.

INSIGHT STAGE: UNDERSTANDING AND REVISING THE NARRATIVE ABOUT MEANING IN LIFE

The goals of the insight stage for MIL work are to help clients become curious about themselves, gain some coherence or understanding of who they are, make sense of past events in relation to present and future events, and construct a more meaningful narrative (i.e., description) about life. In essence, the goal of this stage is to develop a sense of coherence or understanding of the meaning of one's life. By trying to gain insight into clients, by being compassionate, and by remembering that these existential issues are difficult for all of us, the therapist can approach clients with humility, interest, and caring.

While remaining supportive and empathic, therapists can question or challenge clients about leading a meaningful life. But more important, the therapist can foster a sense of curiosity about why clients are not leading meaningful lives (keeping judgments to a minimum). What is getting in their way? What has gone on to defeat them?

Therapists can also help clients make connections between the past and present (e.g., "I lack a sense of mattering because my parents rejected me") and between the present and future (e.g., "Because I now understand that I am a worthy person,

I can accept myself the way I am. I can choose to make changes in my life to reflect my new understanding"). It can be particularly useful to explore family dynamics related to the past, such as the role of religion or spirituality and how the parents dealt with meaning in their own lives and in the family. The therapist can also foster understanding of strengths and limitations and help the client become more self-aware and self-accepting. By understanding oneself more completely, one can make better choices.

If appropriate, the therapist might help the client reinterpret suffering, in particular, trying to make sense of why bad things happen and to reenvision their role in the suffering. As the Buddhist saying goes, "Pain is part of life, but suffering is optional." This work could involve, for example, helping someone understand trauma or oppression. In essence, reinterpreting suffering involves changing one's schemas (see Chapter 2) from the world being an unfair place to accepting and coming to terms with life as it is.

If appropriate, the therapist can also use the therapeutic relationship to deepen the client's insight. By using immediacy to talk about the here-and-now of the relationship, the therapist can provide the client with a sense that the client matters to another person. As Yalom (1980) indicated, the therapist relating to clients authentically can provide the client with an experience of connection and mattering. The therapist can also provide feedback about how the client comes across to the therapist, which might help the client learn about how to navigate relationships better. In particular, resolving problems in the therapy relationship can serve as a model for how clients can resolve problems in their relationships outside of therapy.

Interventions relevant to the insight stage are summarized in Exhibit 5.2. This exhibit summarizes interventions discussed in this chapter; those derived from Cooper (2015), Frankl (1959, 1978, 1986), P. T. P. Wong (1998, 2010, 2012), and Yalom (1980), as well as those supported in our research (Hill, 2016; Hill, Kanazawa, et al., 2017).

Here we continue the example of Kay, whose husband had recently died. During the exploration stage in the first session, Kay identified that MIL was implicated in her depression following her husband's death. In the second session, they moved on to the insight stage.

Therapist: How did you react to what we talked about last week and completing the measure?

Client: I was particularly struck by the question, "I have something I want to accomplish in my life" because I don't have any goals right now. It made so much sense to me to realize that I no longer had a purpose. I realized that at Christmas dinner with my children, I had felt peripheral and irrelevant, that I no longer had a function. I couldn't hear as well as I used to, and it felt like everything was swirling around me. Who am I now without my husband? What am I going to do with the rest of my life? Is it worth living if I don't have someone to share it with?

EXHIBIT 5.2

Interventions for Working With Meaning in Life in the Insight Stage

Intervention	Definition or method
Challenge	Gently point out discrepancies in what the client is saying or doing (e.g., you say you want to find more meaning in your life but you do not talk about it) to help the client gain self-awareness. Perhaps challenge the client's need to achieve rather than just be.
Discernment of meaning or interpretation	Help clients find meaning in the past in terms of creations, accomplishments, or attitude toward suffering. Probe for insight, offer new perspectives, make connections between things in the client's life, conduct a life review, recommend writing a narrative about history, or ask about childhood experiences.
Facilitate finding meaning in activities	Help clients find meaning in activities (e.g., in relationships, creativity, experiences, attitudes toward suffering).
Existential attribution	Ask questions to help clients trace back to fundamental meanings and purposes (e.g., "Why is it important to you to support your mom?" "What is it about helping others that feels good to you?").
Immediacy	Probe or reflect about the relationship between you and the client to help the client become more self-aware and to build, maintain, negotiate, and repair the therapeutic relationship (e.g., "You said that it is important for you to get along better with others to gain more meaning, so I wonder if you'd like feedback about how you come across with me?").

Therapist: You're bringing up a lot of concerns. It sounds like you've done a lot of thinking about this over the past week.

Client: I have. It felt good having a label for what is going on with me.

Therapist: You actually sound energized compared to last week.

Client: I think I am. It helped so much being able to talk about this. I realized how much I have missed having someone to confide in. I have had to hold so much inside for so long, and I felt so tired. I think I was just exhausted.

Therapist: You mentioned last week that you and your husband got into a dance where he dominated, and you allowed him to do that. Could you talk a little more about that?

Client: Hmmm, yeah, good question. I think I was raised with the old gender stereotypes where women are supposed to be submissive and allow their husbands to be the strong partner who takes care of everything. And he was so good at finances and decisions, and he wanted to do all that. It was just easier to let him do everything than to argue with him. But I think my decision-making abilities just kind of atrophied as a result.

Therapist: Where do you suppose all those gender stereotype messages came from?

Client: That's interesting because my father was passive and my mother was dominant but in kind of a sneaky way. She wanted to control me, and I felt that I had to avoid her to have any autonomy. I felt suffocated. I was so angry with her as a teenager. I felt as a young adult that I was making my own decisions. When I met my husband-to-be, we talked about everything, and I felt that we had such a different relationship than my parents did. It was only after a few years of marriage when I started to boil up in rage at his dominating me that we went into marriage counseling. But now that you ask about it, I can see that it goes way back to my wanting to avoid having the kind of relationship my parents had.

Therapist: It sounds like you still have a lot of rage towards your mother.

Client: She was very difficult to live with. I felt so unsupported. I don't even think she knew the real me. She tried to make me over in her own image. I'm not sure I ever did anything I really wanted to do. Even being a special education teacher was something that women of my era could do—you could either be a nurse or a teacher. I liked children, so I guess it felt like a natural path. And it gave me the opportunity to take time off to raise my children, which of course I had to do pretty much on my own because my husband was working 12-hour days. I don't think I ever in my life stopped and thought about what I wanted to do with my life—it just felt like I did what I was supposed to. That's what women of my generation did.

Therapist: That would make me angry.

Client: Yeah, angry, but I'm kind of amazed that I just realized it. I have been so programmed. I was unhappy but didn't realize why.

Therapist: What about your father? Where does he fit in all this?

Client: He was kind of a sad, Walter Mitty type, a very bright guy, but he never figured out what he wanted to do with his life. His mother died when he was young, and he never got much love from anyone. He always seemed so sad and unfocused. He studied to be a biologist, but he never made much of that. He worked in a dead-end job in a clothing store. I don't think my mother respected him. He never had much to say to us kids.

Therapist: So it sounds like there's a distance there, almost like you don't have much of any feeling about him.

Client: I clearly have a lot more anger toward my mother, but I have some anger toward my father that he didn't protect me from my mother, and now that I think about it that, I didn't have much of a relationship with him. I guess we have a lot to work to do related to my parents . . . things I never resolved. I do want to figure out more about how they impacted me so that I'm not always just acting out those same patterns.

Therapist: So this is an ideal time to step back and think more about your past.

Client: Yes, it is. I don't have anyone to answer to at this point. I can do what I want.

Therapist: Do you feel that way, or is it a little scary to think about?

Client: It does feel scary, but I want to give it a go.

ACTION STAGE: CONSULT ABOUT MAKING CHANGES

The goal of the action stage is to help clients decide whether they want to change anything in their lives so that they can gain more meaning. It is typically important that this stage comes after extensive exploration and insight because clients are hopefully ready and eager after such deep work to think about whether they want to change and, if so, in what ways. Premature action could lead to the client rushing around and making changes not solidly based on what the person wants but perhaps on what they think they should want or what others want for them. Not taking action could lead to the client getting stuck in rumination and not changing. In their research, Prochaska, Norcross, and DiClemente (2010) found that embarking on action before spending sufficient time in contemplation and preparation typically results in change that is temporary, which can be demoralizing for clients.

The therapist's task is typically to help clients think about the possibility of change or, in other words, to be a guide or coach in helping clients come to their own decisions rather than being the authority who directs how clients should change to find meaning. As in the other stages, this approach is essentially client centered with the goal of helping clients find a sense of autonomy and self-direction that leads to acceptance and change.

If clients decide it is the right time to make some changes, they might need help with decision making, learning specific behavioral skills (e.g., life skills), assistance with role playing to gain assertiveness skills, or learning emotion regulation (e.g., relaxation, mindfulness). They might also need encouragement and support for the possibility of changing and living more fully. See Hill (2014) for more ideas about how to teach these skills, or consider assigning the Watson and Tharp (2014) text as a self-help guide for clients to make changes on their own.

If appropriate and keeping one's values in mind, therapists might offer suggestions for changes clients could make, or therapists could disclose about change strategies they have used to gain MIL. For example, the therapist might encourage the client to engage in relationships, religion or spirituality, creativity, or hobbies if those are things that seem appropriate for the client.

We, of course, want clients to choose actions that are socially sanctioned. For example, it would be unethical and unwise to help a client become a better serial killer even though that might be his desire. In this way, the therapist is making some judgments and serving as a representative of society (although it is important for therapists to reflect about what they encourage or do not encourage and why).

Likewise, it is important to help clients choose actions that are realistic given their strengths and life circumstances (not everyone can be the President of the United States, a physician, or an astronaut), but therapists can help clients find ways to maximize their unique gifts, talents, hopes, and dreams to find meaning. That said, therapists must also be careful about making assumptions about clients on the basis of stereotypes and biases and thus undersell the client's abilities to find such meaning.

Interventions relevant to the action stage are summarized in Exhibit 5.3. This exhibit summarizes interventions discussed in this chapter; those derived from Cooper (2015), Frankl (1959, 1978, 1986), P. T. P. Wong (1998, 2010, 2012), and Yalom (1980), as well as those supported in our research (Hill, 2016; Hill, Kanazawa, et al., 2017).

We continue with the example of Kay, whose husband had recently died. During the exploration stage, Kay identified that MIL was implicated in her depression following her husband's death. In the insight stage, the therapist and Kay came to some new understandings about how her relationship with her husband was related to

EXHIBIT 5.3

Interventions for Working With Meaning in Life in the Action Stage

Intervention	Definition or method
Dereflection	Shift focus from self-absorption or ruminating to searching for meaning outside oneself (e.g., through group therapy or empathy training).
Encourage engagement	Encourage clients to do what matters to them, promote being, ask what gets in the way of engagement.
Fast forwarding	Ask clients to think about what would happen if they made a particular choice (e.g., "What would happen if you left your husband?").
Gratitude exercises	Help clients find positive aspects of life.
Imagine the possibilities	Ask clients to transcend the present situation and imagine new possibilities (e.g., "If you could do anything you wanted to do after you graduate, what would you do?").
Paradoxical interventions	Prescribe the symptom to help alleviate anxiety and help clients detach from the symptom, view self more dispassionately, and learn to laugh at self so that they can see self more objectively and take mind off ruminating about meaning in life (e.g., ask a client who does not go out in public because of being worried about sweating in front of people to try to sweat more).
Encourage turning to religion or spirituality	Help clients find solace in meaning outside oneself in organized faith or spirituality.
Teach specific skills to help clients find meaning	If clients have deficits, teach relaxation, meditation, or mindfulness, behavior change, assertiveness, and decision making (see Hill, 2014 action stage for more details).

her relationship with her parents. In the 10th session, they moved tentatively to the action stage.

Client: In the last few weeks since we have been talking, I feel so much more like myself. I have energy back. I have renewed vigor for life. I'm talking more with my children, especially my daughter who checks in with me every day now. I feel like I'm ready to make some changes, but I need some help in figuring out the right directions.

Therapist: Okay. I'm up for that. Perhaps we could start by your saying some of the things that have given you meaning in the past? What have you been passionate about?

Client: Well, I used to like working with children, but I think I'm over that. It's nice seeing my grandchildren occasionally, but honestly, I'm ready for them to go home after a couple of hours. I think I've done that enough.

Therapist: I hear you. So what else comes up as you ponder?

Client: What's been playing in the back of my mind is that I used to play the clarinet in the high school band. I really liked that. I liked the music, and I liked being with a group of people making the music. I also used to like singing.

Therapist: So music is something that you've enjoyed before. Tell me more about that.

Client: It's interesting . . . I don't like hearing music as much as I like being part of making it. I loved being fully involved in the music. I didn't like the feeling of having to get the right note all the time, but I loved being a part of the group playing music. And now that I think of it, I liked making up songs for my kids . . . we'd sing silly songs at bedtime . . . they used to love that. And it felt very creative. I liked telling them stories too. I also love reading and would love to be in a book club. I feel like I never talk about what I'm reading, and it would be nice to hear what other people think.

Therapist: So, playing clarinet, singing, making up songs and stories, and book club. All those have a creative aspect. What else?

Client: As I think about it, a common theme is being around people. I really am a people person, and I miss that sense from high school of having a best friend, someone to talk to and share stories with. Interestingly, when my husband was alive, we mostly had couple friends who we would have dinner parties with, and I did not really have friends of my own who I could call.

Therapist: So being around people, and having a best friend stand out.

Client: And the thing from special education is that I like helping others. I don't want to teach special education anymore but maybe some other way of helping others. As I think about it, one thing I have a passion for is the plight of immigrants. There are so many people around the world who have had to leave their countries and find a new way of life. If I'm having this much trouble adjusting after my husband's death, I can't imagine the trauma that people must go through when they have to adjust to a new country and a new language, especially if they are old.

Therapist: I'm hearing a lot of possibilities. And what's cool is that as you talk about these ideas, your face lights up.

Client: Yes, I can see that I have a lot of things I could do.

Therapist: Is there one specific thing that you could check out before we meet next week?

Client: I think I might like to check out helping immigrants get acclimated to moving here.

Therapist: What ideas do you have about how you might do that?

Client: I've heard that a lot of churches sponsor immigrants. I'm not really active in any church, but I might check out the local church and see what they have.

Therapist: You could also check on the Internet to see what you could find.

Client: This sounds exciting. I think I am also going to check out a music group and see what I can find. I might also need to find a little something to supplement my income since social security is not really covering all my expenses, and I'm quickly running through the money that was left after all my husband's health care expenses, but maybe we can talk more about that next time we meet.

Therapist: Sounds great. . . . I can't wait to hear what you find out.

Client: Yes, I'm beginning to feel some confidence that I can make changes and find more meaning in my life. But I'm going to take it slowly and not make any hasty changes. I want to really think through this transition.

Outcomes of Meaning-in-Life Work

It makes sense that if MIL work is successful, clients should have an increased sense that they have meaning in their lives; feel that they matter and have significance; have a sense of purpose and goals for the present and future; have greater coherence in their narratives such that they can make sense out of the past and see connections between the past, present, and future; enjoy thinking about MIL; and have specific sources that provide MIL (see Chapters 1 and 3). Thus, there should be changes for clients on all the subscales of the MILM. They are also likely to have greater self-acceptance, self-esteem, and subjective well-being given that they have constructed a sense of meaning and have greater self-acceptance. We also expect behavioral changes in terms of having more sources in their lives that provide meaning, and thus clients would be engaging in more meaningful activities.

Interestingly, Yalom (1980) suggested that clients might have more anxiety after becoming aware of existential concerns (e.g., death anxiety, isolation). On the basis of this hypothesis, we might expect to see initial increases in existential anxiety, but I also expect to see reductions in anxiety as clients attain greater acceptance, understanding, and coping strategies.

To put it in more statistical terms, we would not expect to see direct decreases in symptomatology or increases in interpersonal functioning (the two most common outcomes typically assessed in psychotherapy) as a function of MIL work. Rather, we might expect that when clients successfully work on MIL in psychotherapy, they improve in terms of subjective well-being and quality of life, which in turn leads to improvements in symptomatology and interpersonal functioning. However, there might be changes in symptomatology and interpersonal functioning if MIL was directly implicated in these concerns and the link was made and understood between MIL and the symptoms.

Conclusion

MIL is one of many things clients want to talk about in psychotherapy. It is not necessarily the most important topic, but it is relevant to focus on in some situations. More specifically, it is typically important to focus on MIL when clients explicitly state concerns about MIL (although sometimes other concerns are more immediately pressing). Other situations in which MIL is often implicated are transitions, violations of expectations, deaths and funerals, depression, interpersonal problems, career concerns, and physical health (covered in more detail in Chapter 8). In contrast, it is typically not advised to focus on MIL concerns when the client expresses a clear preference or need for working on other concerns or does not respond favorably to queries about MIL.

When working with MIL, the background conditions of therapist self-examination and the therapeutic relationship are important to take into consideration. Then, identifying the MIL concern and conceptualizing the role of MIL in the dynamic picture set the stage for MIL work.

One model for working with MIL involves exploration, insight, and action stages, which form a framework for working with many concerns in psychotherapy but is tailored here for MIL. Thus, the therapist helps the client explore the MIL concern in great depth with an emphasis on the underlying thoughts and feelings (exploration stage). Then, the therapist works with clients to gain some new understanding of how MIL fits into their concerns, with an emphasis on connecting the past to the present as well as the present to the future (insight stage). Finally, the therapist helps clients decide whether there any changes they would like to make in life to gain meaning and, if so, how to go about making those changes (action stage).

I stress the need to modify this approach to fit the therapist's style. This model fits my integrative approach but might not fit as well for others. Constructing a personal approach that fits one's style is crucial so that one can be authentic as a therapist.

In addition, the approach must be modified to fit the needs of the individual client. More emphasis on the action stage could be useful for clients who have no goals. In contrast, more emphasis on the exploration stage could be helpful for clients who are adept at setting goals but need help exploring how they can make the best of their lives in the face of pain or adversity. And yet other clients might need more emphasis on the insight stage to work through major emotional conflicts before they can approach MIL issues. Good therapists are thus responsive to individual clients and use whatever interventions work with each client, rather than assuming that particular interventions will be helpful. It can also be helpful to think about specific situations (e.g., depression, career, transitions) that require attention in therapy. I turn to these in the next chapter.

This new approach has to be tested in empirical research. By examining what therapists do after they have been trained in this approach and by testing the effectiveness of various interventions, we will be able to develop a more refined approach for working with MIL in psychotherapy (see also Chapter 12).

Meaning-in-Life Work With Specific Client Problems

6

> The purpose of life is to discover your gift. The work of life is to develop it. The meaning of life is to give your gift away.
>
> —David Viscott, *Finding Your Strength in Difficult Times: A Book of Meditations*

When a person becomes suddenly unemployed or is transitioning back to civilian life after serving in the military or is dying of cancer, questions of meaning in life (MIL) often arise. Because the person's worldview is disrupted, they have some impetus to figure out where they fit in the new world.

Because MIL is often involved in specific problems, it can be useful to consider the role it plays in a person's distress. Specific examples of likely problematic concerns that might involve MIL are a request for a life review, physical health concerns, career decisions, interpersonal problems, transitions (e.g., divorce, leaving the military, immigration, coming out, death of a significant other, trauma), depression, strong religious convictions, imprisonment, and obsessions. For each situation, I describe possible dynamics, offer some ideas for possible interventions (remembering that each client is unique and therapists have to modify treatments to be responsive to the needs of the individual client), and provide a case example. It is important to note that these recommendations are not yet empirically supported because research is lacking. It is also important to note that I lean toward presenting interventions that are humanistic, psychodynamic, and existential in approach, but other orientations (e.g., cognitive behavioral) could be equally useful

http://dx.doi.org/10.1037/0000083-008
Meaning in Life: A Therapist's Guide, by C. E. Hill

in addressing the MIL components of these concerns if they fit with the therapist and client.

Life Review

Some clients come into therapy explicitly stating that they want to review their lives, to reevaluate where they are and where they want to go. The therapist's first task is to conceptualize the client dynamics and understand the request for a life review. If the client is relatively well-adjusted and at a transition point in life, it makes sense to agree to this focus. If other issues seem more pressing (e.g., a marital crisis) or it seems that the client is using the life review as a defense against other concerns (e.g., obsessively ruminating on the meaning *of* life), the therapist might have to focus on these concerns first and then do a life review (after, of course, talking about this process with the client).

In terms of interventions, a life review is not a structured step-by-step activity but often involves looking back, looking at the present, and looking forward. In looking back, the therapist helps the client review what has gone before, construct some coherent explanation or insight about the past, and make peace with the past (i.e., accept, forgive, take responsibility). The therapist might ask clients to write a narrative of their life or construct a timeline. In looking at the present, the therapist can help clients reflect on their current life ("What makes you happy?" "What's working?" "What makes you unhappy?" "What's not working?"). Then the therapist can shift focus and help the client look forward and make plans, always assessing skills for making desired changes and balancing realism and hope. Of course, these three tasks rarely are so distinct; rather, the therapist and client often go back and forth among them.

One example is a 60-year-old European American woman who started therapy because she wanted to do a life review to avoid repeating past mistakes (this case was published in Hill, Gelso, et al., 2013). Her two children were almost grown and ready to leave home, and she was nearing retirement from her nursing career. After her alcoholic husband's death several years previously, she had not dated but was now ready for and wanting a close relationship. Through 24 sessions of psychodynamic therapy, the therapist helped this client explore her past and present and think about what she wanted in the future. One key part of their work was focusing on dreams, which helped the client get in touch with many underlying feelings. For example, in Session 7, the client reported a dream in which she and her deceased husband lived in an apartment with many glass windows. Although the client did not feel comfortable there and wanted to move, her husband had no interest in leaving. The client interpreted the dream as reflecting the differing goals she and her deceased husband had (e.g., she wanted children, but he did not). The dream also helped the client become aware of her lack of trust in men. Because of the dream, she was able to reflect on what she wanted in relationships. Toward the end of therapy, the client on her own initiative wrote out a life review to show the therapist. They talked about what had happened in the past, where she was currently, and what her goals were for the future. Once she finished the life review, this client was ready to terminate therapy with a renewed sense of self and purpose in her life.

Physical Health Concerns

When born with autism or developmental disabilities, when diagnosed with a chronic illness, or when life is disrupted or shortened by accidental injuries, physical illnesses, and terminal diseases, people have to learn to cope with diminished physical and cognitive abilities and circumstances and find meaning. For example, after a brilliant man had a motorcycle accident that left him with paraplegia, he altered his life goals and started on a path of helping other disabled people. When a graduate student contracted a debilitating disease and was unable to complete her doctoral studies, she took a job working 20 hours a week but then had to retire early because she was not physically able to continue even a limited work schedule. After retirement, she had to come to terms with her reduced life circumstances and find meaning in other ways. A client entered therapy because she had Stage 4 ovarian cancer and knew she only had at best a few years to live. She wanted to be happier in the remainder of her life than she had been before. A soldier with a traumatic brain injury from being in a tank near an explosion could no longer function in the military and felt a profound sense of loss of identity and had to cope with the pain of a confused brain. He wondered what the future held for him.

In all these cases, the MIL issue involves figuring out how to find meaning given life circumstances and limitations. For example, when a nurse had to leave her nursing career after having a heart attack, she was devastated because her whole identity had been wrapped up in being a nurse. "If I'm not a nurse," she asked, "who am I?" She had to grieve the loss of her identity and find a new direction in life. (See Chapter 9 for more on this case example.) Clients also have to grapple with the issue of "Why me?" and "Why not me?" given the seeming randomness and unfairness of events.

In terms of an approach to working with clients who have physical health problems, the first step for therapists is self-examination. A major premise in working with such clients is that they are like us in terms of having similar feelings, hopes, and desires, so we as therapists have to deal with our own reactions and biases, whether of superiority, anxiety, overidentification, and wanting to distance ourselves from their pain. For those of us who as teenagers thought we were immortal, the aches and pains of growing older or of discovering a fatal illness can be devastating. Therapists also have to think through their values about issues such as assisted suicide in the case of someone who is terminally ill and medication in the case of someone who is addicted to pain medication because of chronic pain.

A second task is learning more about the physical problem (through consultation or the Internet) to make sure you understand the scope and depth of the problem. It is also important to ask clients to tell you more about their condition to understand their particular problems. In addition, it is useful to ascertain whether clients are getting adequate medical care or whether they need some assistance getting an appropriate referral for medical care.

A third strategy is to listen empathically to the person's concerns to allow them to experience their feelings and grieve their losses. Being able to voice these concerns to an empathic listener and becoming aware of death anxiety can be invaluable for clients. Being asked directly but gently about death and death anxiety can be liberating (and frightening) for clients who defend against such anxieties and rarely talk about them.

As with other concerns discussed earlier, therapists can help clients look back over their lives and identify what was meaningful, think about their present lives and think about what is sustaining, and then look at their hopes and dreams for the future and plot strategies to help them attain their realistic yet lofty goals (to think big within the bounds of obstacles). Finally, specifically labeling and addressing MIL issues is important to help clients begin to think strategically about meaning.

For clients who are dying imminently, one idea might be to encourage them to create a legacy project (e.g., photographs, recipes) so they can leave something behind for their loved ones that reflects who they were and what they valued. One client's legacy project was remodeling her house so that it would be a fit place for her husband and son to live after her death. Others might organize clutter or get rid of junk so that children or significant others do not have to suffer going through their possessions and making decisions about what to save or discard after the death. Others might write a memoir or journal about their recollections.

Let me talk more about the example I gave earlier of the woman who sought therapy for Stage 4 ovarian cancer, which left her with a projection of 4 to 5 years of life. This woman had worked briefly after college but then dropped out of the labor force to raise her only son. She had great anger at her father for dominating and terrifying her throughout childhood and at her husband for dominating her and being difficult to live with. She felt like a failure in life. In response to questions about what brought her happiness, she responded that she loved gardening but could no longer do it because of her physical weakness after the chemotherapy, and she loved reading but could not do it because of a lack of mental focus. I gave her some specific suggestions for how she could cope with everyday life (e.g., hiring help with her house and garden), which was somewhat helpful. What seemed to be more helpful for her once the relationship was built and she trusted me—and some specific problems in daily life were solved—was describing her physical symptoms and medical treatments in detail and talking about her feelings related to death. She talked about what she wanted for her funeral and how she wanted to be buried. She talked about her son and how much she loved him and about her plans to make sure he got a college education; she cried when she allowed herself to realize that in fact her son loved her and wanted to be around her (unlike her relationship with her father). She made plans to fix up her house so that she would leave behind something for her son and husband. What seemed most important for this woman was not identifying how she could change her life and get more social support (although these are certainly important for other clients) but having me compassionately bear witness to her struggle and allow her to have her feelings. Once she felt supported, she was able to go back and explore her feelings about her childhood, accept herself, and then think about how to gain meaning in the future.

Career Concerns

Career is a major identity for many people, providing a sense of purpose and occupying considerable amounts of time (see Blustein, 2008; Brown & Lent, 2005; Savickas, 2012). Without a career, people often lack purpose, flounder about how they fit in society, and have difficulty filling their time, all of which pose major MIL issues.

Throughout childhood, school fills the role of career, with students knowing that their goal is to finish school (whether high school, undergraduate, or an advanced degree program). In college, students have to choose a major to set the direction for their careers. Many people flounder at this point because it is their first major independent life decision after so many things have been dictated for them. Many students in our current era flounder because parents try to pressure them to enter a field in which they can make a lot of money, whereas the student wants to be in a career that is personally meaningful. Once a major has been chosen and the training for it completed (assuming one is accepted into the training program in which one is interested), the person tries to find a job in the chosen specialty, and of course, serendipity and location play a huge role in that.

A colleague at a workshop gave a heartrending example of a bright student who had attended a prestigious university for an advanced degree, only to admit to himself at the end of many years of education that he did not even like the field. Even if one finds a position that is at least relatively suitable, circumstances often intervene such that one becomes unemployed or unhappy with the current position and has to reconsider options. Given that the average length at a job is about 7 years, finding a job is not a guarantee of a lifetime commitment. Then with aging, retirement looms large, and each person has to decide whether and when to retire, how to finance the retirement, and what to do with their time after retirement.

All of these scenarios reflect the typical or standard progression, but life often intervenes. Some people have traumatic childhoods or lack ability and cannot finish high school. Some people opt out of the career path for parenthood and then have to decide if and when to reenter the workforce, often being forced to seek further education to get back into the job market. Some have intractable personality or substance abuse problems that make it difficult to work with others and get satisfaction from their jobs. Some move because of partners and cannot find suitable new employment. Some get injured or contract physical illnesses that prevent them from participating in the workforce (see the previous section). All these possibilities take people off the typical career path and create crises in their lives about how to find identity and meaning.

In terms of interventions, perhaps the most important thing is to ask clients about hopes, goals, dreams, and aspirations. Helping clients sort out what they love doing from what they feel obligated to do or constrained from doing is also useful so that they can begin to understand where pressures to achieve or be in a certain profession originate. Introducing the topic of MIL can also sometimes be a good idea so that clients can talk directly about where and how to get meaning in their lives, whether from career or other sources.

It can also be helpful to develop a thorough career history, alongside an interpersonal history, given that these two strands are often intertwined. Career assessments (e.g., the Strong Interest Inventory), personality assessments (e.g., the Rorschach, the Minnesota Multiphasic Personality Inventory), and intelligence testing (e.g., the Wechsler Adult Intelligence Scale) can also be useful to determine strengths and limitations. A family genogram sketching out different careers and family members' satisfaction with these careers can also be useful to get a perspective on family influences and pressures.

For some clients who have deficits in job-seeking skills, it can be helpful to teach specific skills for decision making and interviewing (see Hill, 2014, Chapter 17). We see a lot of clients at our low-fee community clinic who do not know how to even begin thinking about seeking a job, so along with treating the demoralization, hopelessness, and lack of self-efficacy (see the section on depression), they may need help with specific behavioral strategies (e.g., creating a resume, practicing interviewing skills).

For example, a 50-year-old unmarried African American man who against all odds given a difficult childhood graduated from law school and landed a position in a prestigious law firm where he was subtly but powerfully discriminated against because of his race (see Hill, Chui, & Baumann, 2013, for more details about this case). He developed an addiction to cocaine, which initially helped him cope but then eventually led him to be fired from his job. During and after residential treatment, he spent time exploring what he wanted out of life and came to realize that his passion was for writing rather than the law, so he went back to school and earned a masters of fine arts. During the time in his master's program, he flourished and gained a sense of self-confidence and a solid sense of meaning. Once he graduated, however, he could not find work in his field and again became depressed, which motivated him to seek help. In therapy, we explored his childhood to understand where some of his problematic patterns originated. We also analyzed the cultural environment and looked at the many elements of discrimination that were present in his life and how that affected him. We looked at alternate sources of support and identified how he could work to make money while he poured his considerable energy into writing in his off-work hours. At the end of therapy, this client was more aware that his meaning came from his writing.

Interpersonal Problems

Given that one of the primary sources of meaning for most people is interpersonal relationships (see Chapter 3), it is not surprising that a motivating force for seeking psychotherapy is a lack of interpersonal connections or problems in relationships. Belonging and feeling supported is a crucial source of well-being and MIL for most people.

The first step for therapists is to gather a careful history of the client's interpersonal relationships to be able to form a conceptualization of the problem. What was the client's family history? What was the attachment history? Was there trauma or abuse? Did the client have friends during childhood and adolescence? Does the client lack interpersonal skills?

In terms of assessing interpersonal skills, therapists can also pay attention to their experience with clients. In effect, the therapist has a firsthand experience of how the client comes across. Does the client talk incessantly or not at all, demand that the therapist ask all the questions or not allow the therapist to speak, give too much or too little eye contact, or come prepared to talk or instead complain about being there? Therapists can attend to their internal experience of what it is like to be with the client: Does the therapist feel empathic and warm toward the client, hostile and disgusted, bored and distracted, or sexually attracted and seduced? After considering how much these feelings are sparked by the therapist's issues, the therapist can use these feelings to understand how others react to the client and then conceptualize how to provide a different experience for the client, with the goal of acting differently toward the client than others have in the past and thus help the client have a corrective emotional and relational experience (see also Cashdan, 1988; Castonguay & Hill, 2012; Hill, 2014, Chapter 14; Hill & Knox, 2009; Hill, Knox, & Pinto-Coelho, in press; Safran & Muran, 2000).

Therapists might also work directly to help the client develop better interpersonal, communication, or negotiation skills. It is one thing to figure out what you want or need in life to get meaning, but to negotiate that in regard to another person's needs or wants is difficult. It requires both thinking about oneself and the other without emphasizing either too much. Too much emphasis on the self leads to self-preoccupation and lack of respect for the other, but giving too much to others results in a lack of identity and submissiveness and not being able to reach one's goals. Culture obviously enters in here, with different expectations in different cultures for the roles of parents and children or partners. For example, one Chinese student spoke eloquently about the conflict over feeling a need to please his parents but then feeling resentment about ignoring his own ambitions. Gender role expectations also play a role here, with men in many cultures feeling the right to be dominant and women being expected to be submissive (O'Neil, 2015).

To help clients develop interpersonal skills, therapists might use techniques such as role playing and assertiveness training (see Chapter 17 in Hill, 2014). Group therapy is also often a good option to help people learn about how they come across to others and to gain empathy for others (see Yalom & Leszcz, 2005). Couples or family therapy is also a useful intervention because it enables the therapist to work directly with the system (one of my favorite books of all time is *The Family Crucible* by Napier & Whittaker, 1978).

For example, a married couple sought couples therapy (I thank Orya Tishby for this example, although I have changed some details). The husband was a successful businessman who was dominant in the marital relationship. The wife was submissive in the marital relationship and in her job as a schoolteacher. Through several years of psychodynamic marital therapy, they learned to communicate and negotiate. The wife came to find her voice and realized she did not like being a schoolteacher. What she discovered that she loved doing was interior decoration. They bought a new house, and she decorated it. The husband also retired, and they found mutual happiness and meaning in running a bed and breakfast together in their newly remodeled home.

Transitions

Transitions often stimulate clients' thinking about MIL. As the saying goes, a crisis presents an opportunity. Events such as graduation, going away to college, marriage, having children, miscarriages, divorce, children leaving home, and going away for or returning from vacations all provide opportunities for thinking about the past and the future. In addition, any life experience that illuminates how life is unfair and chaotic or random (e.g., the wrongful conviction of a crime, an advocate for gun control being shot accidentally) leads people to question meaning and their control over events.

At times of transitions, clients are disrupted from their regular routines and are thus more open to questioning how they are living. For example, many people think about quitting their jobs after vacations because they come to recognize that their lives could be different.

In terms of interventions, a primary focus can be on the emotions generated by the transition. The client is at a juncture and needs time to experience the multitude of often conflicting feelings (e.g., sadness about the loss of the past, excitement about new possibilities, terror about the unknown, awareness of the finiteness of life, anger at the unfairness of life). Therapists can help clients experience the depth and complexities of their feelings, understand the feelings, accept the feelings, and modulate or regulate these feelings. Focusing (Gendlin, 1981, 1996) or emotion-focused therapy (L. S. Greenberg, 2015) can be helpful approaches for working with these emotions.

Therapists can also help clients articulate, examine, and modify irrational cognitions (e.g., "I must be perfect; everyone must love me"; see Beck & Beck, 2011). In this process, therapists help clients come to a greater understanding of where some of their problematic thoughts and behaviors originate. Relatedly, therapists can help clients do a life review (connecting past, present, and future; see the Life Review section earlier in this chapter) to readjust values and goals to fit the changed circumstances.

Finally, therapists can help clients think about changes they can make in their behaviors to deal with some of the recurrent patterns. Because routines are disrupted, transitions are an ideal time to help clients think about whether they want to make changes in their lives. If so, clients may need help figuring out the logistics of how to make changes (e.g., they may need skills training, education about possibilities).

Several more specific transitions deserve a bit more attention. Specifically, we focus on divorce, leaving the military, immigration, coming out, death of a significant other, and trauma.

DIVORCE

Transition for the Couple Following Divorce

Divorce is often a difficult transition. Cartwright and Lamberg (1992) eloquently described how it disrupts people's lives. One's very identity can be threatened because of the shift from being part of a couple to being single, from leaving one's home and possessions to having to forge a new life, from having people think of you as part of a couple to seeing you as an individual, from having daily company to facing the absence of the other. In addition, the feelings can range from relief and freedom to grief, humiliation, anger, frustration, regret, and sorrow. Feelings often, however, depend on whether one initiated the divorce or was the one left behind, with the former being laden with freedom and guilt and the latter being laden with hurt and anger. Garfield (1991) found that dreams of being buried alive or lost at sea were common for women anticipating or undergoing divorce. In their study of group dream work for women undergoing the transition of divorce, Falk and Hill (1995) cited some poignant examples:

> A 32-year-old Hispanic woman shared a dream in which she was at the bottom of a muddy, slimy hill. She was trying to climb up a rope but kept slipping back down the hill. The end of the rope was being held by her ex-husband. Although she did not initially report these emotions to the group, her associations revealed that the dream was a reflection of her feelings of distrust and helplessness from the divorce and that the rope was a sign of hope for a way out. Thus, underlying material and the corresponding feelings were now acknowledged and could be worked with in the group setting. Because others shared similar feelings, this working through was beneficial not only for her but for other group members.
>
> A 58-year-old African-American woman who had been married for about 35 years dreamed that she was alone in the kitchen of the house she and her husband had shared. Water began to leak from the faucet, ceiling, and walls. No amount of towels could dry or stop the flow of the water. In the interpretation, she understood that the flow of water symbolized her sense of being out of control since the divorce. She realized that she didn't yet know how to stop the flow of pain.
>
> A 23-year-old African American woman had a recurring dream in which she entered the home of her ex-husband in a good mood, wanting to reconcile. All around the apartment she noticed a great number of fishbowls, all with fish who had died from not being fed. When the woman went downstairs to find her ex-husband, she discovered him with two young, attractive twin girls. With the group's help, she was able to identify feelings of fear, humiliation, and shock during the dream interpretation. A number of other group members identified with the feelings of pain, shame, and humiliation in these dreams and so were able not only to provide validation of the dreamers' feelings but also to gain personal insight. (pp. 38–39)

Dream work was particularly important in helping these women explore their feelings and make sense of their situations. Because they felt supported and gained understanding, they were able to make changes in their lives to gain more MIL. For more discussion of dream work, see Hill (2004).

Transition for the Children Following Parents' Divorce

Parents' divorce can also be troubling for the children, although not always (one student recounted how life was so much better after her parents got divorced because they had so obviously not been meant for each other). For many children, daily life is disrupted when their parents divorce. Students whose parents divorced when the children were in college have also told me that they were distraught because they felt that everything they knew was false, and it was hard to adjust to the new reality. One result of parental divorce can be that children are reluctant to enter into committed relationships for fear of divorce. As with other transitions, therapists can help such clients mourn their losses and then reconceptualize how they gain meaning in relationships and how they can communicate differently with a partner.

LEAVING THE MILITARY

When a person is part of a military team, there is often a special sense of teamwork and purpose. For example, might have joined the army to serve their country, to protect the homeland, or to do their duty. They might have been part of a tight elite group of well-trained individuals who shared a vision of what they wanted to accomplish and formed strong bonds under stressful conditions. To return to regular life can be quite a jolt, given that they no longer have a purpose or a close team oriented toward fulfilling that purpose. When one returns and finds it is not okay to harm the enemy, it can be confusing in terms of shifting morals and values. Being an ordinary civilian can be disconcerting. Other civilians often do not respect or appreciate the sacrifices, leaving the veteran feeling devalued and dislocated. The divorce rate and the suicide rate for veterans are both high. And if the veteran is also disabled from the service, the adjustment can be even more difficult. *The Best Years of Our Lives*, a movie made in 1946, portrays these feelings well for three men who returned from World War II.

Other situations yield somewhat similar experiences. After the 2016 Summer Olympics, there was quite a bit of talk on the news of "What now?" for the returning athletes. For some, nothing in life can compare with the experiences of working toward the Olympics and competing in them.

As with other transitions, therapists can help such clients process the experiences, especially to reexperience the positives and negatives of the past. Therapists can also help clients evaluate current strengths and plan for a new future. Because changes in identity can be so painful, it can be important for therapists to be supportive as well as knowledgeable about what clients are going through.

IMMIGRATION

Immigration is often a difficult transition (Tummala-Narra, 2016). For those who choose to immigrate for a better life for themselves and their children (it gives them a great deal of meaning to do so), detachment from family and culture can be a shock. They also often feel disappointment and loss of everything they have known that has given them meaning. Furthermore, if their children then do not follow their wishes regarding career and romantic ties, parents can feel that they have sacrificed for nothing. Likewise, children can feel upset thinking that if their parents wanted them to have a better life, they should (as one immigrant student told me) let them live their own lives without being so controlling. There is a good example of this transition in the movie *A Fond Kiss*: A Pakistani family immigrates to Scotland and has a crisis when the son falls in love with a Scottish woman and the younger daughter wants to go away to school, both of which violate the parents' expectations and wishes for their children.

Illegal immigrants face additional difficulties given the constant fear of being caught and deported. When parents are illegal and children are legal, there is also the potential of parents being deported with no one left behind to raise the children. Many of these illegal immigrants have fled their countries because of violence and oppression and have lost their home base; many face incredible obstacles surviving in a hostile environment.

Tummala-Narra (2016) noted the importance of helping such clients mourn the losses of their language and culture and deal with traumas that have occurred in their home country and in the process of settling in a new country. Talking about meaning could be particularly relevant for helping people think about their reasons for leaving their home countries and for adjusting to their new country.

COMING OUT

The process of coming out as lesbian, gay, bisexual, transgender, queer, questioning, asexual, or pansexual represents another transition that can cause a person to have a crisis of meaning. Having grown up in a world in which heterosexuals are in the majority, it can be liberating and exciting but also difficult and challenging to come to terms with one's identity and to navigate changes in relationships with family and friends (Hays, 2013, 2016).

As noted in Chapter 1, identity and meaning are closely related constructs, with meaning being a part of the self. Thus, struggles to identify in terms of sexual orientation often parallel struggles to construct meaning. Do we get our meaning from pleasing others and conforming to some societal expectations, or do we examine ourselves and come to an acceptance of who we are?

Talking about the process of coming out and identity with a caring, trusted therapist can be helpful, especially since people often feel isolated and alone. By exploring and gaining insight, people are more likely to feel supported and certain about their decisions and identities.

DEATH OF A SIGNIFICANT OTHER

Another specific type of transition is the death of a significant other, which is often a shock that causes disruption in daily life and to one's sense of well-being. It can also lead to the painful recognition that we also will die given that we are not immortal. For example, when a spouse dies and the partner has been a caretaker during a long illness, the survivor is often left not only with grief about the loss and relief that the person is out of pain but also with a sudden gap in what to do with one's time. For another example, when a good friend dies at a young age, people are often left with haunting memories and an inability to get over the loss. Finally, the death of a child is particularly difficult for most people, not only because of the loss and despair of not having been able to rescue the child but also because it violates the normal expectation that parents should die before children, which leaves parents with the realization that their legacy is not going to be fulfilled in that child.

After the death of a significant other, clients often need a chance to process their feelings. The therapist can facilitate this exploration by asking about memories of the person when alive and well, memories of the death and aftermath, and feelings about the loss and life without the person (see also Neimeyer, 2016). It is important for therapists to remember that feelings at this time are often a complicated mixture of sadness, anger, relief, and survivor guilt. The therapist's task is to help the client explore and accept the complicated and often conflicting feelings. It is also important for therapists to remember that feelings of loss can linger for many years, with some people never wanting to "get over it" but needing to find some way to learn to live with the loss and memories, as Diane Rehm (2017) eloquently described in her book *On My Own* about living after her husband's death. Because the death is also a transition and a disruption for clients, it can be useful to help clients reevaluate their goals for the future and think about what they want to do with the time left in life. Furthermore, because death anxiety can spread from the client to the therapist, it might be helpful for therapists to check in with themselves about whether they are doing what they want to be doing with their lives.

A particularly interesting phenomenon is people who change their whole meaning on the basis of the tragic loss of a significant other. In one example, when a child was murdered, the parents set up a foundation to help other children. In another case when a child was killed by a drunk driver, the parents set up a campaign against drunk driving. Thus, these parents gained meaning by trying to help others in similar situations.

A clinical example is a 35-year-old male client who had nine people die in a 2-year span. He especially grieved his mother, to whom he felt close. He had cared for his mother in the last year of her life, and he felt tremendous guilt because he thought he should have been able to prevent her from dying. With each subsequent death, his defenses crumbled even further, and he lost his ability to cope and process the traumas. He drank excessively to mask the pain. Talking about each death, allowing him to explore his memories, challenging his assumptions that he was in some way responsible for these deaths, and mourning his losses helped him begin to move on. A good relationship with his wife and a satisfying career helped to buffer him, although he continued to struggle with the drinking because it was such an effective tool for masking his pain.

TRAUMA

Another specific type of transition comes through trauma. Experiences such as war, rape, and mass shootings can shake up one's world and worldview and even cause changes in the brain (see Courtois, 2013). These traumatic events often violate our sense of the world as a just, safe, secure, reliable place. After such events, we have to change our ways of thinking to be able to accommodate the horrible event and make some sense (coherence or understanding) of how such things can occur ("Why me?"). In addition to having to make adjustments in coherence, one's felt sense of meaning is often shattered, purpose or goals in life might be affected as one thinks about whether the old things are still relevant at this time of transition, and mattering can be affected if one feels a sense of insignificance or irrelevance in the face of random violence.

Another example is the attack on the World Trade Centers in New York City on 9/11 and the many terrorist attacks since. Nothing like 9/11 had ever happened in the United States, and people did not know how to understand it. They felt frightened and did not know how to organize their lives. The people who were immediately touched by the tragedy were overwhelmed and had their everyday lives disrupted, but others far away from New York City were also confused and panicked about what kind of world we live in and how they wanted to live their lives in the face of such tragedy. Unfortunately, recent terrorist attacks around the world continue to remind us of the fragility of life.

In terms of working with clients who have had their expectations violated, it is often crucial to provide them with a safe space along with acceptance and support with a lack of judgment. Evoking strong emotion is often contraindicated for some trauma clients because they need to be helped to feel less rather than more. For example, in dialectical behavior therapy (Linehan, 2015), clients with emotional dysregulation are encouraged to focus on the here-and-now rather than on larger meanings and emotions.

It is also important, at more of a distance in time, to help these clients examine their assumptions and worldviews (e.g., the world is just, good things happen to people who are deserving, there is a reason for everything that happens, God does not give us more than we can bear). These assumptions often have to be revised on the basis of new information (e.g., the world is not fair, bad things can happen to good people, the universe is often a random place and bad things happen for no good reason). Of course, it is important to remember that changing attitudes is difficult, and it is better for clients to come to these realizations on their own rather than to have the therapist's philosophy shoved down their throats. Thus, being empathic and gentle and asking questions is often far more useful than directing and guiding at this point. In addition, the event that led to the violation of expectations is a kind of transition in life, and so some of the suggestions presented previously for working with transitions can be used by therapists in their work with such clients (e.g., look to the past to understand the past, examine the present to assess concerns, and look toward the future).

A clinical example is of working with a client who had recently been raped. She was frightened of men, and her sense of security was violated. She cried all the time and had a hard time interacting with others. Her experiences with the police were upsetting and shameful; she felt she was being violated all over again because the police did not believe her and even tried to imply that she had been at fault. The therapist to whom this young college student was assigned was a gentle, caring female therapist whose specialty was working with rape victims. Because the client could not even initially talk, the therapist did some psychoeducation about rape and its aftermath and then taught her some breathing and mindfulness exercises. In the second session, the therapist gently asked the client whether she would like to talk and then allowed the client to talk at her own pace. Eventually, after the client talked about the experience, the therapist helped her think of ways she could protect herself in the future (e.g., walking with a friend at night or calling campus security for a ride), and then she helped her think about her violated assumptions and create new assumptions (e.g., "The world is not a safe place so I have to learn how to take care of myself"). Because the client then trusted the therapist, she also began to talk about whether she wanted to stay in college. The client decided she needed some time off to reassess her goals. The therapist helped her find a new therapist in the community with whom she could continue talking about her anxieties.

Depression

Depression is one of the major problems that clients bring into therapy (Lazar, 2010). Depressed clients often feel hopeless and like there is no way out. They may be suicidal. These clients are often painfully aware that they have little going on in their lives, but they also often have tunnel vision, not being able to see beyond the current time to any other vision of the future. Thus, depression clearly involves MIL as an underlying concern.

First and foremost, these clients need to be met with a warm, compassionate, patient therapist who is nonjudgmental and can accept them for themselves. Being heard is very important. This calm, compassionate approach often requires that therapists be self-aware and recall moments of their own angst and work through their depressed feelings in their own therapy so that they can be present and available for the client. Thus, support is especially important initially, with insight perhaps coming later, depending on the client.

When there is suicidal ideation, therapists can also compassionately help the client explore meaning and suicidal ideation. Therapists often fear that talking about suicidal thoughts will encourage the client to commit suicide. But, in fact, the opposite is more often true: Failure to talk about it makes the client feel marginalized and shamed. By talking about their worst fears to someone who listens compassionately, clients often feel less alone and crazy. It is important for therapists not to diminish or negate clients' feelings (e.g., "Don't worry, you'll feel better in the morning") or give false reassurance (e.g., "Everything will be okay" "You have so much to live for") because this can make clients feel unheard and misunderstood. It is also important for therapists to reach out to others for consultation and supervision to avoid feeling overly responsible and to mobilize resources. It is beyond the scope of this book to provide a thorough coverage of suicide risk and suicide assessment, but I refer readers to other excellent texts (e.g., Berman, Jobes, & Silverman, 2006; Konrad & Jobes, 2011).

Therapists can ask clients to talk about what is missing and what was once meaningful, thus helping them reclaim past experiences, recognizing of course that this exploration sometimes leads to great pain as experiences are unpacked and explored. At the same time, the therapist can also help the client relive traumatic events (see the section on violation of expectations in Chapter 2) and grieve over the losses they have encountered and the damage that has been done to them. If appropriate, therapists can share a bit about their own resolved depression to show clients that it is human to feel depressed and that one can get through it.

Therapists could also consider a consultation for possible medication given that some of these problems may have a biological or physical basis. Working together with people who can prescribe is often better than working alone and assuming that all problems can be resolved through verbal therapy. Although antidepressant medications are often not a cure-all, they can sometimes be helpful in lifting the client's mood enough so that psychotherapy can be more beneficial. Therapists might also have to consult with a medical doctor who has hospital privileges if the client has to be admitted to the hospital for close watch. Hospital admission requires considerable clinical skill and compassion and the therapist needs to be seen as siding with the client rather than acting as the overpowering authority.

Finally, it is important to mention the influence on therapists of working in this area. Many therapists, especially novice therapists, have anxiety about working with depression, hopelessness, and suicidal ideation because of fears of emotional contagion: Will clients' despair about lack of meaning infect the therapist? All of us have concerns about lack of meaning and can worry that we will get dragged down into the abyss if we allow clients to talk about these concerns. Being aware of these anxieties and seeking personal therapy, supervision, and consultation is particularly advised here.

An example is of a middle-aged man who sought therapy because he was depressed. His wife left him and took their four children, and soon after starting therapy, he lost his job due to a restructuring of the company. Without his family and career (his sources of meaning), he lost all hope and started drinking heavily and was actively considering committing suicide. He felt his life was full of torment and torture. He told his therapist he had put down a deposit on a gun. His therapist, aware of his duty to protect, asked whether he could call the client's sister. The client agreed, and the therapist asked the sister to accompany the client to the gun store and get his deposit back. The client got his deposit back, taking away access to his weapon of choice. As the client explored, he realized he did not want his children to be negatively affected by a suicide, but he still could not think of how to make his life better. The therapist worked with the client to express his feelings and to think about how to restructure his life. Eventually, the client started a new relationship, got another job, and began drinking less.

Strong Religious Convictions

People who have strong religious convictions often feel they know what the MIL is (to follow their higher power) and that the meaning of life (MOL) is synonymous with the MIL, such that they need to find their MIL by following the MOL. Some people might be quite happy having an MOL assigned to them. Others, however, might have difficulty when they have to hide their true identity to fit in with their religion. Others might despair when they feel that their higher power has given them too much to bear. For example, many people leave their religion when a person close to them has died because they feel that their higher power has abandoned or betrayed them. They lose their faith because they cannot imagine a higher power that allows tragedy to happen. Others, in contrast, might grow closer to their higher power as a way of dealing with grief.

People with strong religious beliefs are often anxious or concerned about talking with a therapist who has a different belief system because they feel that they will not be understood or will be devalued or that the therapist will try to persuade them to abandon their religious beliefs. Likewise, therapists who have different religious beliefs from their clients might have difficulty understanding or valuing their clients' beliefs and might feel a need to argue with them and persuade them of the wrongheadedness of their ideas about MIL.

In terms of interventions, therapists have to be attentive to and aware of their values and not unduly impose them on clients, listen and encourage clients to express their feelings without judgment, and respectfully help clients challenge their thinking while remaining impartial. In particular, therapists might help clients move from an externalized system of beliefs to a more internalized belief system (from operating out of "shoulds" to making personal choices). It is not usually possible to remain entirely neutral, so it might sometimes be best to tell clients about the differences but also assure them that you will try your best to understand and value their beliefs. (See also Chapter 8 about ethical concerns related to values clashes.)

An example is a client who grew up in a Catholic family and was taught not to question but just to accept what the church taught. When this client went to college, her beliefs were challenged. She became aware that others believed in very different ways and started to question her beliefs, particularly because of the church's stance in relation to women (e.g., not allowing women to serve as priests). This client stopped going to mass and gradually lost interest in the church, and as a result, she had major problems in her relationship with her devout parents. After a bitter breakup with a boyfriend, she went to therapy feeling hopeless and not having any anchor in her life. The therapist helped the client examine her values and beliefs. He encouraged the client to pray and seek guidance from a priest who he knew was quite open and understanding. The client reconciled with both her parents and the church. She came to approach her religion in a new way as her choice rather than as a dogma imposed on her.

Imprisonment

When a person is imprisoned and segregated from society, it is hard to feel a sense of worth and that one's life has meaning. Furthermore, if the prisoner committed a horrendous crime, she or he may feel a sense of loss, guilt, shame, despair, and dehumanization. On the other hand, if prisoners are wrongfully convicted, they could feel abandoned by a society that considers them to be of such little value that they are not even gotten a fair hearing. Recent research by Vanhooren, Leijssen, and Dezutter (2015, 2016, 2017) showed that indeed prisoners report a loss of meaning after imprisonment, have lower scores on both Presence and Search scales of the Meaning in Life Questionnaire, and experience distress and deep existential crises with a sense that their lives do not make sense anymore. Vanhooren et al. (2016) presented the case of "Martha," who had been in prison for 15 years. In her reflections on her experiences, Martha said she had struggled with feelings of hopelessness and the temptation to commit suicide. Through the help of a chaplain, Martha felt life was worth living as long as she could mean something to others, which she accomplished by knitting bunnies and donating all the profits to an orphanage. Within the limited possibilities of prison life, she thus created a way to experience meaning.

In terms of treatment, Vanhooren et al. (2017) suggested the importance of social and emotional support and helping prisoners search for new meaning. The authors emphasized helping prisoners learn about coping, make choices, take responsibility for their future, gain insight into their history, gain self-worth, learn about strengths, discover a more nuanced way of thinking, and gain new relational skills, in addition to changing their meaning in life.

Obsessions

Obsessions often serve as a defense against anxiety (McWilliams, 2011), in this case against existential angst. In his brilliant novel *When Nietzsche Wept*, Yalom (1992) provided a fictional example of how a sexual obsession about a patient kept Breuer from confronting his anxieties about aging, death, and the meaning in his work. Only by "chimney sweeping" and continually confronting the existential issues with the support and encouragement of Nietzsche was Breuer able to directly face his fears and choose to live a more meaningful life. Psychoanalysis is thus appropriate for helping psychologically minded clients gain understanding of such obsessions and take more responsibility for their actions. Similarly, in acceptance and commitment therapy (Hayes & Lillis, 2012), therapists help clients face and accept rather than avoid their anxieties.

Conclusion

MIL is implicated in many client concerns, with just a few of these situations highlighted in this chapter (other situations include making bad decisions, losing self, being wealthy or having everything handed to one and not having to search for meaning). Although we do not have empirical evidence yet, it seems likely that MIL work differs depending on the specific problem and the individual client. Overarching considerations are conceptualizing how MIL fits into the client's dynamics and determining how to approach the individual client in terms of bringing up MIL concerns. Of course, we must always be concerned with stereotyping clients, given that each client is unique and therapists need to be responsive to the individual client.

Case Examples of Clients With Meaning-in-Life Concerns

7

The unexamined life is not worth living.

—Socrates (as cited in Plato's *Apology*)

The cases examined in this chapter come from interviews in a qualitative study (Hill, Kanazawa, et al., 2017) described in more detail in Chapter 10. In this qualitative study, we asked experienced therapists in private practice to describe their meaning-in-life (MIL) work with one client who explicitly presented MIL as a concern and a second client who had more implicit MIL concerns (i.e., other concerns were initially more salient, but MIL was an underlying concern and became more salient later in therapy). These cases are thus unusual in that they represent a select segment of the population. It is also important to note that these are not the only types of clients who experience MIL concerns; rather, they represent a few examples of how MIL has been focused on by experienced therapists with specific clients.

I rewrote the interviews to shorten them and make them readable in this format, although I tried to retain the therapists' voices as much as possible. Names and details were changed to protect confidentiality. Therapists whose cases were used reviewed their sections of the chapter to ensure that confidentiality was maintained, cases were presented with fidelity, and details were accurate. At the end of the chapter, I draw conclusions about what we can learn from these cases about how to work with MIL in psychotherapy. The first five cases had explicit MIL concerns; the second set of five cases had more implicit MIL concerns.

http://dx.doi.org/10.1037/0000083-009
Meaning in Life: A Therapist's Guide, by C. E. Hill

Case Examples of Clients Who Had Explicit Meaning-in-Life Concerns

A SPIRITUAL JOURNEY AFTER RETIREMENT

"Bruce" was a married man in his mid-60s who sought therapy because he wanted to make a life change. Dr. A was a 62-year-old female psychologist in full-time private practice. Her theoretical orientation was psychoanalytic–psychodynamic, humanistic–existential, and feminist–multicultural.

Client Background

Bruce had retired after having worked hard in his career and making a lot of money. He wanted to leave the comfortable life he and his wife had built and strike out on a spiritual journey. He was not quite sure what this pilgrimage would look like, but he wanted the freedom to try new things, explore his faith and spirituality, and learn about new faiths. Bruce had some health problems and sensed that his time was limited, so he wanted to live his remaining years in a way that felt meaningful to him. He had lived a lot of his life taking care of other people, raising his children, providing for his family, and helping people. Now, he wanted to try to understand what his life was about and what he needed to do to feel fulfilled before he died. His wife, in contrast, wanted stability and structure, to be around family and friends, and to live in the comfort of their home after her retirement. Given these differences, Bruce and his wife were having a lot of discord and trouble communicating after 45 years of marriage.

Treatment

In his 6-month treatment, Bruce and Dr. A talked a lot about faith, what his faith meant to him, the different ways he explored his faith, the difference between faith and organized religion, the meaning of relationships, and how all these things fit together. They also talked directly about life meaning and his spiritual journey.

The biggest challenge for Dr. A was confronting the possibility that Bruce was using his concerns about meaning in life as a defense against recognizing and dealing with other reasons for doing things. They thus had to talk about whether Bruce was talking about a spiritual journey to hide his attraction to another woman who was interested in going on a spiritual journey with him. To understand and talk about his spirituality, they had to talk about his feelings about his wife and this other woman and how that interacted with spirituality and his sense of life meaning.

Outcomes

Bruce had never been in therapy before and said he had not expected to get as much out of it as he did, particularly in terms of talking so deeply about his feelings and thoughts about spirituality. He was pleased with what he got out of therapy. He returned for another few sessions after terminating so he could talk more about some of the things that were important to him given that he did not have many opportunities to talk about these issues. He was open and talked a lot about his concerns.

In terms of specific outcomes related to MIL, Bruce gained clarity about his spiritual struggles. He was able to sort through what he wanted and to confront himself more explicitly. Dr. A also felt good about the work they did and how they did it. She thought therapy was helpful for Bruce, and she liked being able to be direct with him about the MIL issues.

LIFE REVIEW AFTER A HEART ATTACK

"Stuart" was a 60-year-old man who sought out therapy for a life review. Dr. B, a 50-year-old male psychologist, had been practicing for 28 years in a small private practice in addition to being a professor. He rated himself as moderately high on four theoretical orientations (psychoanalytic–psychodynamic, humanistic–existential, cognitive–behavioral, and feminist–multicultural orientations).

Client Background

After his second heart attack, Stuart was declared dead, but he was brought back to life. He felt he had been given a new lease on life, and he took advantage of the opportunity by coming to therapy for the first time. He wanted to engage in a life review by looking back, looking at his current life, and looking ahead. What had been meaningful, what had been lost? Dr. B indicated that Stuart was not seriously psychologically distressed.

Stuart grew up in the South in the 1950s in a Southern Baptist household in which feelings other than anger were not expressed. His parents were alcoholics, and Stuart also struggled with addiction. Stuart had a limited emotional vocabulary and was unfamiliar with his own affective terrain. He was closed off to his feelings and cut off emotionally. Emotions were equated with weakness, largely as a result of his male socialization process.

Treatment

In this 2-year course of psychotherapy, there were several prominent themes. The work most related to MIL is described here.

Work on Emotions

The first few times Stuart cried in session, he tried to fight back the tears but could not and was thus able to experience some catharsis. An example of this emotion work is a story Stuart told about a trip he took with his parents when he was a young boy. His parents left him alone, and there was a fire at the hotel. Stuart was understandably terrified. When his parents finally appeared, they were drunk. Stuart at first described this event as matter-of-factly as if he had read about it in a newspaper, but the work deepened when he got in touch with his emotions about the experience. Stuart found it meaningful to discover emotions, and emotions became the avenue through which he was able to connect with his daughter and grandkids, leave his current wife, and connect with another woman.

Life Review

Stuart's life review centered on meaning. He told vivid stories about his father and mother. For example, his father never addressed him by name but called him by the same nickname he used with other guys in town and drinking partners. Stuart got the message that rather than being special to his father, he was an annoyance, a pain in the ass. Although his father wanted Stuart to go into a manly profession, his mother instilled in him a love of the arts. With his mother's support, he was able to become a professional artist. Stuart's professional identity was central to his self-identity, so his being an artist was important to him. If he had not had his mother's support and her interest in the arts, Stuart was not sure who he would have been. Interestingly, Dr. B said that MIL work was difficult because the goals in therapy were ambiguous. Stuart did not come in saying he smoked two packs of cigarettes a day and wanted to get down to smoking six cigarettes a day, which would have been easy to measure. How do you know when a life review is complete and whether you did it well?

Dream Work

Occasionally, they explored dreams Stuart brought up in therapy. Stuart seemed to find the dream work useful in trying to understand himself. They explored what might be going on beneath the surface emotionally and what the dreams might be trying to suggest regarding emotions with which he was not in touch.

Encouragement of Creative Expression

Dr. B encouraged Stuart to go into the studio and let loose. Although Stuart was resistant to have his art interpreted and only once brought it in to show Dr. B, his description of it and of the process of creating the art was a nice adjunct to the therapy. Stuart was able to see more of himself through his art.

Systems Work

Dr. B did two sessions of couples therapy with Stuart and his wife (who was in individual therapy with another therapist). Dr. B knew Stuart was struggling with the marital relationship and initiated the idea of couples therapy to get his own sense of the wife rather than relying solely on Stuart's perspective. The wife was manipulative, and Dr. B wanted to work with the system so that Stuart was not just "swimming upstream." The wife came in and was cordial. She tried to team up with Dr. B against Stuart, saying, "I'm so glad you're helping him; he has so many problems." When

Dr. B tried to bond with the wife and get her to work on the relationship, however, she resisted—"No, no, no, not me"—and never returned to the couples sessions. Dr. B thus was able to validate Stuart's reactions to his wife as being a bully. Eventually, Stuart and his wife divorced.

Provided a Rationale or Frame

The work was informed by the idea that people need to integrate and synthesize subpersonalities, like Jung's description of integrating shadow elements and Assagioli's psychosynthesis. Because Stuart was thoughtful and smart, Dr. B presented his goals for therapy so Stuart would have an understanding of the rationale for going into so much exploration. Dr. B thought Stuart would find the rationale consistent with Stuart's wanting to do a life review. Consistent with Jung's ideas, Dr. B believed that a major task in life after the age of 35 is to do a life review and integrate parts of ourselves we have neglected or suppressed. Stuart replied, "Yeah, this is interesting."

Dealing With Resistance

Stuart was resistant a lot of the time. He had a lot of fear and self-loathing, which is why the work took as long as it did. Dr. B let Stuart engage in storytelling because it was safer for Stuart to be on an intellectual rather than an emotional level. Dr. B felt it was a constant balancing act between pushing Stuart to be in touch with his emotions and letting him go and eventually get to emotions on his own. Dr. B felt a need to listen to the stories to develop hypotheses about the emotional content but speculated that there were times he let Stuart go on too much.

Treating Alcohol Problems

Once or twice Stuart gave up alcohol altogether. But at one point his life circumstances were hard when his wife left him before they divorced. It was winter, and he was living in a one-room cabin without heat and hardly any money. He drank to numb himself so he did not feel the pain of the estrangement from his daughter, the divorce, and the disappointment in his father's eyes. It was hard for Dr. B, who felt, "Oh man, all our work may have been undone here." But Stuart got involved with Alcoholics Anonymous, got a sponsor, and realized, "I can't drink. I can't drink, period. I don't have control when I drink."

Outcomes

Stuart developed a relationship with his daughter and grandchildren. His daughter asked him to move closer to her. He partnered with another woman, and they moved to live closer to his daughter. Dr. B thought it was a good outcome and that the case was ultimately successful, with the client having done his life review and gotten a sense of his MIL.

IF I'M NOT A NURSE, WHO AM I?

"Susan," a female client in her 60s, sought therapy because she was feeling aimless. Dr. C was a 55-year-old female psychologist who had been in full-time practice for 13 years. Dr. C rated herself high in psychoanalytic–psychodynamic, humanistic–existential, and feminist–multicultural theoretical orientations.

Client Background

Susan was married, with two grown stepchildren with whom she had distant relationships. As a result of two heart attacks, Susan was on full disability because she could no longer continue her nursing career. No longer being a nurse meant she had lost her community, her identity, her health, and her income. Both of her parents had died recently, and Susan was frustrated that she had not been able to help them more, given that she was a nurse. After her parents died, her family was no longer close. Susan presented with extreme anxiety and agoraphobia as well as depression. She had lost her direction and purpose in life because of the losses. She had no energy and enthusiasm and did not feel like herself.

Treatment

Dr. C believed Susan needed to understand more about her MIL (i.e., why she was living) before she could effectively learn skills to cope with her anxiety. They thus examined Susan's religious beliefs and discovered she no longer had any connection to her religion. They also examined her strong work ethic and discovered that her only source of meaning was her work. In addition, reviewing her parents' deaths in terms of a loss of MIL, specifically the loss of her role as a daughter and caretaker, helped Susan work through her unresolved grief.

Dr. C used questions, clarification, reflection, curiosity, and enthusiasm to help Susan explore MIL. Because Susan was smart and enjoyed a good challenge, Dr. C was able to be gently confrontational, and could also joke, teach, and use more paradoxical interventions than she did with other clients.

Dr. C suggested to Susan that she could create meaning for herself and that this meaning could change over time. Dr. C also shared different ways people find MIL, sometimes by giving examples of people struggling with MIL issues. Susan was surprised to learn of ways to find MIL other than helping others and making a difference in people's lives.

Outcomes

As a result of working on MIL in therapy, Susan discovered she could actively work to create a new MIL and could continue to find purpose in her life by helping others in a different way than she had with nursing. She reconnected with her family, assuming a support role for her nieces and nephews by sending notes of encouragement, money, gifts, and advice. She also saw herself as a patient advocate for members of her extended family—for example, by visiting a rehabilitation center to assess the care her sister was receiving. She also volunteered to speak at her nursing school. Although Susan still struggled with agoraphobia, identifying her goals gave her the motivation to work to overcome the anxiety of crowds and being away from home. She viewed herself as passing on the values and legacy of her much-admired parents.

Focusing explicitly on MIL not only helped Susan deal with her past and current issues but also gave her a framework to cope with her future. Conscious awareness of her MIL and the ongoing need to refine and revise her MIL helped Susan manage the subsequent reemergence of symptoms and her new stressors, such as her deteriorating health. More important, Susan discovered that her MIL was not only a source of motivation but also a source of profound joy, especially in her new role of grandmother to the child of her previously distant stepson.

I NEED TO FIND MYSELF AGAIN

"Claudia," in her late 50s, sought therapy for interpersonal difficulties. Dr. D was a 58-year-old female psychologist in full-time private practice. She rated herself highest in a humanistic/existential theoretical orientation.

Client Background

Claudia worked in the education field as an administrator. She had one daughter and one grandson. Her parents were both still alive, but her father was not in good health. Her first marriage had been difficult because her husband was drug addicted. Shortly after she divorced him, he died suddenly. Her second marriage was to a man who was more a friend to her. They parted after 5 years, however, because the marriage lacked passion. She met her current husband through a spiritual community, and they had been married for over 10 years.

Claudia started therapy because she was triggered by childhood memories due to her parents' failing health and difficulties with a younger brother who was incarcerated for taking advantage of the parents. Her mother was still helping the brother financially, which upset Claudia greatly and brought up memories of not being treated fairly as a child. Given her age, Claudia knew she wanted something more from her life. At the start of therapy, she said, "I need to get back to myself; I need to find myself again." She felt like she was not living her life fully, she was cut off from her emotions, and was not as close to her husband as she wanted to be. She wanted to be close to her mother but did not know how, given her feelings about her brother.

Treatment

At the beginning of therapy, Claudia said she wanted to work on meaning concerns. Dr. D said that the discussion got deep quickly because Claudia was so ready to do this work, and Dr. D could just "go along for the ride."

They talked about her need to reconnect with spirituality. Because Claudia got so angry and frustrated with herself, Dr. D lent her a book on self-compassion. Claudia read the book and was able to apply what she learned and was thus able to be more compassionate with herself.

Dr. D encouraged Claudia to reconnect to things that were helpful for her in the past. For example, when Claudia was exploring what meditation meant to her and how it helped her in the past, Dr. D encouraged Claudia to take up meditation again. Claudia responded positively, "It was some part of my life that was really helpful. It would be helpful for me to try to introduce that into my life again."

Claudia had some meaning in her life. She had a good relationship with her daughter and loved her grandson. Although the daughter and grandson did not live nearby, Claudia made a point of seeing them several times a year. Claudia's work also gave her some meaning, although she felt a lot of pressure to work hard.

What was lacking was her ability to be in touch with her feelings. Most notably with her husband, Claudia was not able to make herself vulnerable and thus felt cut off from her feelings. Dr. D and Claudia talked about how that process had developed over the years. Her abusive first marriage and an emotionally neglectful childhood made her cut off her feelings as a coping strategy and develop a people-pleasing attitude. Feeling that everybody had to like her stopped her from knowing what she was experiencing. Dr. D helped Claudia develop insight in a compassionate way: "It's not surprising that you've learned to cut off your feelings."

Dr. D said that there were no real challenges in working with Claudia in relation to MIL because Claudia was so open and ready to work. She was an insightful, spiritual, and conscious person. No major pathology got in the way, and they had a great relationship.

Outcomes

Dr. D thought Claudia responded well to support. She opened herself up to things that mattered to her. She also became more open to her husband so that his feelings mattered to her and their relationship thus improved. Claudia started to live more fully and allowed herself to have and express her feelings.

WHITE COLLAR CRIME

"Donald" was a 55-year-old physician who had committed Medicare fraud and thus had his life fall apart. Dr. E was a 58-year-old cognitive behavioral therapist psychologist who had been in part-time practice 22 years and was also a psychology professor in a professional school.

Client Background

Donald had gotten caught up in the momentum of getting more and more successful and never said, "I'm breaking the law." He got caught up in a series of small excuses (e.g., "Well, this person did not show up today, so I can bill for a no-show, and Medicare will understand if I billed"), a series of poor choices involving greed rather than sociopathy, and also narcissism (e.g., "I'm really weak and vulnerable and fragile deep down, so I'll do everything I can to be as big, pompous, famous, rich, wealthy, and powerful as I can").

After he was arrested, investigated, and found guilty, Donald lost his medical license, and his wife left him. His world collapsed around him, and he was depressed and discouraged ("What's left that gives me any meaning in life?"). He had been wealthy, successful, and extremely proud of his success, but when he lost the success, he lost all his sources of meaning. He appeared relatively humble at the beginning of therapy, but Dr. E could tell he was looking at the shell of the person Donald once was. When all his meaning was yanked out from under him, Donald came to see Dr. E with no meaning left and a resulting depression.

Treatment

They started talking about meaning in the first session. After hearing Donald's story about the fraud and conviction, Dr. E said, "Well, it sounds like you have lost everything that gave you meaning, and that is why you feel so horrible." Dr. E said that Donald's eyes widened like no one had ever brought that to his attention before, which seemed to give him quick relief. Dr. E added, "We need to figure out where you are going to find meaning in your life." Donald went on to explain that there were some things that gave him meaning, that he had friends and family who cared about him. Spirituality did not come up. Dr. E thought that Donald was less likely to get meaning from God, spirituality, meditating, a monastery, or a temple but more likely to get it from remembering that people still liked him.

The therapeutic relationship was important. When Donald first sat down to talk to Dr. E, he looked like somebody who might as well have said, "I don't think you can help me, but my doctor thinks I should be here." Dr. E asked, "Do you have any questions for me? Anything you need to know before we proceed so you do not sit there distracted wondering about me?" Dr. E said he could tell that Donald was ready to fire some questions at him, checking out whether his credentials and knowledge base were adequate because Donald was absolutely not ready to have a relationship with Dr. E. When Dr. E answered the questions right and seemed to understand how much Donald struggled and how his sources of meaning in life had evaporated, Donald settled in and seemed to become increasingly relaxed. It seemed to help that Dr. E said, "Holy crap, who wouldn't feel lost and confused and frustrated and scared and all those things after all the losses you suffered. We have to figure out what's going to give you meaning now."

Donald had not been completely honest about his legal problems with the people who were close to him. One of his homework assignments was thus to tell these people all he had been through—not just, "I had some trouble with the law, and now I need to take some time off" but that he got probation and had to do public service. Dr. E gave Donald this assignment because he thought Donald had to shift from getting meaning from lots of gold jewelry and fancy cars to knowing that people loved him. He needed to cement the notion "I can get meaning from my relationships; I'll have to really participate more deeply in those relationships; I'll have to test those relationships." Dr. E likened it to prolonged exposure therapy in that if Donald could get closer and was more exposed to the facts, he would be less scared about being involved with humans and would thus find out whether people still cared about him even if he was bad. They went through each person Donald cared about, and Dr. E said, for example, "Is she cool? Would she get this?" Donald replied, "Yes." Dr. E said, "How about your brother? Would he understand?" Donald said, "Yes, he would; he's a really good guy." Dr. E was thus indirectly leading Donald to obtain meaning from the people he claimed were important to him.

In addition, Dr. E probed and asked questions using guided discovery to help Donald explore these issues related to meaning. They further explicitly explored why Donald felt so bad and where he found meaning in his life.

There were some difficulties in the therapy, however, particularly regarding countertransference. Dr. E was baffled that Donald kept talking about how he was still playing golf. It seemed like a big discrepancy to Dr. E for Donald to have nothing left and yet still be going to a country club. Dr. E struggled to understand how Donald could still be attached to a golf and country club when he did not even have a job. Dr. C did not challenge Donald, though, because he was not confident that there was anything wrong with what Donald was doing.

Outcomes

Dr. E thought Donald responded well to his approach. After the first session when Dr. E asked whether Donald wanted to come back, Donald said, "How soon can I come back?" Unfortunately, Donald's narcissism got the best of him, and his desire for immediate adulation ultimately overpowered his desire for his long-term search for meaning.

Case Examples of Clients Who Had Implicit Meaning-in-Life Concerns

BLAME IT ON THE PARTNER

"Jane" was a 73-year-old Jewish woman who initially sought couples therapy because of communication problems with her partner. Dr. F was a 59-year-old female PhD counseling psychologist who had been in practice for 25 years. Her theoretical orientation was relatively eclectic (she rated herself 3 out of 5 on psychodynamic, 4 out of 5 on humanistic, and 3 out of 5 on cognitive behavioral orientations).

Client Background

Jane had been interred as a child in a displaced person camp; she had immigrated to the United States as a child with her father and sister after her mother died. Jane and her lesbian partner began couples therapy because they were arguing and were unhappy with each other. The partner had undergone a serious organ transplant a few years prior but was apparently functioning well again. Jane was angry because she was working full-time and maintaining the household, whereas Jane's perception was that her son and her partner were not doing their share of the chores.

Treatment

At the time of the interview, Dr. F had been working with Jane for about a year. Dr. F first saw Jane and her partner in couples therapy and then shifted to working individually with Jane.

During the couples therapy, Dr. F encouraged Jane to focus on herself instead of constantly doing so much for others. Jane began to realize she had been taking care of others (her children, her husband, her partner) all her life. She had been in Al-Anon and learned she was a codependent enabler and had to start focusing on herself more, but apparently, that message had not been internalized. Jane became aware that it was hard for her to stay with her own experience because her life felt empty without focusing on other people. She felt her life had no point if she was not caring for others and that she cared for others to avoid existential questions about meaning, getting old, and feeling dependent.

Dr. F asked Jane what would happen if she let her partner do some of the tasks. Then, because the partner seemed willing to take on more, Dr. F helped the two of them negotiate the tasks. When Jane let her partner do some of the cooking, however, she started feeling empty and as though life had no meaning.

At this point, Dr. F suggested a shift from couples therapy to individual therapy, during which Dr. F was able to help Jane become aware that her staying so busy was because of all her pain and emptiness. She gained insight that her fears about growing older and feeling vulnerable about no one being there to take care of her had roots in her childhood when she did not have a mother (e.g., she and her sister had to start making dinner from the age of 5).

As they explored, Jane cried a lot, and Dr. F helped her stay with her anger at her partner and son. As they did this, feelings of sadness emerged, and Dr. F helped Jane take responsibility for her part in the situation.

Once Jane was not as busy doing things and taking care of others all the time, she broke down and felt a lot of pain about her life. Jane talked about growing older and not seeing herself as competent and capable. In addition, she feared being dependent on others. Jane felt vulnerable and frequently wondered who was going to take care of her. Much of therapy consisted of allowing space for Jane to ask these questions and experience the related feelings.

Outcomes

Jane responded well to therapy. She felt understood and seemed to consider it a safe place. She began making more connections with her daughter and grandchildren and doing more pleasurable things for herself. When she reverted to a caretaking role with her son, Jane was able to remember the internalized voice of Dr. F challenging her.

CAN'T SLEEP ALONE

"Edna," a female client in her late 70s, sought therapy for anxiety. Dr. D, described earlier in "Need to Find Myself Again," also worked with this client.

Client Background

Edna was fit and in good shape physically and mentally. After having been unhappily married for many years with several children, Edna and her husband divorced because of problems related to his alcoholism. She got a good job working as an administrator for about 10 years and then went back to finish her undergraduate degree in health and obtain an advanced degree in the allied health field. At about the time she finished her undergraduate degree, her mother became terminally ill, so she moved back to be with her mother until she died. Most recently, she had been in a relationship with an older man. After living with him for 10 years, he died suddenly. Although her partner left her a trust fund so she could live in their house for the rest of her life, she still had major financial worries.

When Edna came to therapy about 6 months after her partner's death, she was extremely anxious. She did not know whether she should stay in the house or sell the house so she would have money to use for the rest of her life. She was also having trouble spending the night alone in the house. She spent a lot of nights with her married children in the area instead of spending time in her own place.

Edna was also grieving. She had loved her partner and had built her life around him. There was some regret that they had not gotten married because that would have made the financial concerns easier. Her grieving showed up as a lot of anxiety and fear. Her partner had been a secure base for her, and she felt insecure when he died.

The MIL issue for Edna was trying to figure out what she was going to do with the rest of her life. How was she going to make meaning in these last years of her life? There was a strong caretaker quality to her. She wondered whether she should go and take care of her ailing brother like she took care of her mother, and she wondered how she fit in with her adult children.

Treatment

Dr. D and Edna talked about MIL in terms of trying to figure out what she wanted to do with the rest of her life, especially in the context of her career. She was deciding whether she wanted to keep up seeing clients in her health practice because she did get meaning from that. Edna kept feeling anxiety about doing something. Each week she was hung up with thinking about a different place where she should move. Dr. D encouraged Edna to be patient and give herself time to grieve and not make any big decisions. Dr. D also encouraged Edna to talk in therapy about her partner and sort through his things.

Dr. D brought the topic around to MIL by allowing the client to be more in touch with her feelings and trust herself to make the right decision. One of the more specific strategies that seemed to be helpful was talking about how Edna had made good decisions regarding leaving her husband, leaving her comfortable job where she was making decent money, going back to school, and becoming a health care provider. They talked about all those situations in which Edna had relied on herself and explored what had motivated her to make those decisions.

To work on how Edna was going to make meaning in the future, Dr. D helped her explore the things that had been meaningful to her in the past and how she had derived meaning from these things. Dr. D also helped Edna realistically think about what it was that she wanted to do. Part of it was helping Edna take care of herself because in the past she had often focused on other people like her mother or her children rather than herself. She had to balance the need to take care of others and finding some meaning in that with finding something that was for her. The MIL issues were not urgent for Edna because she did not come to therapy wanting to work on it, so she and Dr. D worked on these issues in a more subtle way, by dealing with her anxiety and grieving first.

Outcomes

Edna was able to get in touch with her emotions, grieve the loss of her partner, and better cope with her loneliness. She was also able to trust herself to make the right decisions about whether to continue working and where to live because she recognized she had made good decisions in the past.

WHY AM I VOLUNTEERING?

"Alice" was a 66-year-old woman whose presenting problems were anxiety and feeling that nothing she did was good enough. Dr. E, described earlier in "White Collar Crime," also worked with this client.

Client Background

Alice volunteered a lot in her church but did not feel she was doing a good job with it. If the task was preparing meals, she said, "I'm not a good cook." If it was washing dishes, she said, "Anybody could do that." If it was singing in a choir, she said, "My voice isn't good enough for that." Clearly, she felt troubled about not measuring up and was comparing herself with other people.

Treatment

None of Dr. E's standard cognitive restructuring techniques (e.g., "What's the evidence? What's another way to look at it?") gave Alice any relief. So Dr. E changed tactics and asked Alice why she was not volunteering at anything else, such as Habitat for Humanity or nonsectarian organizations. In response, Alice paused and thought about why she volunteered at her church. As she told Dr. E about her beliefs in God, Alice realized that only when she was able to see she was serving her God did she get relief. She came back the next time after gaining this insight, and the symptoms were gone. When she walked into her house of worship, it was her and God, and it did not matter whether she sang well or had any particular skills.

Thus, Dr. E directly asked Alice to process the meaning of her work: "What meaning does this work have for you? You could volunteer at a school, or you could teach little kids how to read, but you're at a church, not a school—why?" The therapist guided the client to think through the big picture spiritual or meaning-seeking lens. He suggested that focusing on performance anxiety was focusing on the wrong thing. When a person is completely engaged in what they are doing and not how they are performing or whether they are good enough, they achieve a level of flow. In contrast, if they are occupied with whether they are doing well enough, the physiological response and affective outcome is going to be anxiety and central nervous system activation. Dr. E shifted Alice's attention from "Am I good enough; can I do well enough?" to "I have purpose and meaning, and I'm doing something that matters." It was no longer "I am a screw-up"; rather, it was now "I'm finding meaning from what I'm doing." Her thoughts changed from being focused on self and performance and social comparison to, "Wow, I'm just a teeny molecule in the universe. I'm doing all I can."

Before Dr. E shifted to working with meaning, he said that it was drudgery working with Alice. To everything he suggested, she said, "I've tried that." In contrast, working with MIL presented a perspective to which Alice was more receptive. The challenge was conceptualizing Alice in such a way that Dr. E could figure out how he could help her.

Outcomes

Once Alice felt her volunteering had meaning, she felt at peace with what she was doing. She still struggled with substantial anxiety, but with Dr. E's encouragement learned it was okay to quell her anxiety with prayer.

IS LIFE WORTH LIVING?

"Lanese" was an incest survivor in her mid-20s who had dissociative identity disorder. Dr. B, described earlier in "Life Review After a Heart Attack," also worked with this client.

Client Background

Lanese had an undergraduate degree and was holding down a job. She was functioning okay in her life at the time she started therapy, but she knew she had issues to work through related to trauma. She was socially isolated and was dealing with depression and occasional panic attacks. She had multiple disabilities, some of which were obvious and some that were not visible. The central message communicated to Lanese by her father both verbally and physically was that she did not have the right to exist. Her father told her at an early age that if he had known she was going to have a disability, he would have made sure she had not been born. Lanese attempted suicide five times in the first 2 years of psychotherapy (the therapy had been ongoing for 18 years). She felt suicidal with some frequency and wondered whether life was worth living. MIL was not a central concern when Lanese first started therapy, but it became more central for her over time.

During therapy, Lanese had a number of serious losses. Twice the apartment buildings in which she was living burned down, and she was left homeless without any possessions. She lost pets in one of the fires. She had a major aneurysm and nearly died; the recovery process was long and difficult, calling into question repeatedly whether it was worth it or whether she should just give up. She also had a chronic illness that shortened her life expectancy.

Treatment

Lanese spent a lot of time talking about the traumas she had experienced as a child. She was able to articulate and challenge some of the messages from her father and explore the fact that her mother never intervened. These periods involved intense memory work to help Lanese process her dissociated emotions. The goal was often just to help Lanese get through periods when she felt suicidal.

When Lanese was actively suicidal, Dr. B would remind her of things she had said in the past about what made life worth living. Lanese had recently called Dr. B when in an active suicidal thought process while working through an awful memory. Dr. B told her, "Look, I get that you're suicidal, but that's a permanent solution to a temporary problem." Dr. B also used cognitive behavioral interventions to help Lanese think more rationally, trying to get her not to act impulsively and to recognize the difference between a feeling and a behavior, helping her develop a tolerance for unpleasant emotions. He also helped her distinguish between there and then and here and now.

When they were not putting out fires in the client's life, the work had more of an existential feel. There were stretches of time when Lanese's life was a little calmer, and she was able to engage in reflection. She would bring up questions about whether she had a right to take up oxygen given the messages she had received from her father. She wrestled with these questions before the work began, and she brought them up fairly early on in the work; they would cycle back to them and take them on when she brought them up. For the most part, Dr. B just followed Lanese's lead when she raised the questions, using basic exploration type interventions to explore whether life was worth living. Dr. B also used values exploration, which Lanese found meaningful. Dr. B indicated that Lanese naturally gravitated toward the existential conversations because she was a deep thinker and quite bright. Dr. B typically followed the client's lead on existential issues.

The work was challenging because Dr. B sometimes got drawn into Lanese's despair, feeling he was responsible for keeping her alive. Dr. B was fairly sure that if Lanese had not been in therapy, she would have killed herself. And given the circumstances of her life, Dr. B occasionally wondered whether Lanese would have been better off and wondered whether he had anything to offer her. Dr. B felt it was meaningful work, but he rarely looked forward to seeing Lanese. It was difficult work, and he did not see a tremendous amount of progress.

Outcomes

The changes in the existential conversations were on a cognitive level. Lanese came to realize she had the right to exist and that the messages she heard as a kid were abusive and solely her father's agenda. By the end of therapy, Lanese knew these messages were a reflection of her father and not of her. That realization was a big change. The work helped her internalize that belief deeper and deeper so she did not feel guilty about existing. She was like many kids who are abused who believe that it is their fault or that something is wrong with them. She was able to refute those beliefs cognitively on her own, and the work helped her feel okay about who she was.

AN UNSATISFYING MARRIAGE

"Laurie," about 54 years old, had been in therapy off and on for 10 years with Dr. A (described earlier in "A Spiritual Journey After Retirement"). Laurie sought therapy because she was depressed.

Client Background

Laurie had three children who were close in age, and her work was demanding. She was unsure about what she wanted to be doing with her family and her work and had a lot going on in her life. She and her husband were not getting along, and the marriage was not satisfying.

During the therapy, Laurie became more involved with her children, stopped drinking, and changed jobs, but she continued to have difficulties in her relationship with her husband. Over time it became clear that Laurie and her husband saw life differently, wanted different things out of life, and approached people in their lives differently. In addition, Laurie believed in God, whereas her husband was an atheist. Laurie was caught in the struggle of wanting to live a life that felt more fulfilling to her and not wanting to disrupt the lives of her children because they were important to her. She was afraid that if she challenged her husband, they would not be able to resolve things, and she would have to leave him to live authentically with herself.

The specific MIL issue was that Laurie wanted to live a life that gave her a sense of satisfaction, meaning, and connection with what felt central to her core, which she described as having a lot of kindness toward people and valuing nature and beauty. She had been living her life in a way that matched what was important to her husband rather than what was important to her. Now that her children had left home, Laurie wanted to figure out how to live a life that felt more consistent with who she was and what mattered to her.

Treatment

Laurie talked about MIL in a tangential way, so Dr. A named the issues as looking for meaning, noting that Laurie was looking to be able to live consistently with what was important to her and her values. Having the label of the problem being related to meaning helped Laurie understand what she was struggling with and what created challenges for her. She and Dr. A were then able then to talk more directly and clearly about the things that were important to Laurie.

Outcomes

Dr. A said that Laurie found the exploration to be helpful. Laurie was able to talk more directly about the issues that were central to her and about how to live her life in a way that was more consistent with who she was.

Conclusion

Table 7.1 provides an overview of all the cases presented in this chapter. These cases have to be considered in context. Most of the clients were over 50 and thus may have been more sensitive to the topic of MIL than a younger sample of clients might have been. Several also had health concerns that made them aware of the brevity of life. Similarly, the therapists were over 50 years of age, had considerable experience conducting psychotherapy, and had done a lot of self-reflection about their own MIL issues. From our findings in a survey (Hill, 2016), it seems that experienced therapists are more comfortable than are therapists-in-training about dealing with MIL issues, perhaps because they have had the opportunity to come to terms with their own mortality and choices and thus are not so afraid of allowing clients to talk about these existential issues.

From these examples, it is clear that some clients come into psychotherapy directly and explicitly asking to work on MIL issues. This reflects the data from our survey (Hill, 2016) that about 12% of clients who had MIL concerns explicitly stated them when they started therapy. From these cases, we can see that some clients say they want to do a life review. Others say they want to figure out how to lead more meaningful lives, particularly after a health or near-death scare. Others have had their worlds collapse because of a relationship break-up, loss of a career, or a loss of identity. Thus, therapists can be attentive to explicit statements in the initial sessions about lack of meaning or searching for meaning.

Other clients come into therapy with other pressing concerns that have MIL as an implicit or underlying issue. For example, marital concerns, depression, and anxiety often have an underlying MIL component, but MIL often cannot be addressed until the pressing concern has been at least somewhat resolved. Interestingly, a major theme that arose in the implicit cases presented in this chapter was that of caretaking. Many of the female clients had cared for others all their lives and had neglected their interests and thus felt depleted and unworthy without the caretaking role. Therapists can help such clients examine their need to have their whole identity wrapped up in being caretakers and help them discover other aspects of themselves.

Furthermore, in working with clients for whom MIL is implicit, therapists can listen for underlying concerns related to MIL, label the concerns as MIL, and help

TABLE 7.1

Comparisons Across Cases

Case	Demographics of case	MIL concern	Therapeutic process related to MIL	Outcomes
Bruce and Dr. A: A spiritual journey after retirement	Client: 60-ish retired man; well-adjusted, having marital problems Therapist: 62-year-old woman PhD with psychodynamic/ humanistic orientation	Explicit: After retirement, client was facing death anxiety and wanted to make sure he had lived fully.	Therapist helped client explore MIL concerns, spirituality. Therapist challenged client about his interest in another woman and what that meant about his marriage; helped client gain insight about his struggles and need for meaning.	Client found therapy helpful, became clearer about spiritual struggles and what he wanted out of life.
Stuart and Dr. B: Life review after a heart attack	Client: 60-year-old man; stunted emotionally, with marital problems, alcoholism Therapist: 50-year-old male PhD with an integrative orientation	Explicit: Client experienced a huge scare after a heart attack and realized he wanted to live the rest of his life differently.	Focused on emotions, life review, dreamwork, encouraged creative expression, systems work, provided a rationale, dealt with resistance, treated alcohol problems. The emotions work was really more central than the life review, but emotion work helped client do the life review.	Client developed closer relationships with family and romantic partner. Accomplished life review and had a new sense of MIL.
Susan and Dr. C: If I'm not a nurse, who am I?	Client: 60-ish retired woman; with agoraphobia, anxiety Therapist: a 55-year-old woman PhD with a psychodynamic/ humanistic orientation	Explicit: Client lost her sense of meaning when she had heart attacks and had to quit her nursing career.	Focused on why client was living, examined religious beliefs, examined her work ethic, explored MIL, challenged, used humor, educated, used paradoxical interventions, provided strategies for creating meaning.	Client found new MIL in helping others, reconnected with her family, volunteered, overcame her anxiety.

Claudia and Dr. D: I need to find myself again	Client: 58-year-old professional woman; no serious pathology, having marital problems, emotional cut off, loss of identity) Therapist: 58-year-old female PhD with a humanistic orientation	Explicit: Client lost her sense of self given problems in relationships with partners, parents, and sister.	Explored lack of meaning, reconnected client with spirituality, helped client be more self-compassionate, encouraged client to do meditation, helped client recognize sources of meaning in relationships and work, worked on emotions, supported.	Client opened up, improved relationship with husband, began to live more fully, allowed self to have feelings
Donald and Dr. E: White collar crime	Client: middle-aged male physician accused of Medicare fraud; with depression, narcissistic personality disorder Therapist: 58-year-old male PhD with cognitive behavioral orientation	Explicit: Client lost his identity after losing his job, wealth, and wife.	Therapist answered client's questions, interpreted client's problem as a lack of meaning, understood client, normalized client's emotions, provided specific role-playing to help client get support from friends and family, used guided discovery to help client explore MIL.	Client became invested in therapy and trusted therapist more.
Jane and Dr. F: Blame it on the partner	Client: 73-year-old lesbian woman; having relationship problems Therapist: 59-year-old female PhD with an integrative orientation	Implicit: Client felt empty unless she took care of others.	Therapist encouraged client to take responsibility for her role in relationship problems. Therapist helped client and partner negotiate chores in relationship. Therapist helped client gain insight and acknowledge her own needs. Therapist helped client experience her feelings of anger, sadness, and pain.	Client felt understood; considered therapy a safe place. Client began making more connections with her daughter and grandchildren. Client began doing more pleasurable things for herself. Client was able to internalize voice of therapist to challenge self.

(*continues*)

TABLE 7.1 (*Continued*)

Comparisons Across Cases

Case	Demographics of case	MIL concern	Therapeutic process related to MIL	Outcomes
Edna and Dr. D: Can't sleep alone	Client: woman in late 70s; experiencing anxiety and grief Therapist: 58-year-old female PhD with a humanistic orientation	Implicit: Deciding what to do with rest of life after death of husband and mother and possible retirement.	Therapist encouraged client to be patient and give herself time to grieve and not make any big decisions about what to do with her life. Therapist encouraged the client to talk about her partner and to go through his things. Therapist allowed client to get in touch with her feelings and trust herself to make good decisions, noting that she had made good decisions in the past. Therapist helped client explore motivations for past decisions, what was meaningful in the past, and what she wanted to do, particularly balancing caring for others and caring for self.	Client was able to get in touch with and grieve the loss of husband and cope with loneliness. She was also able to trust herself to make decisions about whether to continue working and where to live.
Alice and Dr. E: Why am I volunteering?	Client: middle aged woman; experiencing anxiety and feeling that nothing she did was good enough Therapist: 58-year-old male PhD with cognitive behavioral orientation	Implicit: Client did not feel she was doing anything important with her life.	Therapist started with cognitive restructuring techniques to help client challenge her depression and low self-esteem. Therapist then shifted to helping client examine the meaning involved in her volunteering.	Once client felt that her volunteering had meaning, she felt at peace with what she was doing. She learned to quell her anxiety with prayer.

Lanese and D. B: Is life worth living?	Client: young adult woman; incest survivor, with dissociative identity disorder, socially isolated, depression, occasional panic attacks Therapist: 50-year-old male PhD with an integrative orientation	Implicit: Questions about whether life is worth living.	Therapist helped client explore childhood traumas and process dissociated emotions. Therapist supported client through suicidal periods. Therapist reminded client of things she had said in the past about what made life worth living. Therapist reminded client that suicide was a permanent solution to a temporary problem. Therapist used cognitive behavioral interventions to help client to think more rationally, to not act impulsively, and to recognize differences between feelings and behaviors. Therapist helped client develop tolerance for unpleasant emotions. When there were not crises, therapist helped client engage in reflection about suffering and whether life was worth living. Therapist used values clarification.	Client came to realize that she had the right to exist and that messages she received as a child were abusive. By end of therapy, client knew that messages were a reflection of her father and not her. She internalized the belief that she did not feel guilty about existing. Client was able to refute beliefs that abuse was her fault. Client felt okay about who she was.
Laurie and Dr. A: An unsatisfying marriage	Client: 54-year-old woman; experiencing depression, bad marital relationship Therapist: 62-year-old female PhD with psychodynamic/humanistic orientation	Implicit: Did client have the right to live life according to her wishes and values or did she have to submit to her husband's values and wishes?	Therapist named the client's issues as involving MIL, noting that client wanted to be able to live consistently with her values. Naming the issues helped Laurie understand what she was struggling with and what created challenges for her. Therapist and client were then able to talk more directly and clearly about what was important to client.	Client was able to talk more directly about central issues about how to live her life more consistently with who she was.

Note. MIL = Meaning in life.

clients begin to explore. Perhaps by just calling attention to the idea of MIL, clients are more able to focus on it. Many people do not have the label, perhaps because we are socialized to think so much about symptoms rather than quality of life issues. Once they are labeled as such, though, clients can begin to focus on this important aspect of life.

It is important to note that the therapeutic relationship was good in all cases, which is not surprising given that we asked for successful cases in the research study. It makes sense that a solid therapeutic relationship is needed for clients to feel safe to explore deep existential anxieties. In the explicit cases, talking about MIL concerns probably helped build the relationship. In the implicit cases, there probably had to be some resolution of the initial problems and clients probably had to trust the therapist to shift from focusing on the presenting concerns to going to the deeper existential levels.

Similarly, outcomes were good across cases, which again is not surprising given that we asked therapists to talk about successful cases. Interestingly, however, the outcomes differed substantially across cases (e.g., improved interpersonal relationships, reduced anxiety, peace, new perspectives), reflecting the diversity of the presenting concerns. It was also interesting that in only a couple of cases did therapists explicitly label the outcomes as involving increased meaning in life or its subcomponents (e.g., purpose). These cases thus provide some anecdotal evidence that a focus of MIL in psychotherapy is at least sometimes helpful.

Interpersonal relationships were a focus in almost all the cases, in terms of causing problems when there were dysfunctions and also in terms of providing meaning. These results make sense and fit with the literature that shows that most people indicate interpersonal relationships are an important source of meaning. For example, Halusic and King (2013) cited research showing that participants spontaneously nominated family or friends as the most important source of meaning in their lives and stated that relationships are an even more fundamental source of meaning than is religion. They reasoned that if "MIL is a fundamental human need, it would make sense that people would turn to close others to satisfy that need, as people tend to look to their community to satisfy most if not all of their fundamental needs" (p. 449). They believed that people feel they are a part of something greater than themselves when they feel a part of the community, and communities transfer cultural beliefs that give order and provide a sense of predictability. Halusic and King (2013) suggested that "people who have environments that support their growth and the realization of their potentials should have more frequent experiences with idiosyncratic sources of meaning and therefore should experience life as more meaningful" (p. 451). Long-term therapy is an excellent place to work on troubled relationships given that a primary component of therapy is the therapeutic relationship (Horvath, Del Re, Fluckiger, & Symonds, 2011).

Interestingly, spirituality was a clear focus for at least three of the explicit cases and one of the implicit cases. These results suggest the utility of helping some clients explore meaning related to spirituality.

Finally, another point that arises from an examination of these cases conducted by experienced therapists is that there are many approaches to working with MIL, including psychodynamic, existential, humanistic, cognitive-behavioral, and integrative. Each therapist approached the topic in different ways, especially by being responsive to the needs of the individual client. Thus, although we can provide some general guidelines as we did in Chapters 5 and 6, it is important to stress that therapists have to be prepared and well-trained for working with MIL but then have to be able to modify their approach to be responsive to the individual client.

In sum, these cases as described by experienced therapists have much to teach us about working with MIL in psychotherapy. MIL work is varied and complex depending on the individual client and therapist.

Multicultural and Ethical Considerations in Working With Meaning in Life in Psychotherapy

8

> Challenging the meaning of life is the truest expression of the state of being human.
>
> —Victor Frankl, *Man's Search for Meaning*

Imagine you are working with a client who is dying of cancer and questioning whether her life had any meaning and is considering suicide. To work effectively with this client, you would have to take cultural and ethical considerations into account. You would need to know about her religious values, you would need to know your ethical obligations regarding how to deal with the suicide threat, and you would need to be aware of values differences so that you do not impose your values about suicide and living a meaningful life—whatever they may be—on her.

This example illustrates that multicultural and ethical considerations have to be taken into account in working with meaning in life (MIL). Therapists must thus be trained and prepared for working with anyone who might walk through their door; they should also be trained and prepared to work specifically with MIL and should be trained in multicultural and ethical issues both generally and in relation to MIL. In particular, therapists need knowledge about MIL, culture, and ethics; they need skills to assess and conceptualize clients as well as to facilitate client exploration, insight, and action; and they need to develop a facilitative attitude to embrace differences in MIL across cultures.

http://dx.doi.org/10.1037/0000083-010
Meaning in Life: A Therapist's Guide, by C. E. Hill

Multicultural Considerations in Working With Meaning in Life in Psychotherapy

Meaning depends on what culture(s) one is exposed to (see also Chapter 2). As an example, if you grew up in India, you probably were exposed to ideas about universalism and putting family first when developing meaning, whereas if you grew up in the United States, you may have been exposed to the idea that you should develop your meaning for yourself individually.

When developing our meaning, we start with the influence of our parents, then become exposed to peers who may have different values, and then typically move on to learning about other cultures and people as we become adults and as our cognitive capacities increase. As adults, we have the opportunity to evaluate what we have been exposed to and decide what values we choose to hold onto, although we are always heavily influenced by early cultural teaching. Thus, all of our thinking about MIL is necessarily embedded in what we have been exposed to in our culture(s).

PERSONAL REFLECTIONS EXERCISE

To prepare for this section, take a minute to think about your cultures, given that all of us have many aspects to our cultures. Use the following questions to identify what your cultures are. Mark which aspects of your culture seem most salient to you when you think about MIL:

- What races or ethnicities are you?
- What are your national and regional origins?
- What is your relationship status?
- What is your parenting status?
- What kind of family values and beliefs did you grow up with?
- In what cultures did your mother grow up?
- In what cultures did your father grow up?
- How similar are you to your mother or father in terms of values?
- What developmental experiences influenced your worldview?
- How have you changed since childhood regarding your values and beliefs? How have these values and beliefs been informed by your family, and how do they differ? What experiences caused you to shift?
- What is your age cohort?
- What, if any, physical, intellectual, or developmental disabilities do you have?
- What is your religion or spirituality?
- What is your socioeconomic status (lower, middle, upper class)? How is your socioeconomic status different from when you were growing up?
- How do you identify in terms of gender and sexual orientation?
- What are your political affiliations?
- What groups, clans, or tribes do you most identify with (think of religious, professional, or neighborhood groups)?

Now consider how these cultural variables influence your thinking about MIL. Note that you could have received different messages from different parts of your culture (e.g., from one's religion vs. one's professional affiliation). Consider the following:

- What messages did you receive about MIL as you were growing up?
- What values are placed on searching for, reflecting on, prioritizing, and having MIL in your cultures?
- In your cultures, is MIL constructed by the individual, is it to be discovered from outside oneself, or is it a given that one must conform to?
- How consistent are your beliefs about MIL across the different aspects of your cultural inheritance?

For me (see the Prologue to this volume), growing up in a religious home led to my initially developing meaning through religion, but then learning to think for myself and my training as a psychologist led me to change my thoughts about MIL. Had I been African American or a child of immigrants from China, I certainly would have had different meaning. My colleague from Korea, Professor Eunsun Joo, gave the example of how Koreans do the "right thing" their whole lives and then are suddenly lost when they retire; as a result, there is a high suicide rate among Korean elders.

THEORY ABOUT CULTURE AND MEANING IN LIFE

In their writing about meaning and culture, Chao and Kesebir (2013) relied on Baumeister's (1991) definition of *meaning* ("Shared mental representations of possible relationships among things, events, and relationships"; p. 15), which aligns with our coherence component of MIL. They then went on to define culture as a "shared network of meaning that is produced, distributed, and reproduced among a group of interconnected individuals" (p. 317). Thus, for them, culture is a network of meaning, including norms, values, and beliefs that are sustained by members of the culture and in cultural institutions and practices. For example, news, fairy tales, urban legends, architecture, and art all provide evidence of one's culture.

There are two types of meaning, according to Chao and Kesebir (2013), both of which are imparted and influenced by culture. *Small-m* meaning involves comprehensibility, or detecting and expecting patterns or associations (e.g., Thursday follows Wednesday, rules about social interactions). *Capital-M*-meaning involves matters of significance and worth and how things fit into larger values and meaning systems (e.g., contemplating MOL [meaning *of* life] and MIL).

Thus, Chao and Kesebir (2013) concluded that meaning and culture are intertwined in that "culture rests on meaning, whereas meaning exists and is propagated in culture" (p. 317). Thus, the pursuit of meaning occurs within the context of culture, and the act of defining and redefining meaning (largely through language) helps to redefine the culture. In other words, everything we think about MIL is constrained by what we have learned within our culture, but we also help to push the limits of culture by thinking in new ways about meaning.

Chao and Kesebir (2013) said that like fish in water, our meaning systems surround us and influence us. We are often so used to these meaning systems, however, that we are not even aware they exist. We thus view our world through our cultural lenses regardless of whether we are aware of them, such that we often cannot even imagine initially living other ways. For example, when I first visited Taiwan I was struck by the obvious awareness that the Taiwanese have different customs and beliefs and that there are other ways to live; yet at the same time, I was impressed by some fundamental similarities especially in terms of emotions.

Many of our cultural meanings are invisible, taken for granted, and not even questioned (Kitayama & Markus, 2000). For example, we might be so accustomed to gender roles that we do not even question whether there are other possibilities. Although cultures are often invisible, they are also diverse and dynamic and constantly under construction, as people participate in building and changing culture (Chao & Kesebir, 2013).

According to Chao and Kesebir (2013), cultures exist because of adaptive survival functions (e.g., in some cultures in which people do not conform with the cultural proscriptions, they are shunned and die; Frank & Frank, 1991). Basic human needs are met through the cultural ability to use, communicate, and transmit meaning. Psychological needs are met through culture by providing a sense of self-worth to those who fit the societal norms, rules, standards, ideals, and ideologies. Cultures that are insistent on members following the cultural norms are considered *tight cultures* (e.g., Japan), whereas cultures that are more heterogeneous and tolerant of deviation are *loose cultures* (e.g., the United States; Triandis, 1989). It is important to note that people tend to follow cultural norms more closely when their meaning systems and existential security are threatened. By conforming to the norms at such times, people gain a sense of existential security and have a sense of self-worth and meaning.

Perhaps the major cultural construct that distinguishes cultures is the universal (collectivist) versus individual (Tummala-Narra, 2016). The emphasis in many Eastern and African cultures is on the family, focused on harmony, collectivism, and respecting elders. In contrast, the emphasis is on the individual for many European and American cultures. So, for example, a universal or collectivist perspective is that young people should succeed for the glory of the family and should not focus as much on their own needs. Women, for example, may not be allowed to have much autonomy in the collectivist cultures (e.g., women in the Sudanese culture are not expected to get an education or come up with their own meaning). In an individualistic culture, by contrast, the young person is expected to grow up and leave home and achieve independence and autonomy, and men and women are often allowed to have equal rights. Constructing one's own sense of MIL is expected more often in an individualistic than in a universalistic society. Conversely, accepting the family's definition of meaning is more expected in Eastern cultures.

Another relevant point is that spirituality and religion are more likely to be viewed as appropriate ways to cope with problems in living in some cultures than others. For example, Hines and Boyd-Franklin (2005) described how religion has been important for African Americans since the time of slavery as a way of dealing with so much suffering. In contrast, church attendance has been dropping rapidly in Europe.

Another important cultural difference involves psychotherapy more specifically. Different cultures have different views about mental illness and mental health. In some areas of rural India, for example, people who are what we might label schizophrenic are allowed to live freely in the community and are given small jobs even if the parents pay for the opportunity for them to work so they can feel like valued members of the community. In contrast, in the United States, people with schizophrenia are shunned and relegated to mental hospitals or group homes or to living under bridges. Another example is that Eastern cultures value "being" in terms of mental health, whereas the American culture values doing or achieving (Yalom, 1980). Relatedly, different cultures and religions have different views about death (e.g., burial vs. cremation) and what happens after death (e.g., that the only life is here on earth vs. the existence of an afterlife).

Another cultural difference involves customs around meals. Some cultures (e.g., French) value spending long hours socializing with family and friends over meals, whereas in other cultures (e.g., North America) meals are often eaten quickly and alone while working. Another example is that North American individuals tend to project their emotions onto others (e.g., "If I feel angry, others must feel angry too"), whereas East Asians project complementary emotions onto others (e.g., "I feel angry, and others are fearful"; Cohen & Gunz, 2002).

Relatedly, although facial expressions of basic emotions are universal, the rules about how and when emotions should be displayed vary across cultures (Matsumoto & Ekman, 1989). In one study, Olympic Games athletes initially all showed universal microexpressions of joy when they won and sadness or contempt when they were defeated, but later displays of emotions were governed by cultural norms, with strict emotional regulation for athletes from collectivist cultures and more open expression for athletes from individualistic cultures (Matsumoto & Willingham, 2006; Matsumoto, Yoo, & Fontaine, 2008).

Interestingly, the motivation to seek meaning and positive regard seems to be universal, but the way that these motives are achieved varies across cultures (Chao & Kesebir, 2013). Some Eastern people might seek to gain meaning by pleasing family rather than self, whereas others in more Western cultures might seek to gain meaning by enhancing self rather than others.

SPECIFIC CULTURAL EXAMPLES RELATED TO MEANING

To illustrate the influence of culture, I provide two examples. Many more could be offered, but these two serve as a starting point.

Young, Straight Adult Working Class Men

A perhaps surprising group that has been written about recently as particularly having problems with meaning, are straight, White, working class, young adult men (Levant & Wong, 2017; O'Neil, 2015; Thompson & Bennett, 2015; Y. J. Wong, Ho, Wang, & Miller, 2017). Although once the most privileged group, these young adult men are now struggling with both physical and mental problems. Their unemployment level is far higher than the rest of the adult population. Alcoholism, substance abuse, and suicide are at epidemic levels, with some calling these *despair deaths*. Cultural changes appear to be influencing these changes because these men feel they have no place in our society and sense that their masculinity is under attack. Gender norms that encouraged them to be tough, dominant, self-reliant, not emotionally expressive, and avoidant of traditionally feminine behaviors no longer work for them, leaving these men depressed, anxious, and stressed. New methods are needed to help these men find meaning, especially given that traditional verbal psychotherapy is not typically well-received by them. The book *Hillbilly Elegy* (Vance, 2016) provides a moving account of one man's journey away from the lower socioeconomic class and into the upper classes through hard work and an Ivy League education, the stress such a shift imposed, and how he was still left with the remnants of his early life.

Japanese Versus American Young Adults

As noted earlier, Asian and Western cultures are quite different, particularly in that Asians adhere more to a universalist position of regarding family and others first, whereas Americans strive toward independence. Steger, Kawabata, Shimai, and Otake (2008) suggested that because meaning is derived within the context of culture and culture is an important source of values, expectations, needs, and meaning, we would expect differences between Asian and American scores on measures of meaning. O'Donnell, Shim, Barenz, and Steger (2014) summarized related cross-cultural research using the Meaning in Life Questionnaire (Steger, Frazier, Oishi, & Kaler, 2006; see also Chapter 11, this volume, for more description of this measure). Interestingly, in studies in the United States, scores on the Presence scale were on average higher than scores on the Search scale, and the two scales were negatively related. In contrast, in Asian samples, Search scores were higher than Presence scores, and the two scales were positively related. Steger et al. (2008) suggested that the difference in the results might be because of the individualistic and analytical cognitive style in the West compared to the collectivist and dialectical style in the East.

These results also suggest that Presence and Search might be interpreted and valued differently in Asian versus Western cultures. Steger et al.'s (2008) explanation for these findings was that people in an independent culture find it important to feel good about themselves and thus think they have meaning and do not need to search for it. They suggested that searching for meaning and not thinking you have meaning is more socially accepted in Japan than in America. Steger et al. suggested that Japanese people are more comfortable with contradictions than are Americans because they think in a more holistic or dialectical manner.

IMPLICATIONS FOR PSYCHOTHERAPY

It is profoundly important for the therapeutic endeavor that we can never understand another person's culture and background completely. We only see others through the lens of our own experiences. It is easy to make assumptions about others, either that they are like us (the ingroup) or not like us (the outgroup). The reality of cultural differences has several major implications for therapists.

Increase Cultural Awareness

We can increase our cultural awareness and cultural competence, or our ability to navigate among cultures. Knowledge, skills, and awareness are all important when talking about cultural competence (D. W. Sue et al., 1982; S. Sue, 1998). Therapists have to understand different meaning systems, be aware of our assumptions and assumptions in other cultures, and act in appropriate ways so we can help clients from different cultures.

Chao and Kesebir (2013) noted that being exposed to different cultural traditions increases one's awareness of the role of culture in thoughts and behaviors, such that one can begin to interpret the world through different cultural lenses. Thus, much as bilingual people can switch between languages, a multiculturally aware person could switch between meaning systems when appropriate. For example, one might stress harmony more with clients from Chinese culture, whereas one might stress individuality more with clients from a North American culture. Of course, mental health professionals would not automatically apply such cultural rules but would check with clients about their needs, reactions, and perceptions, thus recognizing the vast heterogeneity among individuals within cultural groups.

It is also important for therapists to note, as discussed earlier in this chapter, that when one's identity and values are under threat, individuals hold on to the meaning structures more tightly and react against others. This construct is similar to countertransference (Gelso & Hayes, 2007) and suggests that when therapists' issues are brought to the surface, they well could act out against the needs of clients.

Therapists must become knowledgeable about other cultures. To become familiar and comfortable with other cultures, therapists can

- live in or travel to other countries,
- read novels or watch movies about other cultures,
- talk with people from other countries and ask about their experiences,
- read the abundant professional literature about culture (e.g., Comas-Díaz, 2012; Hays, 2016; McGoldrick, 2008; Tummala-Narra, 2015),
- attend workshops (e.g., many states in the United States now require continuing education focused on culture), and
- obtain supervision or consultation with someone from another culture and/or someone who is knowledgeable about other cultures.

Importantly, therapists should not assume that all stereotypes or features of a given culture fit a specific person. For example, just because a client says she or he is Muslim does not mean that the particular client espouses a particular view on MIL. It is always useful to remember that differences among groups are larger than differences between groups (i.e., there are more differences among men and women than there are differences between men and women) and to remember that people come from multiple cultures, some with conflicting values. Thus, after familiarizing oneself with stereotypes about cultures, therapists must remain open to learning about the individual's unique culture.

Use Culturally Appropriate Skills

In terms of specific therapeutic skills, my experience presenting talks around the world is that exploration skills (e.g., open questions, reflections of feelings) seem to be fairly universally valued, albeit to different degrees according to theoretical orientation. In contrast, people seem to have very different reactions to the insight and action stages according to their culture. Here, I focus on some potential differences for therapist use of direct guidance and immediacy.

In terms of direct guidance, some cultures want the therapist to be the expert and provide direct guidance, whereas other cultures prefer that the therapist facilitate clients' coming to their own conclusions. In Hill (1989), I provided a poignant example of problems that occurred when a female Chinese client wanted direct guidance from her African American therapist who preferred psychodynamic techniques. Joo, Hill, and Kim (2017) noted that although Korean clients often explicitly ask for direct guidance, they do not want to be told what to do but rather want to be offered suggestions and encouraged to arrive at their own conclusions.

Immediacy refers to talking about the therapy or the therapeutic relationship directly in the here and now. Although proscribed in many cultures (e.g., Asian), talking openly about the relationship can be helpful for clarifying expectations and resolving problems if therapists are mindful of adjusting the flow of the discussion to the comfort level of the client (see Hill, Spangler, Jackson, & Chui, 2014; Spangler et al., 2014).

Attend Directly to Culture in Relation to Meaning in Life

Therapists can listen attentively to clues about culture in what clients talk about in general and more specifically in relation to MIL. Therapists can also ask directly about the influence of culture in terms of the client's MIL. For example, if an Iranian woman is reluctant to discuss MIL, the therapist might ask how MIL is viewed for women in her culture.

Have Culturally Appropriate Attitudes

In terms of attitudes, the most important is perhaps an openness to different cultures and worldviews. People are endlessly interesting, and one of the benefits of being a therapist is getting a chance to experience vicariously what other people's lives are like. Rogers (1957) gave us the notions of nonjudgmentalness and unconditional positive regard, which enable us to listen and encourage the client without judging.

A recently developed construct that has great relevance is cultural humility, which involves taking an other-oriented stance, being open to explore identities and experiences, and trying to understand the client's reality (Hook, Davis, Owen, Worthington, & Utsey, 2013). The emphasis is on being curious and open. Intrapersonally, it involves a willingness and openness to reflect on oneself as an embedded human being and having an awareness of one's limitations in understanding others' cultural background and viewpoints. Interpersonally, it involves an other-oriented approach with regard to aspects of an individual's cultural background and identity as a way of understanding, being respectful and considerate of a person's experiences, being genuinely interested in understanding the person's perspective, not acting in a superior manner, and not assuming that much is already known about this person. Recent research has shown that clients' perceptions of their therapist's cultural humility were positively related to the working alliance and perceived improvement in therapy across a broad range of domains (Hook et al., 2013, 2016).

Ethical Considerations in Working With Meaning in Life in Psychotherapy

Because existential issues are fundamental human issues involving values and choices, ethical issues are certain to arise in working with clients. Thus, therapists need to not only be aware of their own biases and beliefs but also to be knowledgeable about ethical standards (see *Ethical Principles of Psychologists and Code of Conduct*; American Psychological Association, 2017). Ethical principles for therapists (see Chapter 3 of Hill, 2014, for more detail) include the ideas of *autonomy* (i.e., the right of the client to make choices and take actions, as long as these do no harm), *beneficence* (i.e., the intent of the therapist to do good and to be committed to the growth and development of clients), *nonmaleficence* (i.e., ensuring that our interventions and actions do not hurt others), *justice* (i.e., believing in fairness and equality of opportunities and resources for everyone), *fidelity* (i.e., keeping promises and being trustworthy in relationships), and *veracity* (i.e., telling the truth).

I hope all therapists will take the ideas of ethical standards seriously. These are not standards imposed on us by stern overlords but rather aspirations our communities have crafted and agreed on to guide us in difficult situations. They represent the wisdom of many therapists who have struggled with these issues and often learned from having lived through painful situations. When we as therapists are faced with difficult issues for the first time, we often do not know how to respond. By having studied these principles and learned from the experiences of others in advance, we are more likely to be able to handle situations thoughtfully when they occur and engage in good decision making. Importantly, ethical guidelines cannot address the specifics of any given situation completely because situations that arise are often complex and idiosyncratic. Rather, therapists are expected to work through ethical dilemmas systematically by applying the ethical principles and seeking consultation.

In this section, I describe two ethical concerns that seem most related to working with clients about MIL: (a) clashes in values and (b) competence. I then briefly describe a model of ethical decision making.

VALUES CLASHES IN WORKING WITH MEANING IN LIFE

The primary ethical concern in working with MIL involves a clash of values between the therapist and client. Consider the following scenarios:

- Your client is Catholic and believes that his meaning comes from God, whereas you are an atheist and believe that meaning must be constructed.
- You are a professional woman who obtains much of your meaning from your career, whereas your female client spends much of her time shopping and pleasing her husband, who dominates her and does not allow her to have any independent thoughts.
- Your client is angry, wants revenge on his brother who he feels wronged him, and is collecting guns and planning an attack because that would make him feel like a man, whereas you do not believe in guns or violence.
- Your client is dying but refuses treatment that might help her live and wants help with assisted suicide, whereas you believe in the sanctity of life.
- Your client is on a crusade to close the borders of the country and deport all illegal immigrants, whereas you believe your country has a moral duty to welcome immigrants.
- Your client supported a political candidate whom you opposed.
- Your client wants to abolish abortion, whereas you firmly believe in a woman's right to choose what happens with her body.
- Your client has no interest in meaning or insight and just wants to coast along in life without much direction (could be considered existentially indifferent), whereas you believe people should find a sense of meaning in their lives.

All these situations pose ethical dilemmas. Should you impose your values about religion, whether meaning is discovered or constructed, the roles of women and men, the sanctity of life, immigration, abortion, sexuality, and meaning and insight (not to mention global climate change, nutrition, exercise, communication, relationships, arts and entertainment, etc.)? How do you navigate helping a client when their values so clearly differ from your own?

The ethical principle of autonomy is implicated here. Clients have the right to choose how they want to live their lives, as long as they do not harm others (There is an ethical obligation to warn if the client is in danger of harming self or other.). Our role as therapists is to provide a listening ear so that clients can thoroughly explore their thoughts and feelings and think about the antecedents of these thoughts and feelings (particularly in terms of family values and experiences), help them think about current stressors and relationships, help them think through the possible consequences, and help them figure out what they want to do in terms of MIL. These are client-centered objectives and require us as therapists to facilitate clients in becoming aware of and accepting their instincts.

However, when clients have different opinions, values, and choices, we often feel conflicted and anxious. Our thinking and values are challenged and threatened. We might feel a need to convince the client to alleviate our conflicts and shore up our beliefs. Furthermore, client's choices are sometimes self-defeating or potentially harmful to others and society, so we have to consider what our obligations are to our communities.

What can we do with the anxiety and confusion raised when clients have different opinions, even though we are supposed to encourage them to think for themselves? Introspection, personal therapy, supervision, and consultation are invaluable in raising self-awareness. Self-awareness helps us keep a balance and enables us to determine what issues are the client's and what issues are our own. Self-awareness thus helps us stay out of the way so that clients can find a solution to their problems with our support. Furthermore, consultation helps us determine what to do when clients' choices are in opposition to the "societal good." I particularly recommend consulting with professional organizations and licensing bodies in such situations to help determine your ethical and legal obligations.

COMPETENCE TO HELP CLIENTS WHO HAVE MEANING-IN-LIFE CONCERNS

A related fundamental ethical assumption is that we should be competent to help our clients with their concerns. Being competent requires that we have knowledge, skills, and awareness related to the topics under consideration. Thus, for MIL, therapists have to know the literature about MIL, have skills to work with it, and be aware of their own issues related to the topic. In addition, because MIL is implicated in so many other problems (e.g., depression, career concerns) and these vary by culture, therapists also have to have knowledge, skills, and awareness about these other concerns and about culture. Therapists also have to think about the intersectionality of all these variables because they so clearly are not separate variables. Reading theory and research related to these topics is a beginning; supervision and personal therapy can then help therapists apply the literature to individual clients.

COPING WITH ETHICAL CHALLENGES

The current thinking about ethical challenges is that it is how you think about the challenges that matters rather than having the answer about the "right" way to handle the ethical situation (Knapp, Youngren, VanderCreek, Harris, & Martin, 2015). Therapists thus have to incorporate the aspirational ethical guidelines into their personal guidelines and think through each ethical situation as it arises. Therapists can engage in reading, personal therapy, supervision, and consultation to gather information and think through the ethical dilemma. It is important to emphasize that we cannot remove values from our work because it is not possible and it would result in a sterile, meaningless approach. Rather, we have to be aware of our values and not impose them on clients. As an example, I heard a talk by a Christian therapist who freely admitted that she based her work on Christian values. She did not demand that clients agree with her but thought they had a right to know her values. Because of her openness about her values, Christians may have felt comfortable seeking help from her, but others might not have.

One model of ethical decision making I have found useful is the A-B-C-D-E model (Sileo & Kopala, 1993). To describe this model, let us take the example of a married male client who wants to have an affair, but who you strongly believe is obsessing about another woman as a means of avoiding dealing with his own mid-life crisis.

- In the *assessment* step, you work to identify the ethical dilemma in terms of the client's status and resources and your values and feelings (e.g., the client is a well-adjusted adult in a dysfunctional marital relationship that he has little interest in exploring; you have a strong reaction to the idea of this client having an affair, and you feel a little impatient that your client does not value probing deeper into his marital relationship).
- In the *benefits* step, you evaluate what is most likely to benefit the client, the therapeutic relationship, and significant others (e.g., the client might initially feel excited about having an affair, but you worry that there would be a disruption to his marital relationship, and you worry that he is looking to you for affirmation of his choices rather than thinking them through).
- In the *consequences and consultation* step, you consider the consequences that could result from the possible actions. You might consult with a supervisor who could help you sort through the ethical, legal, emotional, and therapeutic concerns (e.g., the supervisor helps you identify that your strong reactions to the client might be due to countertransference related to your father's having multiple affairs when you were a child and suggests that you go back to therapy to help you understand those values about relationships so that you do not act out with your client and to ponder your concerns about MIL; the supervisor also helps you become aware that it is important for you not to impose your values on your client).
- In the *duty* step, you consider to whom you have a duty (e.g., in this case, it is fairly obvious that your duty is to your client rather than to the wife, although there might be a duty to warn if the client was threatening the wife with physical violence).
- Finally, in the *education* step, you review what you have learned about ethics to make sure you are doing the right thing. Hence, in this situation, the ethical course of action for you as a therapist is to work on your countertransference concerns in your own therapy to maximize your ability to listen to the client, treat him respectfully, and tailor your interventions to help him think about his choices.

Conclusion

Therapists have to be aware of multicultural and ethical considerations in working with MIL in psychotherapy. They can immerse themselves in the literature about multiculturalism and ethics and learn all they can about these topics. In addition, therapists can learn about the specific multicultural and ethical concerns from the individual client and modify the treatment to be responsive to that client's needs. Therapists can also profit from introspection, personal therapy, supervision, and consultation when issues related to multiculturalism and ethics related to MIL arise. But we also have to be careful not to stereotype individuals from different cultures on the basis of our research because that can be just as discriminating as having no knowledge about different cultures. All of us have cultural insensitivities and ethical lapses, so the intent here is not to blame and criticize but to help all of us grow in awareness so that we can be better people and better therapists. These are certainly not easy issues, and all of us are constantly struggling to become more aware and sensitive.

9 Finding Meaning in Life
A Self-Help Guide

> The meaning of life is not to be discovered only after death in some hidden, mysterious realm; on the contrary, it can be found by eating the succulent fruit of the Tree of Life and by living in the here and now as fully and creatively as we can.
>
> —Paul Kurtz, *Toward a New Enlightenment: The Philosophy of Paul Kurtz*

This self-help model for working with meaning in life (MIL) is similar to the model presented in Chapter 5 for therapists working with clients on MIL. The major difference, of course, is that you are doing it on your own without the opportunity to discuss it with someone who can help you challenge your ideas and give you a different (though not necessarily more valid) perspective. As with dream work (Hill, 2014), I think that working on your own to find meaning makes sense and is indeed what most of us do, but I strongly urge self-helpers to seek professional help when they get stuck (e.g., cannot think of ideas), ruminate too much (e.g., obsess about the "right" answer), sink into despair and cannot see a way out (e.g., become anxious or depressed about there not being a meaning of life), or would just enjoy talking with another person who is also dedicated to reflecting about meaning (of course, finding a good therapist is key to making therapy productive).

http://dx.doi.org/10.1037/0000083-011
Meaning in Life: A Therapist's Guide, by C. E. Hill

Preliminary Steps

In preparation for working on MIL using a self-help approach, I start with two suggestions. First, get prepared. Second, assess where you are currently regarding MIL.

READ THROUGH THE WHOLE BOOK

Having knowledge about the topic of MIL can be invaluable as a starting point. As you read this book, engage thoroughly with the text: Write questions about what you read, determine which ideas you like, and challenge the ideas you dislike. Focus particularly on Chapters 4 through 8 to get an idea of what the therapeutic process would look like and hear stories of other people who have struggled with this topic. Also, read this whole chapter before starting so you have a road map of what this self-help project might entail.

ASSESSMENT OF LEVEL OF SELF-AWARENESS

I particularly recommend taking the Meaning in Life Measure (MILM) and comparing your results with published data (see Chapter 11). You can also assess your goals for life by writing down possible goals and evaluating how you are doing now on these goals and your aspirations. Another helpful activity would be to write an obituary for what you imagine you would like to have said about you at the end of your life. In addition, you can create a timeline where you indicate the year you were born and the year you project that you might die, with important markers in between (e.g., marriage, children). Finally, you can make a list of things that bring you pleasure versus things that bring you meaning. Once you have completed these exercises, it might be helpful to write a self-assessment of your strengths and weaknesses, talents, and goals.

Stages of the Model

Once you are ready, I suggest you engage in three stages. The first stage involves exploring MIL, the second involves insight, and the final stage involves action.

EXPLORATION

In your notebook or on your computer, write your answers to the following questions and prompts. Try not to do too many at once; do not think about what someone else would want you to say, but try to be as honest with yourself as you can. Write and then read what you have written both immediately and again at a later time and reflect on whether you still feel as you did. At the end of your writing about each question or prompt, makes notes about what you think you were feeling when you wrote it (e.g., angry, sad, hurt, scared, pleased, curious). Try to imagine someone else reading what you wrote and responding compassionately; what would that other person say (e.g., "You must have been so scared")?

- What are the beliefs in your cultural background (e.g., religious or spiritual background) about MIL? In what ways do you agree and disagree with these beliefs?

- What were your parents' beliefs about MIL? How did they live out these beliefs? Who are you most like in relation to beliefs about MIL?
- Write down any recent dreams you have had. What do you think is the meaning of these dreams in relation to your current quest for MIL?
- In what ways do you think you matter or have significance? Perhaps look back to what you wrote in response to the obituary exercise and reflect about whether you still agree with what you wrote.
- What were your goals in the past? Which have you accomplished? Have you done anything that matters?
- What are your current goals? How are you doing on those?
- What are you passionate about in your life?
- On a daily basis, what do you do that gives you meaning?
- Are you in a career that provides you with meaning? If not, what was the impetus that got you into this career?
- Write about relationships and what role they play in your meaning.
- In what way does creativity play a role in providing you with meaning?
- What role does religion or spirituality play in providing you with meaning?
- Describe the suffering you have had in your life. What meaning do you make of this suffering? What have you learned from the suffering?
- Write about the role of physical disability, physical illness, physical attractiveness, and physical complaints as influencing your feelings about MIL.
- Write about death and death anxiety. When do you think you will die? How will you die? What will happen after you die?
- Reflect about loneliness and isolation.
- Think about freedom—do you have a choice in determining what you do with your life, or is it predestined for you?
- Is your meaning given to you by a higher power, or do you have to construct your own meaning? Do you feel any conflict between these two ideas?
- When do you feel most engaged in life?

After engaging in these writing exercises (assuming it has been a few weeks since you started this exploration process), write down now what you have learned. What are you surprised to learn about yourself? What are your growing edges?

INSIGHT

This is where the process could become difficult because it is hard to get outside oneself and get a new perspective, especially if you tend to be hard on yourself. Again, if you can, you might seek professional help for this stage.

First, go back to some of the things you have written and challenge your ideas. Are there discrepancies in what you said? Are there some things you said just because you have been told them and not because you necessarily believe them? What do you imagine that a wise, gentle, compassionate person would say to you to give you a new perspective?

You answered some questions in the exploration stage about culture and parents. Now let us dig a little deeper. What role did your culture and parents play in your thinking about MIL (e.g., "My parents were Italian and taught us that family comes first and that sitting around the dinner table for long meals was important, so my MIL now revolves around close relationships, listening, and loyalty" or "As a member of the gay community that values freedom of expression, I derive meaning from the opportunity to fight for causes important to me; I need to speak my mind, or life seems meaningless"). Where do you think your parents' thinking came from (e.g., "They were both scared of facing life—my mother was abused and did not think much of herself; my father had to leave home and fend for himself at an early age")? In what ways did they suffer and pass their suffering along to you (e.g., "On the one hand they wanted me to succeed because they were immigrants and were not able to; on the other hand, they seemed frightened of me doing better than them and no longer wanting to be around them")?

How do you see your past as influencing who you are now (e.g., "My parents did not treat me well, so I have minimal self-esteem and have always done less than expected" or "My parents expected so much of me because I was the firstborn, and I cannot live up to that")? How much do you feel that you are the master of your destiny (e.g., "I have been dominated my whole life and am scared to think on my own" or "I never had any guidance and just feel that I am floundering")?

You can also ask yourself how you see your future? What are your goals and ambitions?

At this point, you have probably spent a few weeks thinking about how you got to where you are now. Perhaps write a narrative summary trying to make sense of your life in terms of how you got to where you are. How does your past connect with the present? How does the present connect with your future and where you would like to be? Perhaps write a memoir about a specific theme in your life and how you have been transformed because of incidents in your life.

ACTION

There are several steps to this stage. Perhaps try to do one step in a given session.

Think About the Possibility of Change

We are going to think first about the possibility of change rather than rushing into making changes. Here are some questions to start you thinking. Please again write your answers.

- What do you imagine it would be like to have a different ______ (choose what it is you think would perhaps help you gain more meaning: career, passion, hobby, pastime, spouse, house, or neighborhood)?
  - In what ways would the change give you more or less meaning?
  - What are the positive aspects of changing? What might you gain?
  - What are the negative aspects of changing? What might you lose?
- What are the positive forces that would help you change?
  - Who would be happy for you if you had more meaning in your life?
  - What resources do you have at your disposal to make changes?
  - Think about your strengths (e.g., money, age, talents, education) that could help you change.

- What are the barriers to change?
  - Who would be upset if you had more meaning in your life?
  - How would others try to keep you from changing?
  - Think about realistic barriers to change (e.g., money, age, talents, education). Make sure to determine whether these things are realistic because of external pressures or because of a lack of self-esteem (if the former, you may have to cope or readjust goals; if the latter, you may have to work on building your self-esteem; again, think of seeking professional help).
  - What would you have to sacrifice to make changes to get the meaning you would like to have?

Now that you have gone through these writing exercises, ponder carefully whether you still want to change or whether there are too many drawbacks. It is your choice whether you want to change or stay the same. Think about how you would advise someone else in your situation. Write a narrative summary of your thoughts about changing or staying the same.

Goals for Changing

After completing the exercises about the benefits and barriers to changes and if you have made a decision to change, it is time to make as exhaustive a list as possible of things you could change in your life to help you get more MIL. At first, I suggest you simply make a list of all the ideas you can think of without judging whether the ideas are any good. You might set a timer for 5 minutes and try to come up with as many ideas as you can, ranging from the easy ones to the outlandish, crazy ones. You might also ask others for suggestions, keeping in mind that these are all just suggestions at this point. For example, a list for a 20-year-old person might include the following:

- Go back to school to get my BA degree and become a medical technician.
- Become a hairdresser.
- Take a year off and go around the world.
- Volunteer to work with children who have autism.
- Go to see my grandmother more often.
- Repair my relationship with my mother.

In contrast, a list for a 70-year-old person might include:

- Volunteer to help housebound elderly people by reading to them daily.
- Join a book club.
- Apologize to my daughter and try to develop a better relationship with her.
- Take a course in philosophy at the local college.
- Get marriage counseling.
- Write a novel.

Once you have all the possibilities listed, write a few sentences about why each option appeals to you and what the positive forces and barriers are to achieving this goal. Then, give it some time and come back and reexamine your list and your thinking—has anything changed?

Choose a Goal

Are you ready to make a change? If so, choose the top option and strategize how you would go about doing this. What are the requirements, supports, and barriers? The Internet, of course, is an excellent place to start to look up information, but you can also ask others who might know something.

Start the Change Process

The book on self-directed behavior change by Watson and Tharp (2014) is an excellent resource for how to go about making specific behavior changes. It is important that you take small steps. Changing is hard, and many people try to do too much at one time. Always remember to take "baby steps," but get started. Also, remember to reinforce yourself for taking action, and remember that reinforcements differ for each person (e.g., for one person taking a warm, relaxing bath would be reinforcing, whereas for another taking a long walk might be reinforcing).

If you feel defeated at this point, again I recommend seeking professional help. There may be some unconscious blocks that make it difficult for you to change. Perhaps someone else can help you determine what is going on.

Reevaluate

After trying out your new goals for a while, it is time to reevaluate. Has your life changed for the better? Are you feeling more of a sense of mattering, more goals, more coherence? Perhaps engage in the self-assessment again (retake the MILM) and compare your results with those from before you started this journey. Think about what worked in this process and what did not work. Write about your experiences. Try not to be self-devaluing, and use the reflection process as a way of learning more about who you are and what works and does not work for you.

If things are better for you, that is wonderful. If you have experienced no change or feel worse, it might be time to seek professional help. Again, it is hard to do this work on your own and to see yourself with objectivity.

Conclusion

A fair amount of literature shows that far more people engage in self-help than in psychotherapy and that self-help has at least as good or better outcomes than therapist-administered psychotherapy, especially for depression, anxiety, and mild alcohol abuse (Mains & Scogin, 2003; Scogin, Bynum, Stephens, & Calhoon, 1990). I use and recommend self-help. I like to work through things on my own, and I also really value talking with my husband, grown children, friends, and colleagues about my search for meaning. And I have profited tremendously from more than 30 years of psychotherapy with a wonderful therapist. We can use lots of different avenues to learn about ourselves and grow.

Here are a few gentle hints to help in this process:

- Set aside an hour a week to engage in this process; this will allow you to commit yourself to the process and make sure you take it seriously.
- Make sure you have a quiet spot and will not be interrupted or distracted.
- Write down what you learn so you can go back over your notes.
- Do not rush through the steps; take plenty of time to ponder and reflect.
- Be gentle and compassionate with yourself—reflecting about meaning is hard.
- Talk about your ideas with friends and relatives.
- Seek spiritual guidance if that fits your values.
- Seek professional help if needed.

Good luck on your journey!

RESEARCH ON MEANING IN LIFE III

Our Research at the University of Maryland on Meaning in Life

10

You can't connect the dots looking forward; you can only connect them looking backwards.

—Steve Jobs, *Stanford University Commencement Address, 2005*

Investigating meaning in life (MIL) is challenging because it is an amorphous construct and an inner experience that cannot be directly observed. However, it is one of the most fascinating constructs around and well worth the struggle of figuring out how to handle it.

An extensive body of research now exists on MIL, much of which is in social psychology, developmental psychology, personality psychology, positive psychology, and logotherapy, with some current work in meaning-centered psychotherapy. This body of work is well summarized in several recent handbooks (Hicks & Routledge, 2013; Markman, Proulx, & Lindberg, 2013; Shaver & Mikulincer, 2012; P. T. P. Wong, 2012; P. T. P. Wong & Fry, 1998), and a selective review of this literature is presented in the first three chapters of this book.

In this chapter, I review the studies my research teams and I have conducted thus far on MIL to illustrate how my thinking on MIL developed. The first studies focused more broadly on the construct of MIL, whereas the latter studies focused on working with MIL in psychotherapy. A summary of findings across studies can be found at the end of the chapter. Implications for future research can be found in Chapter 12.

http://dx.doi.org/10.1037/0000083-012
Meaning in Life: A Therapist's Guide, by C. E. Hill

What's It All About? A Qualitative Study of Undergraduate Students' Beliefs About Meaning of Life

We (Hill, Bowers, et al., 2013) conducted a qualitative study of undergraduate students' beliefs about meaning of life as a part of a small undergraduate honors course on consensual qualitative research (CQR; Hill, 2012). I wanted to select a topic that undergraduates could relate to, and indeed they loved talking about meaning. All the students were seniors struggling with what to do next with their lives and wanting to make a difference in the world, so this topic struck a chord with them.

It is interesting, looking back on this initial experience, that we used the term *meaning of life* (MOL; the belief about "the" cosmic meaning for all people living), whereas I soon came to realize that what we were actually interested in was *meaning in life* (the personal construction of a meaningful life). Fortunately, our undergraduate participants did not make such fine distinctions either and responded according to their thoughts about their personal meaning. In later studies, we used the term MIL given that our questions were more about personal than cosmic meaning (see Chapter 1).

The purpose of this study was to examine undergraduate students' beliefs about MOL. We had several specific questions. How did students define MOL? What were their theories and attitudes about MOL? What were their goals in life? What limitations did they experience to attaining their goals in life? What were their sources of meaning? How did they develop MOL?

BACKGROUND AND PROCEDURES

Of the 10 students in undergraduate psychology classes at a large public mid-Atlantic university who volunteered to be interviewed, nine were female and one was male, with a mix of racial and ethnic backgrounds (five European Americans, two Hispanic Americans, two Asian Americans, one African American). Participants completed the Meaning in Life Questionnaire (MLQ; Steger, Frazier, Oishi, & Kaler, 2006) and the Sources of Meaning Profile (SOMP) before the interview to prompt their thinking about meaning. Each 1-hour interview was conducted in person by one of the 10 undergraduate students (all of whom had been trained in interviewing skills) in the qualitative research class. The interviewees' scores on the MLQ and SOMP were similar to those of the larger population of students on campus. Hence, although the sample was small, it seemed to be relatively representative of the population of students at this large public university. In this section, I describe results that emerged for more than half the sample (what is called a typical finding in CQR).

DEFINITIONS AND THEORIES ABOUT MEANING OF LIFE

We noted that although participants seemed intuitively to know what MOL was and easily talked about many aspects of it, they had a hard time defining MOL, and thus no typical definition emerged. In terms of components of MOL, they typically cited needs for (a) passion, (b) to be a good person with morals and values, (c) for balance or moderation, and (d) for happiness.

In terms of theories about meaning, participants suggested that MOL is individual and personal and differs for each person. One person said, "The meaning of life could mean anything for anyone. It could just mean, like, going to school, getting good grades. To someone else, it could mean obtaining happiness. To someone else, it could mean getting the job." Furthermore, these participants talked about the role of meaning in society and about people who had challenged their ways of thinking. They suggested that MOL changes over time and is fluid (e.g., "When we are children what brings meaning to our life is far different from when we are elderly"). Finally, they thought that meaning is internally driven or constructed rather than externally driven or discovered.

GOALS (STATED AND IF NO LIMITATIONS)

These students had clear goals in life. They wanted to gain a good education and career, contribute to society and help others, have a family, be happy and satisfied with having lived a good life, and engage in self-improvement, self-actualization, and self-care. However, they also noted that a lack of resources (e.g., money, connections) and personal limitations (lack of brilliance, lack of motivation) were barriers to attaining these goals. When asked what their goals would be if there were no barriers or limitations, students still wanted to contribute to society and help others, but fewer wanted an education or career, and more wanted leisure, fun, travel, or hobbies. These results reflect that few of us can do what we truly would like to do and that we have to work within constraints to find our meaning.

DEVELOPMENT OF MEANING OF LIFE

In terms of the development of meaning, these undergraduate participants said that their meaning had been triggered by life-changing experiences and by being exposed to new ideas. One participant, for example, talked about how traveling to impoverished countries as a child had exposed her to "things that were just unfair, like kids asking for money . . . stealing, doing drugs," which pushed her "to try to make a difference." They also said that development was triggered by negative experiences such as loss, trauma, and discrimination. One participant was able "to be more empathetic" to others because of surviving a medical problem.

In terms of specific changes in MOL over time, participants talked about shifting to being more independent in their thinking and shifting to more meaningful pursuits. This process involved growing from being children and adolescents to becoming adults and taking more control of their lives. They cited parents as being a big influence in these changes.

SOURCES OF MEANING

Participants spoke most enthusiastically and at length about personal relationships as a source of meaning. Relationships provided for personal development, allowed for helping and affecting others, provided support and belonging, yielded happiness or fun, and were a source of learning for the students.

Participants also spoke at length and enthusiastically about altruism and helping others as a source of meaning. Participants said that helping others felt good and that they liked being needed. They also spoke about the opportunity to better society and give back. Furthermore, they noted that helping others fulfilled a calling or expectations (which is perhaps why most were psychology majors).

Other sources of meaning involved work and career (e.g., it made them happy to do what they loved and valued, they liked being able to have an impact on others, work or career satisfied the need to succeed or achieve), growth or self-actualization (e.g., participants talked about the drive to achieve or be the best and the importance of creativity), and the pursuit of happiness (e.g., participants found meaning in having fun).

Participants seemed somewhat ambivalent about religion as a source of meaning. On the one hand, they said that religion provided meaning through providing morals, values, comfort, and security. But on the other hand, they also either said that religion did not give them meaning or they questioned whether it gave them meaning. Our sense was that participants had not quite worked out the role of religion and spirituality in their lives.

CONCLUSIONS FROM THE QUALITATIVE STUDY WITH UNDERGRADUATE STUDENTS

Our experience interviewing these undergraduates was very different from Baumeister's (1991) experience that "the issue of life's meaning is too unnerving for people to try to say anything sincere or serious, and so nervous laughter seems the only safe response" (p. 4). He also cited Freedman's (1978) research interviewing people about what made their lives meaningful and happy, which found that people were reluctant to say anything. Furthermore, they noted that when people were interviewed in groups, they evaded the questions and made jokes, became emotional, and clammed up. They suggested that people were more willing to discuss intimate sexual matters more than meaning and happiness.

In contrast, our interviewees were quite open and eager to talk about MOL. They got involved with the topic. They had clearly pondered this topic and found it meaningful. They also, however, found it difficult to articulate their thoughts. They found the topic to be abstract and hard to "grab onto." We suspect that our semistructured method of interviewing helped interviewees feel safe and valued, making it easier not to feel judged even though they could not articulate all their thoughts.

A summary of the results revealed that MOL developed as a result of life-changing events. Students' goals were somewhat socially determined (e.g., get an education and career, help others, have a family, be happy, engage in self-improvement, have fun, and have financial stability). They perceived barriers to doing what they wanted in life, primarily from a lack of resources and personal limitations. If there were no barriers, students said they would still want to help others, but they would focus less on education and career and more on leisure, fun, travel, and hobbies. Relationships were a major source of meaning, allowing students a sense of belonging, mattering, fun, learning, and growth. Helping others was also a major source of meaning, providing both self-oriented ("feels good") and other-oriented ("make the world a better place") meaning. Finally, students were ambivalent about the role of religion and spirituality as a source of meaning.

What's It All About? A Qualitative Study of Meaning in Life for Counseling Psychology Doctoral Students

We conducted another study (Hill, Spangler, Jackson, & Chui, 2014) in the subsequent year as a part of another CQR class. Our goal was to extend the findings from the undergraduate students to a sample of doctoral students. We figured that doctoral students might have different thoughts about MIL given that they were further along in their career paths and had chosen to go into a helping profession. More specifically, we wanted to know how these students defined and thought about MIL and personal sources of meaning. We also wanted to know about professional sources of meaning, specifically what meaning these students gained from doing therapy, research, and teaching, all activities that were a large part of their doctoral training. Furthermore, we wanted to know how these students worked with MIL with their clients in psychotherapy.

BACKGROUND AND PROCEDURES

Interviewees were 10 female doctoral counseling psychology students. Half of the participants were European Americans, and half were of Asian descent, four being international students and one an Asian American. Interviewees were given the interview protocol ahead of time and completed the MLQ, Purpose in Life Test, and SOMP before the interview to prompt their thinking about meaning. The 1-hour interviews were conducted in person by 10 undergraduate students (all of whom were trained in interviewing skills) from a qualitative research class. Compared with a large sample of undergraduate students at same university, doctoral student participants scored significantly higher on the Presence subscale of the MLQ but similarly on the Search subscale of the MLQ. In this section, I describe the results that emerged for more than half the sample (typical or general findings).

DEFINITION OF MEANING IN LIFE

Participants defined MIL as having goals, a sense of purpose in life, or a reason for living. For example, one person said that MIL is "fulfilling some sort of purpose," and another said that MIL is "purpose . . . there's a reason why you're here, like you made an imprint in whatever shape or form . . . you just had some kind of impact in life." Thus, these doctoral students had a clearer idea of the definition of MIL than did the undergraduates in the previous study.

REFLECTIONS ABOUT MEANING IN LIFE

These students said that the topic of MIL was important to them, and they actively searched for and reflected about it. One person said, "I've always thought about meaning in life . . . I was an oversensitive child in many ways because I had all these questions about why we are alive, why do these things happen to some people." Another said, "I just spend a lot of time to think about my MIL."

Although they all liked to think about MIL, they said that the time spent thinking about it fluctuated depending on what else was going on in their lives. One person said, "It comes and goes." Another said, "It crosses my mind when certain things happen, like if I'm struggling or if I'm having a really positive experience."

DEVELOPMENT OF MEANING IN LIFE

These participants thought their MIL had developed partly as a result of positive experiences. These experiences included such things as helping others (e.g., "People who were never talking to anyone opened up to me . . . I have a gift; I think I should do this"), family ties, hobbies (e.g., "I'm a violinist, and that was sort of my way of finding meaning . . . because the creative outlet was really important"), travel, and being independent (e.g., "Travel helps me reflect on what's really important and what I care about").

Second, they cited negative experiences as influencing their development of MIL. Crisis, trauma, stress, and the ending of relationships all caused them to think about meaning. One participant said,

> I was in a natural disaster that left me very scared of certain weather conditions . . . A lot of trauma happens in countries that aren't really equipped with mental or medical care, so to be able to go in and help in those situations feels really important to me.

Another cited death of loved ones (e.g., "Any experience I've had with death has really impacted my reflection on meaning of life").

Third, transitions and choices stimulated their thoughts about MIL. One person said, "I studied abroad . . . and being away from home for the first time . . . gave me a sense of independence . . . I've always felt that my meaning in life was really based on the risks I took." Another said, "I didn't really feel like the work [in a job in the business world] I was doing mattered in any way that was important to me [and wanted to change to something more meaningful]."

Finally, participants reflected on how their MIL was shaped by culture. For example, one person said, "Moving back and forth between [an Asian country] and the U.S. has driven a lot of me thinking about what's important to me, who I am." Another emphasized the role of collectivism: "It's really coupled with this idea that the group is important; it's not just me and my meaning in life." Another talked about cultural beliefs about helping others:

> I grew up in a relatively well-off upper-middle-class area, it was a lot about being thankful and grateful for what you have . . . made me want to go into a helping profession . . . that's a way I can do something for the world.

PERSONAL SOURCES OF MEANING

A big source of personal meaning for these female doctoral students was relationships. On the positive side, relationships provided meaning because of mutual caring and acceptance (e.g., "So much of what makes life worth living is feeling connected to others"), personal growth and insight (e.g., "The best romantic relationships that I've had have been the ones that really push me and propel me forward to become a stronger and better person individually"), and values (e.g., "[It was] instilled [in me] that helping other people . . . was so important"). On the negative side, relationships also sometimes detracted from meaning. Participants were distressed when they lived far away from loved ones or when they ended important relationships (e.g., "Breakups are so hard for me because I feel a lack for the other person, but maybe the other person doesn't feel a lack for me, so I feel I'm not special").

Personal growth was also a source of meaning for these counseling psychology doctoral students. They specifically mentioned emotional well-being and self-care (e.g., "learning something, doing something productive"), travel and fun (e.g., "It's really important for me to experience other cultures and to see how other people live"), and religion and spirituality (e.g., "I love going to any kind of spiritual community because suddenly I'm surrounded by people who ask these questions why are we alive, what can we give, why does suffering occur?").

PROFESSIONAL SOURCES OF MEANING

These therapists were in at least their third year of doctoral training and had been engaged in providing psychotherapy, conducting research projects, and teaching psychology classes for at least two years, so they had ample experiences that allowed them to reflect on how each of these activities provided meaning. According to what they said in their interviews, these doctoral students derived both self-oriented and other-oriented meanings from all three activities, but the specific meanings differed across the three types of activities.

MEANINGS DERIVED FROM BEING A THERAPIST

In terms of self-oriented meanings, these doctoral students described both a sense of feeling fulfilled and having obtained self-efficacy from being a therapist and providing psychotherapy (e.g., "To be able to kind of just sit with someone and share in that moment I think is very powerful, and I think that it gives me personally a lot of meaning"). They also said that being a therapist provided personal growth and insight (e.g., "It definitely helps me learn about who I am"). Finally, they said that being a therapist provided a sense of connection and intimacy (e.g., "I'm realizing how much, how important it is for me to just feel connected to people—to feel like I can share a bond with people, to feel like I can hear them, and to feel heard and to feel listened to").

In terms of other-oriented meanings, the doctoral student therapists derived meaning from helping individuals. For example, one person said,

> There is just something meaningful about sitting down with somebody and helping them to understand themselves a little bit better, open up things that feel a little bit painful or scary, and making connections and having a better understanding of why things are the way they are and what might be holding them back.

The doctoral student participants also felt good being able to help on a more cosmic level, such as making a difference in the world. Thus, they suggested that changing an individual can help change the system. For example, one person said,

> If it's fulfilling something for the world and not just for me, then that's meaningful. So if I'm having some kind of an impact on other people . . . that will trickle down. . . . If I have a client who is really angry and I make them feel better, and they're not angry anymore, I've improved their life but also improved their environment.

MEANINGS DERIVED FROM BEING A RESEARCHER

In terms of self-oriented meanings, participants indicated that conducting research fostered creativity and intellectual curiosity. It allowed them to use their intellectual capabilities and feel self-efficacious. One person said, "I can do whatever I want, in any way I want, and no one's going to say anything about it. . . . I can create something new; I can contribute."

In terms of other-oriented meaning, these doctoral students described how research could contribute to knowledge and thereby hopefully eventually change the world. One person said,

> The idea of research is that theoretically you could impact a lot more people if you were able to do psychotherapy research that helped us understand the process better or helped to understand how change happens or what people need or how different people react in different ways to different interventions.

MEANINGS DERIVED FROM BEING A TEACHER

In terms of self-oriented meanings, participants said that being a teacher feels good, is fulfilling, and is gratifying. One person said,

> Being a teacher gives me a sense that I can impart knowledge or skills and to be able to really encourage people and foster their curiosity and creativity. I really like trying to have a classroom where people feel like learning can be fun, and learning can be a place to ask a lot of questions and to challenge, things like that. I think that gives me great sense of purpose and meaning.

Teaching also afforded other-oriented meanings. For example, these doctoral student participants (all of whom had been teaching as a part of their doctoral program) reported that teaching provided meaning because they were able to inspire or help individual students grow and develop (e.g., "You expose students to ideas, to thoughts, to different ways of looking at the world; I think that gives meaning to my life"). Teaching psychology also provided meaning by allowing these students to contribute to society and fight for social justice (e.g., "If I teach somebody something and then they go tell their friends, like I taught a diversity class, and so I felt like that was having like a social impact even though it was just teaching a few people . . . connected to the world, the larger world").

INTERVENTIONS USED IN THERAPY TO WORK WITH MEANING IN LIFE

We asked a rather broad question: "How do you work with clients regarding MIL?" In retrospect, we might have obtained more specific answers had we asked about a specific client. At any rate, the participants said they explored components of MIL (e.g., goals, purposes, dreams, career paths, passions, identity, motivation), but they did not use the term *meaning in life* in their work with clients. Several examples illustrate what they said:

- "I probe them or try to push them to try to think beyond what other people think cause that's what they always focus on and, you know, just kind of live a little, but not live a little like go do crazy things but live a little like why don't you tell me what your dreams are, why don't you tell me what would be meaningful for you."
- "Helping them find what's important to them, who they are, what shapes who they are, who they want to be."
- "It comes out in the form of motivation, so we'll talk about what motivates them, and a lot of times part of students' problems are that they feel unmotivated, so I think when we're talking about what matters to them, what motivates them, what their goals are, that's kind of like a meaning in life conversation."
- "I tend to go for their passion, if that makes sense. If there's something over a decision or something, I want to know what path feels right to them and why, and what path is going to make you happiest or give you the meaning in life and that kind of thing."

The second major way these doctoral student therapists worked with MIL in working with their clients in psychotherapy was to explore other problems that have MIL as an underlying component. In other words, the therapists suggested that if the other problem (e.g., low self-esteem, anger, depression, eating disorder) were resolved, the client would have more MIL. They thus focused on the MIL issues as a part of the larger problem. Again, several examples illustrate this idea:

- "So someone might have very low self-esteem, so they can't think their life has any meaning, then I'd work on the self-esteem part of it. Say someone has anger issues, so they constantly hurt other people and don't feel like their life has meaning, so I'd work on the anger."
- "When someone comes in, and they're feeling really depressed, that might mean that their life doesn't have much meaning, and so why is that? And if it looks like they're moving in that direction of having purpose or a calling or

something to get out of bed for in the morning, like, that's I think a good marker of healing."

- "Some of the clients in the groups that I work in, we do talk about meaning in life because they are people that struggle with eating disorders and also people who struggle with obesity. So there is a fundamental question that is always in the room: What is it going to take to make you stop doing these harmful behaviors that ultimately will probably lead to your death? So that's a meaning in life kind of a question."

CONCLUSIONS FROM THE QUALITATIVE STUDY WITH DOCTORAL STUDENTS

These counseling psychology doctoral students actively searched for MIL and enjoyed talking about it, but like the undergraduate students, they said it was difficult to articulate their thoughts. Although important and meaningful, MIL is a hard topic to define and think about. For these doctoral students, MIL, which they defined as having a purpose or goals, developed from positive and negative life experiences, with transitions and experiencing different cultures being particularly poignant triggers (recall that four of the 10 participants were international students). As with the undergraduate students, relationships and personal growth were important sources of meaning. Specific to this sample was that participating in therapy, research, and teaching all provided self-oriented and other-oriented meaning, although the meanings were slightly different according to the activity. In terms of actually working with clients in psychotherapy, the doctoral student therapists indicated that they did not use the term MIL or work directly with MIL in their work with clients, but rather focused on purposes, goals, motivations, and other problems for which MIL seemed to be an underlying concern.

Although we had started this study hoping to find some cultural differences given that half the sample was European American women and the other half was of Asian origin, we did not find many noteworthy differences. The lack of differences may have been because of the small sample size or because all participants were doctoral students in counseling psychology at one university and shared similar values, but it may also be that we did not ask the best questions to get at cultural differences.

Meaning in Life in Psychotherapy: The Perspective of Experienced Psychotherapists

We conducted a study (Hill, Kanazawa, et al., 2017) with eight undergraduate psychology students in a qualitative research course (Yoshi Kanazawa co-taught this class with me). Our goal was to extend the findings from the doctoral students to experienced therapists. We speculated that experienced therapists might have different thoughts about MIL given that they were more experienced in life and in conducting psychotherapy. More specifically, we wanted to investigate what meaning these experienced therapists gained from providing psychotherapy and their beliefs about the role of MIL in psychotherapy. We also wanted to know, following up on the study about how doctoral students worked differently with clients who had explicit and implicit MIL concerns, how these experienced therapists worked with clients who explicitly presented MIL concerns and how they worked with different clients for whom MIL was more secondary and implicit.

BACKGROUND AND PROCEDURES

Because past experiences have suggested that experienced therapists are more likely to talk openly with colleagues than with undergraduate students, Yoshi Kanazawa, Sarah Knox, and I (all professors) conducted the interviews. To be eligible to participate, participants had to be PhD-level psychologists, work with MIL in their practices, and be willing to talk about their work with MIL. Participants were given the interview protocol ahead of time so they could prepare for the recorded 2-hour telephone interview. For the portion of the study on MIL work with specific clients, therapists were asked to select successful cases of clients whom they were currently seeing or with whom they had mutually terminated within the past 6 months and with whom they had worked for at least eight sessions. They were also asked to select one such client who explicitly presented an MIL problem and another who sought help for something else but for whom MIL was an underlying concern.

The seven male and six female therapist participants, all European American, were on average about 56 years old and had been in practice 26 years. They rated themselves as believing in and adhering most to a humanistic–existential–experiential theoretical approach (average of 4 on a 5-point scale), with moderately high ratings on psychoanalytic–psychodynamic (average of 3.5 on a 5-point scale) and cognitive–behavioral (average of 3.2 on 5-point scale) approaches. I report only those results that emerged for at least half the sample (considered typical or general in CQR language).

PERSONAL SOURCES OF MEANING IN LIFE FROM BEING A THERAPIST

These experienced therapists reported gaining both self-oriented and other-oriented meaning from being a therapist. They felt rewarded, gratified, satisfied, and fulfilled by providing therapy. One person said, "It brings out the best in me." Another said, "When I do a session of psychotherapy, I never have to question whether or not that's meaningful or whether that activity inherently has meaning. It's just really important to me." Conducting psychotherapy also provided these therapists with the opportunity to continue to develop personally, emotionally, and intellectually. One person said, "When I'm with a client, I'm never bored, or very, very rarely bored, and even that is interesting to me." Being able to be in close, intimate relationships was also of value to these therapists. One person said, "It involves being humanly connected to another person in fundamentally important and significant ways." Indeed, these comments indicate that therapists gained a lot personally from conducting therapy.

In terms of other-oriented meanings, the experienced therapists derived meaning from helping individuals and alleviating suffering. It gave one person meaning to "help alleviate their suffering in some way, help them see their lives differently or from a different perspective, help them have more love and compassion for themselves, and see themselves as more than their struggles." It was also important for these therapists to make the world a better place; by helping individuals, they believed there was a ripple effect of making things better incrementally. One person said, "Maybe psychotherapy could affect a person, could affect a family, could affect bigger systems."

In reflecting about the developmental trajectory of changes in how they worked with MIL in therapy over time, one therapist summed it up nicely, saying, "The meaning I derive from doing therapy has not changed from when I was a novice therapist, but now I'm more likely to obtain the meaning because I'm less anxious and more skilled at working with clients." This statement is a good way of putting it. We can tell from our study with undergraduate psychology students that they wanted to help others, so that desire was there early on. What does change, though, is the ability to help people make deep and significant changes in their lives.

ROLE OF MEANING IN LIFE IN LIFE AND PSYCHOTHERAPY

Although perhaps not surprising because they volunteered to participate because they worked with MIL in psychotherapy, these experienced therapists believed that seeking and finding MIL is the essence of humanity (e.g., "The nature of being alive and human is to struggle with thinking about meaning"). Given this belief, it then follows that they also believed that MIL is a component of all client problems and must be addressed at least to some extent in therapy (e.g., "MIL is pervasive and global and needs to be a part of the healing process"). Relatedly, they viewed having MIL as a positive diagnostic sign and not having MIL as a sign of psychological distress (e.g., "[MIL reflects] a sense of purpose, understanding, and acceptance of self, recognition of one's own strengths and limitations"). Thus, these therapists believed that MIL work was central to the work of psychotherapy.

That brings us to the question of how they worked with MIL with clients. Importantly, therapists indicated they would not work with MIL in therapy if other client problems were more pressing and needed immediate attention but that once these more pressing issues were at least partially resolved, they might shift to include work with MIL (e.g., "I never really think of MIL as a primary issue; to me, it's always a secondary issue; . . . to me, depression is primary and issues of MIL are secondary"). Therapists also, however, emphasized that sometimes it is crucial to focus explicitly on MIL, especially when the client has concerns related to relationship problems, trauma or loss, depression, or suicidal ideation or attempts. For example, one said,

> It certainly came up around 9/11. What's our role in the world? Are we doing the right things? Do we have a right around how we treat people? Do we have a right to expect others to treat us in certain ways?

These results suggest that, in general, therapists first attend to the client's most pressing immediate concern, whether it be depression or MIL. They noted, however, that therapists had to be attentive to the underlying role that MIL might play in all problems even if they did not necessarily initially address it directly. Thus, they suggested that MIL concerns are always there, but whether they are a focus of the work is a matter of what is most salient and pressing at the moment.

WORKING WITH CLIENTS WHO HAVE EXPLICIT AND IMPLICIT MEANING-IN-LIFE CONCERNS

In the doctoral student study (C. E. Hill et al., 2015), students stated they rarely worked directly with MIL in psychotherapy. We thought that perhaps doctoral students had not focused on MIL directly because of a lack of experience or because of anxiety related to dealing deeply with difficult concerns. We suspected that a selective sample of experienced therapists who liked to work with MIL would be more comfortable directly addressing the topic with appropriate clients than were the less experienced therapists (C. E. Hill et al., 2015). Indeed, we found that these experienced therapists did work with MIL more frequently and explicitly at least with some clients (labeled here as explicit MIL cases), although as indicated in the previous section, they also approached MIL more indirectly with some clients (labeled here as implicit MIL cases). See also Chapter 7 for more detailed descriptions of some of the explicit and implicit cases from this study.

Description of Clients

The prototypical explicit case was an older man or woman who had experienced a life-threatening physical health crisis that compelled them to seek therapy to make sense of the remainder of their lives life, get more satisfying interpersonal relationships, and deal with psychological distress. This client typically initiated talking about MIL issues by specifically asking for help with MIL (e.g., asking for a life review).

In contrast, the prototypical implicit case was a middle-aged woman who had been in long-term psychotherapy for psychological distress. MIL concerns were initially less salient for this person than were other psychological stressors. The topic of MIL came up gradually over the course of therapy after extensive probing and exploration of other concerns.

Meaning-in-Life Concerns

MIL concerns were expressed primarily as a lack of purpose, which occurred equally often in explicit and implicit cases. After a major health scare with her heart, one client was

> suicidal with some frequency and wonders if life is worth living . . . she very nearly died, and the recovery process was long and very difficult for her. It called into question repeatedly whether it was worth it or if she should just give up.

A second MIL concern was relationship issues, which was reported as occurring more often in the implicit than in the explicit cases. Events such as the loss of a loved one or a divorce prompted these clients to think about their lack of connection and meaning and what they could do to ease their pain. One client, who was estranged from her son, mother, and husband, was unsure of "how to connect or what it means to truly feel connected."

The third type of MIL concern was identity issues ("Who am I?"), which were more predominant in the explicit than implicit cases. Especially after the loss of a loved one or a job, clients had to rethink who they were and how to redefine their identities. One person who lost her nursing job because of a major illness had to completely restructure how she thought about herself. Clients often felt their lives as they had known them were shattered, and they did not know how to put them back together again.

Interestingly, MIL issues were more evident in relationship problems for implicit problems, whereas they were more evident in identity issues for explicit than implicit problems, with lack of purpose being equally distributed. Thus, therapists might have to search more for MIL when clients are talking about relationship issues, whereas it might often be clearer in problems related to identity and lack of purpose.

Therapist Interventions for Working With Meaning-in-Life Concerns

Four types of interventions were identified by the experienced therapists. The first three types were used almost equally with clients with explicit and implicit MIL concerns, whereas the final type was used more with implicit than explicit concerns.

First, therapists used insight-oriented interventions to help clients understand the role MIL played in their lives. One therapist helped the client explore how childhood patterns were playing out in his relationship with his wife. Another therapist helped her client try to understand how the issues she was struggling with were related to issues about how she found meaning in her life.

Second, therapists supported clients in their struggles to talk about and find meaning. They were empathic, compassionate, and responsive to client needs. One therapist indicated that she needed to be supportive for a long time with her client because of the depth of the client's trauma and pathology.

Third, action-oriented interventions were used to encourage clients to make changes and improve their lives, thereby gaining meaning. For example, several therapists encouraged clients to become more engaged with family as a way of gaining meaning.

Finally, therapists used exploratory interventions to help clients explore their issues at length until underlying MIL components were identified. Therapists asked questions and restated and reflected feelings to help clients think about and begin to label their concerns. Once clients identified MIL as a concern, they also used the other interventions (insight, support, action) to help them with MIL.

Thus, therapists used a wide variety of interventions with clients to facilitate MIL work. These interventions spanned client-centered, psychodynamic, and behavioral approaches, suggesting that many approaches can be helpful in MIL work. Of course, further research investigating interventions in ongoing therapy is needed to replicate these findings.

CONCLUSIONS FROM THE QUALITATIVE STUDY WITH EXPERIENCED THERAPISTS

These experienced therapists had thought deeply about MIL both for themselves and their clients. As with the doctoral student therapists, these experienced therapists gained both self-oriented and other-oriented meaning from being therapists. It was so well stated that they were more likely at this stage of their careers to gain meaning from their work because of being skilled and experienced. They believed in the value of working with MIL in psychotherapy. Furthermore, although they thought that MIL underlies all concerns, they stated that therapists have to be sensitive to and responsive to clients' willingness to work on MIL instead of forcing MIL work on clients. In contrast to the doctoral student therapists who seemed almost reluctant and nervous about working with MIL with clients in psychotherapy, these experienced therapists seemed to embrace MIL work. They used a combination of insight-oriented, supportive, action-oriented, and exploratory interventions to work with MIL but used more exploratory interventions initially if MIL concerns were more implicit or underlying and needed work to draw out.

This was a selective sample of therapists chosen because they liked to work with MIL concerns. But the results suggest that at least some experienced therapists might be more comfortable working with MIL concerns than are doctoral student therapists.

Therapists' Perspectives About Working With Meaning in Life in Psychotherapy: A Survey

The survey study (Hill, 2016) came about as a direct result of the previous three qualitative studies on MIL. We wondered how much the results of the study on experienced therapists would generalize to practicing therapists. Given that all the previous studies had used small samples, we thought a survey method might help us gain a broader perspective on MIL work in psychotherapy. More specifically, we wanted to know whether some therapists are more likely than others to work with MIL in psychotherapy, whether some clients are more likely than others to be attracted to MIL work, who initiates MIL work, what interventions are used, what the consequences are of MIL work, what training therapists have had in working with MIL, and how competent therapists feel about working with MIL.

BACKGROUND AND PROCEDURES

We developed the survey on the basis of our past findings and the literature about working with MIL in psychotherapy (e.g., Frankl, 1963; P. T. P. Wong, 2010; Yalom, 1980). A total of 212 practicing therapists, ranging from doctoral students to experienced therapists, all of whom were currently working with clients, completed the 20-minute online survey. On average, these therapists were moderately high on all three major theoretical orientations (an average of 3.8 on a 5-point scale for the humanistic–existential–experiential orientation, an average of 3.6 on a 5-point scale for the cognitive–behavioral orientation, and an average of 3.3 on a 5-point scale for the psychoanalytic–psychodynamic orientation).

WHICH THERAPISTS WORKED WITH MEANING IN LIFE?

Of the 212 participants, 129 had a recent MIL case to describe, whereas 83 did not have a case to report in which they had worked with MIL. Thus, 61% of the sample had recently worked with MIL in psychotherapy. Given that the sample probably valued MIL work more than did therapists who chose not to participate in this study, this estimate might be high compared with average therapists.

Those 129 who had recently worked with a client with MIL concerns, compared with the 83 who had not worked with MIL, were more likely to be postdoctoral psychologists rather than trainees, to be older, to be more experienced, to be more humanistic–existential–experiential in orientation, to have had more MIL training, and to feel more competent in MIL work. Thus, it appears that some therapists are more likely than others to work with MIL in psychotherapy. It may be that therapists are more at ease with working with MIL as they gain more personal and professional experience. They may seek out more training and be more humanistic in their approach and thus feel more competent and passionate about MIL work. And perhaps because they are comfortable working with MIL, their clients feel safe and willing to bring up such topics.

WHAT TYPES OF CLIENTS PRESENTED WITH MEANING-IN-LIFE CONCERNS?

The clients reported on were diagnosed as primarily having internalizing issues (e.g., depression, anxiety), interpersonal issues (e.g., relationship issues), and career issues (e.g., unemployment, retirement). They were less often judged as having physical health issues (e.g., cancer) or externalizing issues (e.g., anger, substance abuse). Perhaps MIL is most easy to identify in the former areas, or such clients are more receptive to MIL work.

WHO INITIATED MEANING-IN-LIFE WORK IN PSYCHOTHERAPY?

According to these therapists who had worked with MIL in psychotherapy, only 12% of the clients explicitly labeled MIL as an issue coming into therapy. Rather, clients talked about related issues and agreed with the MIL term once the therapist suggested it (53%); MIL came up after considerable probing and exploration of other topics (28%), and MIL came up because of an extreme situation or issue (e.g., loss of loved one; 8%). Thus, these results confirm the findings from our previous studies described earlier that MIL is often an implicit rather than an explicit concern in therapy.

INTERVENTIONS FOR WORKING WITH MEANING IN LIFE IN PSYCHOTHERAPY

We provided therapists with a list of 20 possible interventions we culled from our previous studies and the literature (particularly Yalom, 1980, and Frankl, 1959). We asked participants to rate, using a 7-point scale, how much they used each of these 20 interventions in their work with the identified client with MIL concerns.

The three most highly rated interventions were (a) offered support; (b) helped examine thoughts, feelings, and behaviors to discover hopes and goals; and (c) facilitated exploration of MIL cognitions and experiences. Thus, what therapists did most to work with MIL in psychotherapy was support the client and facilitate client exploration. These results emphasize the need for safety and a good relationship when discussing such a deep, personal topic as MIL.

Moderately highly rated interventions were (a) helped find meaning in creativity, experiences, and interactions; (b) probed for insight into MIL concerns; (c) offered new perspectives on MIL; (d) helped clients understand they were not alone in having MIL concerns; (e) modeled meaningful engagement in the present moment; (f) provided interpretations about MIL; (g) helped find meaning by directing clients to change their attitude toward unavoidable suffering; (h) shifted self-focus to searching for meaning outside oneself; (i) helped define specific action plans; (j) helped find meaning in suffering; (k) challenged assumptions about MIL; (l) provided gratitude exercises; (m) encouraged turning to religion or spirituality to find MIL; and (n) self-disclosed personal struggles related to MIL. Thus, therapists used a wide variety of interventions, probably dependent on what they were familiar with and what they thought the client needed. These interventions were primarily insight oriented (a, b, c, d, f, g, j, k) and action-oriented (a, e, i, l, m), which suggests that these might be particularly appropriate depending on the specific client. These results also support the findings of the previous study (C. E. Hill et al., 2015) that experienced therapists use a range of interventions from a variety of theoretical approaches for MIL work.

The only intervention rated low on the 7-point scale was paradoxical interventions. We speculated that therapists either did not know much about this intervention or they thought it was not particularly appropriate for working with MIL.

CONSEQUENCES OF WORKING WITH MEANING IN LIFE IN PSYCHOTHERAPY

Using a 7-point scale, participants were asked to rate how much each of 10 different consequences had occurred for the MIL work with for the specific client. All 10 consequences were rated moderately high, suggesting that they occurred moderately often. These consequences were (a) symptom change, (b) focusing on meaningful, positive aspects of life, (c) more actively engaging in meaningful activities outside therapy, (d) improved interpersonal relationships, (e) more actively engaging in psychotherapy, (f) identifying specific things or people who provide MIL, (g) expressing that MIL work was helpful, and (h) gaining understanding of the role of MIL in life.

These results suggest that MIL work was effective, although of course, this was not a controlled clinical trial so we cannot claim causal effects.

Two of the interventions (helping clients find meaning through creative accomplishments and modeling meaningful engagement) were strongly related to the consequences (indicating that the more the intervention was used, the higher the consequence was rated as having occurred). Twelve other interventions were modestly related to consequences. In contrast, five interventions (helping clients define action plans, exploring cognitions and experiences related to MIL, shifting self-focused attention, paradoxical interventions, and challenging assumptions) were not related to any of the consequences. Although correlational rather than causal evidence, these findings provide hypotheses that can be tested in further research.

We can integrate the findings about the frequency of use of interventions with the correlations of the interventions with consequences. These results suggest that the best interventions for working with MIL are those that are supportive, exploratory, encouraging of creative accomplishments, and modeling meaningful engagement.

CONCLUSIONS FROM THE SURVEY STUDY WITH PRACTICING THERAPISTS

Several take-home points came from this study. First, therapists worked with MIL in psychotherapy more often if they were older, experienced, humanistic–existential in orientation, had more presence of MIL themselves, and were trained in working with MIL. Second, clients rarely explicitly labeled MIL as a concern at the start of therapy but were more likely to consider MIL as a component of their problems after exploration. Third, clients who have MIL concerns most often also had internalizing, interpersonal, and career concerns, suggesting that MIL might be an underlying factor in these concerns. In contrast, clients who had MIL concerns were less often reported to also have physical health concerns and externalizing concerns. Fourth, there was a wide repertoire of therapeutic interventions that were used to work with MIL, with those used most often involving support and exploratory activities. Fifth, MIL work was viewed as having moderately positive consequences.

Thus, this study replicates some of the findings of the earlier qualitative studies. It suggests that at least some therapists work with MIL with at least some clients and that such work is moderately effective. Finally, this study provides ideas that can be followed up in investigations of ongoing psychotherapy (e.g., looking more specifically at how MIL work is initiated and conducted).

Meaning in Life As an Outcome in Psychodynamic Psychotherapy

Given that our previous studies had used interviews and surveys with therapists about their experiences related to working with MIL in psychotherapy, we decided to extend the inquiry to actual psychotherapy. Thus, we conducted a study to determine whether scores on the MLQ (Steger et al., 2006) changed over time for community clients in open-ended psychodynamic psychotherapy in a psychology department training clinic (Hill, Kline, Aaron, King, & Kivlighan, in press). The focus of the study was whether change in MIL occurred across time in psychodynamic treatment-as-usual (i.e., treatment was not focused in any structured way on meaning, and therapists had not received specific training in MIL) and whether any such changes corresponded sequentially with changes in psychological functioning (symptoms, interpersonal functioning, and social role performance).

The 34 adult community clients who were participants in the study all had at least eight sessions of psychodynamic psychotherapy with doctoral student therapists-in-training. Of the 34, five (15%) had mentioned MIL issues in their intake interviews, which corresponds closely to the 12% noted in the Hill (2016) survey of practicing therapists.

In thinking about these results, note that the MLQ Presence subscale assesses a sense of having meaning in one's life, whereas the MLQ Search subscale indicates that one is searching for or trying to find meaning. In past research, Steger et al. (2006) showed that Presence was associated with positive psychological functioning, quality of life, and well-being, whereas Search was associated with negative psychological functioning and depression.

The results for changes in MIL over time varied according to initial levels. Those clients who started therapy high in Presence decreased during the middle of therapy and then increased toward to end of therapy back to their initial level (a U-shaped curve). In contrast, those clients who were initially low in Presence increased and then decreased (an inverted U-shaped curve). Thus, it appeared that their initial experience of having meaning in their lives was disrupted during the intensity of the middle therapy and then reconsolidated toward the end of therapy. We suspected that the sense of meaning was different toward the end of therapy, but wondered whether the MLQ was capable of picking up subtle differences given that Presence provides only a broad assessment of MIL.

Results differed for the Search scale. Those clients who started high on Search decreased and the leveled off over time, whereas those clients who started low increased and then leveled off over time. Thus, the groups differed at the beginning but were closer to each other by the end, suggesting that most clients reached a moderate level of searching for meaning.

Another interesting finding was that changes in psychological distress preceded changes on the MLQ. Thus, when clients improved in psychological distress during one 8-week period, they subsequently gained in Presence and decreased in Search in the subsequent 8-week period. In contrast, when they decreased in terms of psychological distress during one 8-week period, they subsequently declined in Presence and increased in Search during the subsequent period. The opposite direction was not found, such that changes on the MLQ did not systematically lead to changes in distress. These results show that change in distress leads to change in meaning but change in meaning does not lead to change in distress. If these results are replicated, the implications for practice are that therapists should focus first on distress and then later on meaning.

Summary of Results Across Studies

COMPARISONS ACROSS ALL STUDIES ON MLQ SCORES

Table 10.1 shows a comparison across studies on the MLQ (Steger et al., 2006) subscales of Presence and Search. For Presence, we see a clear difference across samples related to age and experience level, such that the undergraduate sample (Hill, Bowers, et al., 2013) scored lower than doctoral students (C. E. Hill et al., 2015), and doctoral students scored lower than the experienced therapists (Hill, Kanazawa, et al., 2017). The sample of 212 therapists (Hill, 2016) scored between the doctoral students and experienced therapists and had a much higher standard deviation, which makes sense given that participants in this sample ranged from doctoral students to experienced therapists.

In contrast, Search scores were lower at higher age and experience levels. Thus, undergraduate students had the highest Search scores and experienced therapists the lowest. Perhaps because the experienced therapists were engaged in careers they loved and had reflected deeply about meaning issues, they had little need to search actively for meaning.

These data for the MLQ are consistent with findings reported in O'Donnell, Shim, Barenz, and Steger (2014) for other large samples. Thus, our samples were at least somewhat representative of the larger populations (which is always reassuring with small samples in qualitative studies).

COMPARISONS ACROSS THE UNDERGRADUATE AND DOCTORAL STUDENT STUDIES

Because some similar questions were asked, we could make some comparisons across the undergraduates and doctoral student studies. More specifically, we could compare them regarding definitions of MIL, development of meaning, and sources of meaning. See Table 10.2 for a comparison of findings.

Definitions

Undergraduate students had no typical definition of MIL and actually confounded it with other constructs such as values and happiness. In contrast, doctoral students had more awareness that MIL is related to goals, purpose, and reason for living. These differences may be related to the greater exposure of doctoral students to the literature in psychology.

Development of Meaning

Both undergraduate and doctoral students indicated that they developed MIL as a result of positive life experiences (e.g., travel, new ideas) and negative life experiences (e.g., loss, trauma, death, discrimination), stressing the importance of such experiences in causing an individual to pause and think about life and meaning. In addition, the doctoral students added that transitions and choices and cultural

TABLE 10.1

Means and Standard Deviations for Presence and Search on the Meaning in Life Questionnaire

	MLQ-P		MLQ-S	
	M	*SD*	*M*	*SD*
Hill, Bowers, et al. (2013) undergraduate students in psychology classes, *N* = 10	23.6	4.9	26.0	6.8
Hill et al. (2014) doctoral counseling psychology students, *N* = 10	28.6	2.6	24.6	9.4
Hill, Kanazawa, et al. (2017) experienced therapists, *N* = 13	30.1	2.8	20.1	8.4
Hill (2016) therapists ranging from doctoral students to experienced therapists, *N* = 212	28.9	4.8	23.7	7.1

Note. Scores on the MLQ can range from 7 to 70. High scores on the MLQ-P indicate high levels of the presence of MIL; high scores on MLQ-S indicate high levels of search for MIL. MIL = meaning in life; MLQ = Meaning in Life Questionnaire; MLQ-P = Meaning in Life Questionnaire Presence subscale; MLQ-S = Meaning in Life Questionnaire Search subscale.

TABLE 10.2

Comparison Between Undergraduate Student and Doctoral Student Samples in Terms of Definitions, Theories, Development, and Relationships as a Source of Meaning

Domain	Undergraduate psychology students (Hill, Bowers, et al., 2013; *N* = 10)	Doctoral psychology students (Hill et al., 2014; *N* = 10)
Definition of MIL	No typical definition emerged (some students talked about needs for passion, having morals and values, balance and moderation, and happiness)	▪ Having goals ▪ Having a sense of purpose in life ▪ Having a reason for living
Development of meaning	▪ Positive life experiences (e.g., new ideas or experiences) ▪ Negative life experiences (e.g., loss, trauma, discrimination)	▪ Positive experiences (e.g., helping experiences, travel) ▪ Negative life experiences (e.g., crises, stress, trauma, death) ▪ Transitions and choices ▪ Cultural influences
What relationships provide as a source of meaning	▪ Personal development ▪ Helping or affecting others ▪ Support and belonging ▪ Happiness and fun ▪ A source of learning	▪ Mutual acceptance and caring ▪ Personal growth and insight ▪ Nurturing values
Personal growth as a source of meaning	Yes	Yes
What religion or spirituality provides as a source of meaning	▪ Morals or values ▪ Comfort and security ▪ Does not give meaning	▪ Positive benefits ▪ Searches for MIL in religion or spirituality

Note. Results reflect data that were at least typical (i.e., emerged for more than half of each sample). MIL = meaning in life.

influences contributed to their development of MIL. These latter results are not surprising because the doctoral students were older and had gone through more transitions than had the undergraduate students. Furthermore, half the doctoral students were of Asian origin, and four were international students who had moved to the United States for doctoral study. These international students had experienced firsthand the effects of culture and thus had more to say about it. All the doctoral students had also studied extensively about culture in their multiculturally oriented program, which may have made them more aware of cultural influences. These findings reinforce the notion that people often do not think about meaning when life is just going on, but when something out of the ordinary happens, they get triggered into thinking about what it all means. For example, the death of a significant other often forces a person to think about that person's meaning to them, the person's legacy, and also what they want their legacy to be.

Sources of Meaning

Undergraduate students were asked specifically about relationships, altruism, work and career, growth and self-actualization, the pursuit of happiness, and religion and spirituality as sources of meaning. In contrast, doctoral students were asked more broadly about personal and professional sources of meaning.

Table 10.2 shows a comparison of findings for sources of meaning between the undergraduate and doctoral student samples. There was enough data to enable comparisons across the domains of personal relationships, altruism and helping others (although this finding is discussed in the next section), personal growth, and religion and spirituality.

Personal relationships were described as big sources of personal meaning for both the undergraduate and doctoral student samples. Specifically, the undergraduate students said that relationships provided meaning through personal development, helping others, support and belonging, happiness, fun, and learning. For doctoral students, relationships provided meaning through mutual acceptance and caring, personal growth and insight, and nurturing values. These results reflect the human need for connectedness and attachment (Bowlby, 1969, 1988) and the growing literature showing that relationships are the biggest source of meaning (Halusic & King, 2013).

Personal growth was also noted by both the undergraduate and doctoral samples. These data fit with the choice of psychology for a major and career. In our university, psychology is one of the largest majors, with many students choosing to major in it even though most do not go on to graduate school and become psychologists. These findings about personal growth might reflect the common notion that students major in psychology to learn about themselves.

Religion and spirituality were more mixed as sources of meaning. Undergraduate students said that religion provides morals, values, support, and comfort but also noted the negative and repressive effects. Doctoral students were more positive, although they often referred to it as spirituality rather than religion. In the culture at large in the United States, religion is on the decline, and people sometimes also replace religion with psychology. The research, however, showing high correlations between religious and spiritual beliefs and meaning (Steger et al., 2010) gives pause.

COMPARISON ACROSS THREE SAMPLES FOR MEANING DERIVED FROM HELPING OTHERS

Table 10.3 shows a comparison across the undergraduate, doctoral student, and experienced therapist samples regarding meanings derived from helping others and altruism. All had self-oriented and other-oriented meanings that they derived from helping others. In other words, it was not only gratifying to help others and thereby hopefully change the world, but it also felt good and fulfilling to be able to use their empathic talents in the service of helping others.

Limitations

Although these studies represent a number of samples and methods, major limitations were that samples were small, not representative of the population (there was an overrepresentation of White, European American participants), and centered in the United States. Thus, the findings have to be replicated in other samples more representative of age, gender, race and ethnicity, education, and cultural context. As with most studies, further research is needed to determine the generalizability of findings.

TABLE 10.3

Self-Oriented and Other-Oriented Meaning Gained From Helping Others or Being a Therapist

Domain	Hill, Bowers, et al. (2013) Undergraduate psychology students ($N = 10$)	C. E. Hill et al. (2015) Doctoral counseling psychology students ($N = 10$)	Hill, Kanazawa, et al. (2017) Experienced therapists ($N = 13$)
Self-oriented meanings	▪ Feels good or needed ▪ Fulfills calling or expectations	▪ Feels fulfilled or efficacious ▪ Personal growth or insight ▪ Allows for connection and intimacy	▪ Enjoys and feels fulfilled ▪ Personal growth ▪ Allows for connection and intimacy
Other-oriented meanings	▪ Bettering society and giving back	▪ Helping others ▪ Making a better world	▪ Helping others and alleviating suffering ▪ Making a better world

Note. Results reflect data that were at least typical (i.e., emerged for more than half of each sample).

Conclusions From Our Research

Although these studies have limitations, they provide some ideas about how MIL can be investigated using a number of different methods (qualitative interviews, surveys, and quantitative methods using standardized measures in psychotherapy). We have found a number of take-home messages in this line of research. I list them here in bullet form to highlight the findings, roughly in order of the studies presented in this chapter.

- Undergraduate psychology students, doctoral counseling psychology students, and experienced therapists loved talking about MIL and found participating in the research to be meaningful. This topic is one that people (at least those in the psychology field) find personally relevant and important.
- MIL develops through positive and negative life experiences. People seem to think more about meaning when there are disruptions in their lives.
- Personal relationships and helping others are big sources of MIL.
- Helping others, research, and teaching all provide both self-oriented and other-oriented meaning for doctoral students in counseling psychology
- When MIL is more implicit than explicit, clients might have to spend more time in exploration. Once MIL has been identified as a topic worthy of attention in psychotherapy, a variety of insight-oriented, action-oriented, supportive, and exploration interventions seem to be helpful.
- The most helpful interventions for working with MIL in psychotherapy tend to be those that are supportive, exploratory, and insight oriented.
- Therapists who were more likely to work with MIL in psychotherapy were older, more experienced, and more humanistic–existential in theoretical orientation; had training in MIL; and felt more competent in working with MIL.
- Regarding initiation of the topic of MIL in therapy, only 12% of clients explicitly initiated MIL, whereas 81% talked about related issues before identifying MIL as an important focus.
- MIL work results in a variety of moderately positive consequences.
- Clients in psychodynamic psychotherapy go through a period of disruption during the middle of therapy regarding their experiencing of meaning (they drop if they started at a high point, but they increase if they started at a low point), but this reverts back to initial levels by the end of therapy. In terms of search, clients end up at a more moderate level as a result of therapy.
- Changes in psychological distress during psychodynamic psychotherapy lead to changes in meaning in life, such that when clients get better regarding psychological functioning, they subsequently feel more presence of meaning and are less likely to be searching for meaning. However, if they get worse regarding psychological functioning, they subsequently experience less presence of meaning and start to search for more meaning.

Measurement of Meaning in Life

11

> There are two ways to think about all this. One way is that life is absurd to start with and that only a madman goes out and tries to change the world, to fight for good and against evil. The other way is that life is indeed absurd to start with and that it can be given meaning only if you live it for your ideals, visions and poetic truths, and despite all the skepticism of all the Sancho Panzas in the world, saddle up whatever worn out horse you've got and go after those visions.
>
> —Leonard Bernstein, "Fantastic Variations (*Don Quixote*)"

To study meaning in life (MIL), it helps to have psychometrically sound measures that adequately assess the construct. With a good measure, researchers can compare the construct with other related constructs, determine how one sample compares with other samples, and study change over time.

In this chapter, I briefly review some of the existing measures to determine how well they assess the construct of MIL in contrast to related constructs. Then, I describe a measure we developed to more precisely assess our definition of MIL as presented in Chapter 1.

Existing Measures

Brandstätter, Baumann, Borasio, and Fegg (2012) reviewed 59 measures that had been developed to assess MIL. Thus, we can see that the construct of meaning has been popular, with many researchers trying to figure out how to capture its essence.

http://dx.doi.org/10.1037/0000083-013
Meaning in Life: A Therapist's Guide, by C. E. Hill

It is important to note that these measures vary widely in what they assess, reflecting the lack of consistency in the definitions of MIL. For example, a number of measures assess sources of meaning rather than presence or experience of meaning (these measures are reviewed in Chapter 3). Other measures include items of well-being and search, which are related factors and perhaps antecedents or consequences of MIL, rather than components of MIL itself. By including items that measure constructs other than MIL, precision is lost and the constructs become muddy.

Another concern is that most of the measures are self-report. It makes sense to use a self-report format given that MIL is an inner experience that cannot be observed by others. But we must recognize the limitations to the validity of the construct given that participants completing these measures may not understand the definition of MIL, might not have thought deeply about MIL, and might not spend an adequate amount of time thinking about and responding to items on a self-report measure.

These measures are presented in chronological order of when they were developed. This ordering makes sense given that more recent measures seemed to build on trying to correct limitations in previous measures.

THE PURPOSE IN LIFE TEST

Crumbaugh and Maholick (1964) developed the Purpose in Life Test (PIL) to measure Frankl's (1959) ideas about purpose in life. This measure seems to be the first standardized measure of MIL and was widely used for many years.

In his extensive review of the PIL, Yalom (1980) noted that the construct validity of the PIL is problematic because it is not unidimensional (i.e., it measures other constructs in addition to meaning). He noted that seven items assess purpose and mission, six items assess life satisfaction, three items assess freedom, one item assesses fear of death, one item assesses contemplation of suicide, and one item assesses the perceived worthwhileness of one's life. Yalom argued that life satisfaction and consideration of suicide are conceptually related to MIL, but they are not MIL. Similarly, it seems to me that freedom, fear of death, and worthwhileness of life are related constructs but not MIL. Another concern noted by Yalom is that the PIL is highly related to social desirability (correlation of .57 with the Marlowe Crowne Social Desirability Scale), suggesting that people may have a hard time responding negatively to the items. Furthermore, Yalom cited research showing that people from different cultures interpreted some of the PIL items differently (e.g., the *empty* in "My life is empty" was interpreted by ghetto residents as referring to empty stomachs, by commune residents as losing one's ego in meditation or bliss, and by engineers as dullness). Thus, Yalom concluded that the PIL seems to be value-laden and based on assumptions inherent in the Protestant work ethic, making it hard to have a high level of confidence in it.

A number of factor analyses have been done on the PIL. To cite just one that demonstrates the typical finding that the PIL is not unidimensional, McGregor and

Little (1998) found two factors of Happiness (with six items) and Meaning (with three items), with other items not loading on either of the two factors. In their study of the personal projects of undergraduate students, the Happiness scale was significantly correlated with students being involved in projects for which they felt a sense of efficacy (projects were achievable and likely to be successful), fun (projects were pleasant and enjoyable), and support (trustworthy others supported them on their projects). The Meaning scale, in contrast, was significantly correlated with projects that were rated high in integrity (projects were consistent with their core values, commitments, and self-identity).

Despite the psychometric problems, Yalom (1980) concluded that some validity had been established for the PIL. Notably, people with psychiatric problems, delinquency, drug and alcohol abuse, high neurosis, social introversion, sexual frustration and maladjustment, and hedonism scored low. In contrast, people with religious beliefs and values, conservatism, antihedonism, idealism, low death anxiety, involvement in organized groups, positive worldview, goal orientation, self-transcendent goals, and vocational goals scored high.

Thus, although widely used and possessing some validity, the PIL has a number of problems. Perhaps the most troubling problem is that it includes items assessing variables other than MIL. It would appear to be more of a measure of quality of life than a more specific measure of MIL. That said, it was an excellent start to try to assess the construct of MIL, and by building on the results, other researchers were able to develop better measures.

LIFE REGARD INDEX

The Life Regard Index (LRI; Battista & Almond, 1973) is a 28-item measure of personal meaning, developed with the assumption that each person has beliefs about what is meaningful. Battista and Almond (1973) developed this measure to get at their ideas about life regard, which they thought results when a person commits to a concept in their lives that allows them to understand existence and that also supplies the person with reasonable, valued goals. Making progress toward those goals provides a sense of fulfillment. Thus, they developed the LRI to have two subscales (Framework and Fulfillment) that form a higher order MIL construct (each subscale has seven positively worded and seven negatively worded items). Framework assesses how much a person has a perspective or life goals on which to build a personal meaning system or set of goals for life. Fulfillment assesses the extent to which the framework or life goals are being fulfilled.

Steger (2007) criticized the LRI as having items that were confounded with passion, energy, and general happiness. Similarly, McDonald, Wong, and Gingras (2012) were concerned that the Fulfillment subscale might be confounded with the construct of life satisfaction. Furthermore, Steger noted that previous research had shown an inconsistency of results regarding the factor structure of the LRI. Using a new data set, Steger could not confirm the factor structure proposed by Battista and Almond (1973). In an exploratory factor analysis, they derived three scales, only one of which seemed pertinent to MIL. Even that scale, however, contained items related to passion and contentment in one's life. The other two scales contained content relevant to lack of clarity about values and goals.

Hence, although used relatively widely, the LRI seems inadequate for assessing MIL. As with the PIL, the items seem to be confounded with other constructs, making it difficult to claim that it is assessing just MIL.

SENSE OF COHERENCE SCALE

The Sense of Coherence Scale (SCS; A. Antonovsky, 1983, 1993) is a 29-item measure of coherence, which A. Antonovsky thought was the essence of MIL. It has three subscales: Comprehensibility (assessing the degree to which the world is perceived as ordered, predictable, and explicable), Manageability (assessing the degree to which a person can cope with life events and meet challenges), and Meaningfulness (assessing the degree to which a person views life as important and challenges as worthy of commitment). A. Antonovsky (1983, 1993) reported internal consistency for the full scale of .82 to .91 and test–retest reliability of .63. The SCS has been found to be positively related to health (A. Antonovsky, 1983), positively related to emotional closeness in the family and stability of the community and negatively associated with state anxiety (H. Antonovsky & Sagy, 1986), as well as positively related to health and well-being (Korotkov, 1998).

Unfortunately, in their reanalyses, Chamberlain and Zika (1988a) were not able to replicate the factor structure of the SCS. Rather, they identified seven components, with several components being problematic in terms of relating to the proposed constructs of coherence and MIL. In addition, Sammallahti, Holi, Komulainen, and Aalberg (1996) argued persuasively that the SCS measured coping disposition rather than meaning in life. Thus, the SCS does not appear to be promising as a measure of MIL.

In addition, although I have conceptualized coherence as a major component of MIL (see Chapter 1), it seems limiting to consider coherence as the only component (ignoring felt sense, mattering, and purpose or goals). But perhaps most important, the items do not seem to measure just coherence. Hence, the SCS is also limited as a measure of MIL.

THE MEANING IN LIFE QUESTIONNAIRE

Steger, Frazier, Oishi, and Kaler (2006) criticized previous measures of MIL for including items that are confounded with other variables. For example, they noted that the PIL and LRI contain items about suicide and mood, which probably account for the high correlations of these measures with measures of negative affect, positive affect, and life satisfaction. They noted that measures of MIL are needed that are not confounded with the correlates, antecedents, and consequences of MIL. Furthermore, Steger et al. pointed out that the factor structures of the PIL and LRI have varied from study to study, causing difficulties in interpreting results. Finally, they noted that existing measures do not account for search for meaning, which they believed is a crucial component of MIL given Frankl's (1963) idea that searching for meaning is a fundamental human motivation.

Steger et al. (2006) thus sought to develop a better measure of MIL, which they defined as "the sense made of, and significance regarding, the nature of one's being and existence" (p. 81). They believed this definition encompassed previous definitions, allowed participants to define meaning using their own criteria, and was consistent with the idea that individuals construct their own meaning.

The Meaning in Life Questionnaire (MLQ) includes a subscale of Presence, which refers to the amount of meaning one feels in life. An example item for Presence is "I have discovered a satisfying life purpose." Two of the items reflect coherence and three reflect purpose, but none of the items reflect the mattering or significance part of their definition. The MLQ also has a subscale measuring *search*, which refers to how much one is actively looking for or seeking to find meaning (e.g., "I am always looking for my life's purpose"). Steger et al. (2006) found good factor analytic support for the MLQ with internal consistencies for the subscales of Presence and Search ranging between .82 and .87. The two subscales were slightly negatively correlated, $r = -.19$, indicating that they are independent constructs. MLQ-Presence was positively correlated with measures of life satisfaction, positive emotions, intrinsic religiosity, extraversion, and agreeableness but negatively associated with depression, extraversion, and neuroticism. In contrast, MLQ-Search was positively associated with neuroticism, depression, and negative emotions.

In their review of the massive literature using the MLQ, O'Donnell, Shim, Barenz, and Steger (2014) noted that the MLQ was the most widely used measure of meaning. The MLQ has been translated into more than 30 languages, with the two-factor model being supported in several countries in addition to the original U.S. samples. For some of our findings using the MLQ, see Chapter 10.

Brandstätter et al. (2012) concluded that Steger et al.'s (2006) MLQ was the most psychometrically sophisticated measure. In fact, they evaluated the MLQ as having a perfect score given its rigorous development and robust psychometric properties. This conclusion fits with my less systematic review in this chapter of some of the existing measures.

Although the MLQ is highly regarded and widely used, it also has some problems. The first problem is that, as noted earlier, the Presence scale does not include items related to felt sense or mattering/significance. Second, it seems questionable to me to include Search as a component of MIL, especially given that it is not significantly related to Presence. In fact, in more recent studies (e.g., Martela, Ryan, & Steger, 2017), Search is not included when MIL is assessed and related to other constructs.

BAUMEISTER'S MEANING MEASURE

Baumeister, Vohs, Aaker, and Garbinsky (2013) created a simple, global, three-item measure of meaningfulness that seems to capture a global or felt sense of meaning. The internal consistency of this measure was >.94 and the 5-week test–retest reliability was .76. Furthermore, as reviewed in Chapter 1, Baumeister et al. were able to differentiate happiness and meaning using this simple three-item measure and a parallel measure of happiness.

This measure of meaningfulness seems to be useful for a quick assessment of the general construct of meaning and certainly fits well with the felt sense component described in Chapter 1. It does not, however, seem as useful for assessing the other components of meaning such as coherence, mattering/significance, purpose/goals, and reflectivity.

MULTIDIMENSIONAL EXISTENTIAL MEANING SCALE

As a part of their conceptual paper on the tripartite model of MIL, George and Park (2016) briefly described the Multidimensional Existential Meaning Scale (MMES), developed to assess the three components of the tripartite model (comprehension, purpose, and mattering). They indicated that exploratory and confirmatory factor analyses substantiated a three-factor model and that the MMES was correlated as hypothesized with existing measures of meaning. Without a further description of this measure, however, it is difficult to evaluate its adequacy.

Critique of Existing Measures

Many measures have been developed for assessing MIL, including others not reviewed in this chapter. But there are a number of problems with the existing measures. First, some measures assess the presence of or the experience of having MIL (e.g., the PIL, LRI, SCS, and MLQ-Presence, MMES), some assess sources of meaning, and others assess search for meaning (e.g., the MLQ-Search). In addition, as noted by Steger et al. (2006), many of the early measures (e.g., the PIL) had problems with content being related to other variables (e.g., well-being, life satisfaction) in addition to MIL. A further problem is that correlations among measures are not high (see Steger et al., 2006), which again suggests that they measure different constructs. Many of these problems seem to be related to a lack of clarity in the definition of MIL. We are left with confusion about the definition and operationalization of MIL. Of the existing measures, the most promising appear to be the MLQ and MMES. These measures, however, do not assess MIL as we defined it in Chapter 1.

Our New Measure: The Meaning in Life Measure

As we began to research MIL, we were concerned about the problems noted earlier with the existing measures. We were particularly dissatisfied that the existing measures did not fit our conceptualization of MIL (as consisting of an overall sense of meaning with five components of felt sense, mattering/significance, purpose/goals, coherence, and reflectivity; see Chapter 1). Our construct of felt sense is similar to Baumeister's three-item global meaning measure (see earlier). A. Antonovsky's measure of coherence (SCS; 1983, 1993) seemed to tap the coherence construct, although not all the items on the SCS are related to coherence. We liked the Presence scale of Steger et al.'s (2006) MLQ as a measure of presence of meaning, but were concerned that, as noted earlier, it included only purpose and coherence and thus did not measure mattering and felt sense. It also included a Search subscale that was not correlated with the Presence subscale. Finally, none of the existing measures captured the construct of reflectivity, which we think is important because pondering about MIL seems likely to be a part of valuing or experiencing MIL.

It thus seemed that a new measure was needed to assess the five components of felt sense, mattering/significance, purpose/goals, coherence, and reflectivity. Thus, in Hill, Kline, Miller, et al. (2017) we created a new Meaning in Life Measure (MILM).

THE MEANING IN LIFE MEASURE

We were not exactly sure about the structure of the MIL construct. Hence, we set out to develop a measure that could include either three (felt sense, mattering/significance, purpose/goals, coherence, and reflectivity) components as in the tripartite model, four components (adding felt sense to the tripartite model), or five components (adding both felt sense and reflectivity to the tripartite model).

Development of the Meaning in Life Measure

To this end, we developed a large set of positively and negatively worded items for all five components on the basis of the literature. We asked 25 psychologists and psychologists-in-training to place each item in the best-fitting component. Interestingly, many items could not be placed under a single component, indicating that there was already some difficulty separating the components. Next, we conducted extensive exploratory factor analyses on the resulting 24 positively and negatively worded items. Because we speculated that the poor fit was due to wording effects (given that half of the items were positively worded and half were negatively worded), we dropped the negatively worded items and found support for a two-factor model: Experience (including all the felt sense, mattering/significance, purpose/goals, and coherence items) and Reflectivity. To make the shortest measure possible, we selected the highest loading items representing each of the four constructs for the Experience scale and retained all four items on the Reflectivity factor. Additional analyses showed this shortened eight-item measure to still be a good fit for the data. Confirmatory factor analyses in a new sample replicated the two-factor structure. Exhibit 11.1 shows the eight items for the MILM. Internal consistency was .85 to .87 for the total MILM, .82 to .84 for Presence, and .86 for Reflectivity across two samples.

Further tests of validity indicated that the MILM-Experience (MILM-E) was strongly positively related to the MLQ-Presence scale (MLQ-P; Steger et al., 2006), an established measure of MIL, providing evidence that the MILM-E and MLQ-P assess a similar construct. In contrast, the MILM-Reflectivity (MILM-R) subscale was only moderately related to the MLQ-P and MLQ-Search, indicating that they were assessing related but independent constructs. Unfortunately, we did not have another measure of reflectivity to compare the MILM-R with directly, but we can infer from these data that it is measuring something related to but different from these other measures.

EXHIBIT 11.1

Meaning in Life Measure

Instructions: Please take a moment to think about what makes your life feel important to you. Please respond to the following statements as truthfully and accurately as you can. Remember that these are subjective questions, and there are no right or wrong answers. Circle the number that best fits how you feel about each item.

	Strongly disagree			Neutral			Strongly agree		
1. I will be remembered.	1	2	3	4	5	6	7	8	9
2. I can make connections between events in my past and present.	1	2	3	4	5	6	7	8	9
3. I have something I want to accomplish in my life.	1	2	3	4	5	6	7	8	9
4. I experience my life as meaningful.	1	2	3	4	5	6	7	8	9
5. I think about what gives me meaning.	1	2	3	4	5	6	7	8	9
6. Meaning in life is a topic I value.	1	2	3	4	5	6	7	8	9
7. There are times in my life when I think about what it all means.	1	2	3	4	5	6	7	8	9
8. I often reflect about issues related to meaning in life.	1	2	3	4	5	6	7	8	9

Note. All eight items are included in the Total Scale. Items 1, 2, 3, and 4 fit on the MILM-Experience subscale; Items 4, 5, 7, and 8 fit on the MILM-Reflectivity subscale. Scale scores can be calculated by summing the items and then taking the average across items for the scale (i.e., dividing the sum by the total number of items).

In terms of convergent validity, the MILM-E and MILM-R were related in expected ways to related constructs. For example, moderately positive relationships were found for both subscales with subjective well-being, extraversion, conscientiousness, agreeableness, openness, and social desirability (both self-deception and impression management), whereas moderately negative relationships were found for both subscales with depression and emotional stability.

We also found some demographic effects, although all these differences were small. The MILM-E was slightly higher for women than men, older than younger people, individuals with higher income than lower income, and for married people with children than for single people without children. In addition, the MILM-R was slightly higher for women than men.

Copy of the Meaning in Life Measure

A copy of the MILM is shown in Exhibit 11.1. A table summarizing the range of average scores (67% of the samples fall within the range shown for each scale) for adults across the age span of 18 to 80 years and from undergraduates at a large public university is presented in Table 11.1. You can compare your scores with those in Table 11.1 by noting whether you fall below, within, or above the range presented for each scale for the best comparison sample. Please recall that many groups of people (e.g., those not from the United States, older people, people under 18) are not well represented in these data, so readers should interpret the results with caution.

TABLE 11.1

Meaning in Life Measure and Meaning in Life Measure–Reflectivity Scores for U.S. Public University Undergraduates and U.S. Adults

	M	*SD*	Low	Average	High
Undergraduates at a large public U.S. university					
MILM-T	6.98	1.23	<5.75	5.75–8.21	>8.21
Males (*n* = 123)	6.80	1.42	<5.38	5.38–8.22	>8.22
Females (*n* = 349)	7.05	1.15	<5.90	5.90–8.20	>8.20
MILM-E	7.45	1.34	<6.11	6.11–8.79	>8.79
Males (*n* = 123)	7.29	1.49	<5.80	5.80–8.78	>8.78
Females (*n* = 349)	7.50	1.28	<6.22	6.22–8.78	>8.78
MILM-R	6.52	1.55	<4.97	4.97–8.07	>8.07
Males (*n* = 123)	6.32	1.74	<4.58	4.58–8.06	>8.06
Females (*n* = 349)	6.59	1.47	<5.12	5.12–8.06	>8.06
U.S. adults (ages 18–80)					
MILM-T	6.94	1.39	<5.55	5.55–8.33	>8.33
Males (*n* = 152)	6.61	1.36	<5.25	5.25–7.97	>7.97
Females (*n* = 243)	7.14	1.37	<5.77	5.77–8.51	>8.51
MILM-E	7.13	1.51	<5.62	5.62–8.64	>8.64
Males (*n* = 152)	6.74	1.54	<5.20	5.20–8.28	>8.28
Females (*n* = 243)	7.39	1.43	<5.96	5.96–8.82	>8.82
MILM-R	6.74	1.71	<5.03	5.03–8.45	>8.45
Males (*n* = 152)	6.48	1.67	<4.81	4.81–8.15	>8.15
Females (*n* = 243)	6.90	1.73	<5.17	5.17–8.63	>8.63

Note. 67% of participants fell within the average range. If the score is below the range, then ratings are lower than the average person in this sample. If the score is above the range cited for a scale, ratings are higher than the average person in this sample. Note, however, that these samples might not be representative of the population. For the undergraduate sample *N* = 473; for the adult sample *N* = 401. One and six subjects, respectively, did not identify their gender and were excluded from the analyses of gender. MILM-E = Meaning in Life Measure–Experience; MILM–R = Meaning in Life Measure–Reflectivity; MILM–T = Meaning in Life Measure–Total.

Interestingly, across all samples for the MILM, participants scored higher on the Experience scale and lower on the Reflectivity scale. Thus, most people think they have goals in life but are less sure whether they can make sense of their lives. These results suggest that people are perhaps less interested in thinking or pondering about meaning than being assured that they have meaning.

SUMMARY OF FINDINGS ABOUT THE MEANING IN LIFE MEASURE

We were able to develop a psychometrically sound measure of MIL. This measure has strong construct validity, as assessed through exploratory and confirmatory factor analyses, and correlations with the MLQ, another measure of MIL. It has high internal consistency and test–retest reliability. In addition, it has moderately strong relationships in the directions expected with related constructs of subjective well-being, personality, depression, and social desirability.

Conclusion

A variety of self-report measures have been developed to assess MIL. The most promising of these existing measures is the MLQ (Steger et al., 2006) because it has excellent psychometric properties. In addition, we recommend our newly created MILM, a psychometrically sound measure that fits our conceptualization of the experience of and reflectivity about MIL. The MILM can be used to examine MIL more carefully and determine its antecedents, correlates, and consequences. Ideas for research are presented in the next chapter.

CONCLUSION IV

Future Directions 12

The meaning of life is just to be alive. It is so plain and so obvious and so simple. And yet, everybody rushes around in a great panic as if it were necessary to achieve something beyond themselves.
—Alan Watts, *The Culture of Counter-Culture: Edited Transcripts*

The topic of meaning in life (MIL) is enjoying a surge of both theoretical and empirical interest in psychology. This growing recognition in psychology of existential issues and internal experiences is, in my mind, a welcome advance. Given the universality of concerns about MIL, it is refreshing to see more emphasis on the topic.

It is still disconcerting, however, to realize how far we are from coming to some clear understanding of the construct of MIL (see Chapter 1). Is it a single dimension of an intuitive felt sense of meaning, is it a tripartite construct (coherence/comprehension, mattering/significance, and purpose/goals), is it four dimensions (felt sense, coherence/comprehension, mattering/significance, and purpose/goals), or is it five dimensions (felt sense, coherence/comprehension, mattering/significance, purpose/goals, and reflectivity)? If MIL is indeed a cluster of highly interrelated constructs, can we distinguish it from other closely related constructs (e.g., subjective well-being, belonging, engagement in life, search for meaning)? Are the sources of meaning more important than the MIL itself? These are all questions that have to be considered by future researchers.

http://dx.doi.org/10.1037/0000083-014
Meaning in Life: A Therapist's Guide, by C. E. Hill

Research on Meaning in Life

Given that the construct of MIL is abstract and complex and much of the writing about MIL has been in the realm of philosophy and theory, conducting research on MIL is challenging. One could argue, on the one hand, that research is not important because the topic is one that fits more in the realm of spirituality and faith and, as such, is more unknowable, and science can destroy the essence of it. On the other hand, research, although imperfect, can help us clarify our definitions and assumptions. Although I am painfully aware of the limitations of research, I also believe it can help us advance our thinking, as long as we remain aware of its limits. In this section, I provide some ideas about future directions in the hope of stimulating others to think about what they could do.

RESEARCH ON THE CONSTRUCT OF MEANING IN LIFE

There seems to be some consensus that MIL is composed of at least mattering/significance, purpose/goals, and coherence/comprehensibility (see Chapter 1). In addition, I have suggested the importance of adding felt sense and reflectivity. A number of other components have also been suggested for consideration (e.g., self-esteem, happiness, well-being, engagement, identity), and it would be good to clarify exactly what MIL is composed of and what the related constructs are. Some researchers have combined the presence of MIL with other constructs such as sources of meaning, search for meaning, and meaning of life. Without a clear definition, it is difficult to have a conversation about MIL; it is like a Tower of Babel with everyone talking about something different and hence not communicating. Given that our measures of MIL depend on our definitions, we must thus start with clarifying the conceptual definition of MIL. I offered such a definition in Chapter 1 (felt sense, mattering/significance, purpose/goals/engagement, coherence/comprehensibility, and reflectivity), and we based our measurement of MIL on that definition (see Chapter 11). Hopefully, this bold assertion will be followed by others advancing this work by clarifying the definition even further and developing better measures (always recognizing that any such measurement is an imperfect approximation of the construct). With better measures of MIL, we can pursue better research on MIL.

Research on the interrelations among the five components (felt sense, mattering, goals, coherence and reflectivity) of MIL is of great interest. Can we develop a profile for each person? Is there an ideal balance across the components for mental health and well-being? If one component is enhanced, do all components follow? Is there a sequence that can be identified among the components, such that reflectivity leads to a felt sense, which leads to coherence/comprehensibility, which leads to purpose/goals, which leads to mattering? Or is it a different sequence? Or is the sequence different for each person?

Another direction is examining the antecedents of MIL and its components. What leads one to feel they have MIL? King, Heintzelman, and Ward (2016) argued persuasively on the basis of their research that if people are in a positive mood, they rate themselves as having MIL. How do we understand this connection if MIL and positive mood are not the same thing? Does a positive mood allow us to see that we do have MIL and sources of MIL in our lives? Likewise, what are the consequences of feeling a presence of MIL? Is it always a good thing or are there some negative consequences? What is the theoretical and empirical relationship between presence of meaning, search for meaning, reflectivity about meaning, and prioritizing about meaning? Have we captured all these different aspects or is there something we are missing?

RESEARCH ON THE NATURE OF MEANING IN LIFE

A related definitional concern involves clarification of the nature of MIL. I asserted in Chapter 1 that MIL is essentially a positive and healthy striving. And in Chapter 3, I asserted that there are some healthy sources of MIL (e.g., helping others) versus some neutral sources (e.g., avidly watching television, being a devoted sports fan, obsessively keeping busy) and some negative sources of MIL (e.g., being a serial killer). Considering the nature of MIL to be a positive, healthy striving involves a value judgment (e.g., who gets to decide the value?). I think this topic has to be addressed head-on in the literature lest we again muddy the topic completely by considering anything to be MIL and a source of MIL.

E. O. Wilson's (2014) theory about meaning based on a biological perspective has some interesting implications for research (see Chapter 1). Wilson posited that our human brains developed because of the dialectic between altruism within groups and competition between groups. Although this tension between ingroups and outgroups may have worked well in primitive societies, it does not work so well in our modern cultures. Research to figure out how to help people balance the tension between helping those we love and keeping others at a distance is sorely needed if we are to survive on this planet.

RESEARCH ON THE DEVELOPMENT OF MEANING IN LIFE

A number of exciting theories have been proposed for how MIL develops (e.g., terror management theory, violation of expectations, attachment, self-determination, life experiences, cognitive development; see Chapter 2). Research comparing these theories is an important direction for future research. Of course, clear definitions of MIL are needed before this comparative research can be accomplished, however, to ensure that we are investigating the development of MIL as opposed to overall development. Such research can take place in the laboratory, as much of the research on terror management theory has, but it also has to be conducted in naturalistic settings.

SOURCES OF MEANING IN LIFE

As noted in Chapter 3, a number of measures of sources of meaning have been developed. Problems were identified, however, in that many of these have conflated presence of meaning and sources of meaning and have labeled many things as sources of meaning that seem to be sources of things other than meaning (e.g., pleasure). Thus, a new measure of sources of meaning is needed that fits the five components of MIL as proposed in Chapter 3. Then, future investigations could be done using such a measure to determine how to help people increase their probabilities of gaining meaning from different sources.

STUDY OF MEANING IN LIFE WITH DIFFERENT POPULATIONS AND CULTURES

A research direction that comes from our initial research with undergraduate psychology students is the study of MIL in other populations. It would be interesting to interview undergraduate students from other majors (e.g., business, engineering) to determine differences in definitions, development, and sources of meaning. At the other end of the spectrum, it would be interesting to interview retired and terminally ill people to see how they derive meaning when work is no longer part of the equation.

Furthermore, the interesting questions raised about MIL and culture (see Chapter 8) yield important questions that beg for further research. If we have to locate the definition of MIL within specific cultures, then the definition I provided earlier (in Chapter 1) may be only applicable to culture in the U.S. It may be that we need culture-specific definitions and measures. This area of research could be vibrant as we struggle to determine what is universal versus what is culture specific in the definition of MIL.

RESEARCH ON WORKING WITH MEANING IN LIFE IN PSYCHOTHERAPY

Now that we have some basic knowledge about MIL, I think that some of the most exciting and important work that has to be done is in applications to psychotherapy. We have to know so much more about how to work with MIL in therapy, how to assess the changes in MIL as a result of therapy, and how to train therapists to work with MIL.

Process of Working With Meaning in Life

There are many ideas for studying MIL in the psychotherapy setting. Now that we have some basic research about how therapists think they work with MIL in psychotherapy, we need more research about the actual process of working with MIL in psychotherapy. One possibility would be research within research clinics. If all sessions are recorded, therapists and clients could indicate after sessions whether MIL was discussed. In those sessions in which clients or therapists have indicated that MIL was discussed, clients and therapists could be interviewed about their experiences discussing MIL; trained judges could observe and code the process and consequences of MIL work, much as how dreamwork has been studied in psychotherapy (see Hill, Gelso, et al., 2013). It would be particularly illuminating to determine whether some interventions are better for working with different client problems, as suggested in Chapter 6. It would also be interesting to determine how therapists shift from working with psychological distress to working with meaning, as was suggested in the Hill, Kline, Aaron, King, & Kivlighan (in press) study.

Outcomes of Meaning in Life Work

As noted in Chapter 5, we need further research examining changes in the five components of MIL (felt sense, mattering/significance, purpose/goals/engagement, coherence/comprehensibility, reflectivity) as a result of working with MIL in psychotherapy. In extending the research using the Meaning in Life Questionnaire (Hill, Kline, Kivlighan, Borkowski, & King, in press), it would be interesting to investigate changes in these five components over time, changes in MIL in relation to psychological distress, and changes in sources of meaning. Researchers might also examine how results differ by client problems and therapist interventions.

It would also be interesting to determine whether changes occurred in constructs that are related to MIL. For example, in our development of the Meaning in Life Measure (Hill, Kline, Miller, et al., 2017), we found positive correlations with subjective well-being. We would also expect that after successful work on MIL, clients would have greater self-acceptance and self-esteem.

Interestingly, Yalom (1980) suggested that clients might have more anxiety after becoming aware of existential concerns (e.g., death anxiety, isolation). According to this hypothesis, we might expect to see increases in existential anxiety, but I would guess that existential anxiety increases and then stabilizes or decreases when there is more acceptance of such anxiety and more coping strategies are developed.

Finally, it would be interesting to investigate changes in the more standard outcomes of psychotherapy: symptomatology and interpersonal functioning. There might be some interesting mediational processes, such that the attainment of MIL leads to changes in interpersonal functioning, which leads to changes in symptomatology. Or it could be more specific to changes in subtypes of MIL, such that increases in mattering leads to better interpersonal functioning, which leads to increases in goals, which leads to decreases in symptomatology. We can certainly guess that all the variables are intertwined, but learning more about the sequential processes would be interesting.

Training Therapists

Finally, once we know something about how to best work with MIL in psychotherapy, it would be important to investigate methods for training therapists about how to work with MIL in psychotherapy. As with dreams, therapists often feel anxious about and incapable of working with MIL because of a lack of specific training. Thus, we have to help them feel comfortable knowing what to expect and how to do this work.

Developing New Theories About Working With Meaning in Life in Psychotherapy

Once we have a better idea of what interventions are helpful for working with MIL with different types of clients, a treatment approach could be developed and compared with other treatments to determine the overall effectiveness of meaning-centered psychotherapy. This new approach could be compared with existing structured meaning-centered approaches, described in Chapter 4 (typically based on logotherapy or existential psychotherapy).

Of particular interest would be work on methods for increasing client reflectivity about MIL. McWilliams (2004) suggested that one of the key features of psychodynamic psychotherapy involves the therapist being curious about clients' dynamics and encouraging curiosity in clients about their dynamics.

Conclusion

To move this field forward, we need more theorizing about the construct of MIL, more work in developing therapies to help clients work with MIL, and more research on the topic. Interestingly, this topic attracts attention from across the spectrum of psychology (social psychology and developmental psychology, as well as counseling and clinical psychology) in addition to attention from philosophy. The intersection of interests can help us expand our thinking about this topic and hopefully enrich the field. This topic is of great interest to many of us personally, and I hope that many young psychologists take the thinking to new levels of understanding.

The ideas I mention here are just for heuristic purposes, to spark others to think about possibilities. I hope that people will develop their own ideas and move the field forward and that in 50 years we will have many new theories about MIL and an abundance of supporting empirical evidence.

References

American Psychological Association (2017). *Ethical principles of psychologists and code of conduct* (2002, Amended June 1, 2010, and January 1, 2017). Retrieved from http://www.apa.org/ethics/code/index.aspx

Andersen, S., Chen, S., & Carter, C. (2000). Fundamental human needs: Making social cognition relevant. *Psychological Inquiry, 11*, 269–275.

Anderson, M. L., Goodman, J., & Schlossberg, N. K. (2012). *Counseling adults in transition: Linking Schlossberg's theory with practice in a diverse world* (4th ed.). New York, NY: Springer.

Antonovsky, A. (1983). The sense of coherence: Development of a research instrument. *Newsletter and Research Report of the W. S. Schwartz Research Center for Behavioral Medicine, 1*, 11–22.

Antonovsky, A. (1988). *Unraveling the mystery of health*. San Francisco, CA: Jossey-Bass.

Antonovsky, A. (1993). The structure and properties of the sense of coherence scale. *Social Science & Medicine, 36*, 725–733. http://dx.doi.org/10.1016/0277-9536(93)90033-Z

Antonovsky, H., & Sagy, S. (1986). The development of a sense of coherence and its impact on responses to stress situations. *The Journal of Social Psychology, 126*, 213–225.

Arndt, J., Landau, M. J., Vail, K. E., III, & Vess, M. (2013). An edifice for enduring personal value: A terror management perspective on the human quest for multilevel meaning. In K. D. Markman, T. Proulx, & M. J. Lindberg (Eds.), *The psychology of meaning* (pp. 49–69). Washington, DC: American Psychological Association. http://dx.doi.org/10.1037/14040-003

Battista, J., & Almond, R. (1973). The development of meaning in life. *Psychiatry, 36,* 409–427. http://dx.doi.org/10.1080/00332747.1973.11023774

Baumeister, R. F. (1991). *Meanings of life.* New York, NY: Guilford Press.

Baumeister, R. F., & Vohs, K. D. (2002). The pursuit of meaningfulness in life. In C. R. Snyder & S. J. Lopez (Eds.), *Handbook of positive psychology* (pp. 68–618). New York, NY: Oxford University Press.

Baumeister, R. F., Vohs, K. D., Aaker, J. L., & Garbinsky, E. N. (2013). Some key differences between a happy life and a meaningful life. *The Journal of Positive Psychology, 8,* 505–516. http://dx.doi.org/10.1080/17439760.2013.830764

Beck, J. S., & Beck, A. T. (2011). *Cognitive behavior therapy: Basics and beyond.* New York, NY: Guilford Press.

Berman, A. L., Jobes, D. A., & Silverman, M. M. (2006). *Adolescent suicide: Assessment and intervention* (2nd ed.). Washington, DC: American Psychological Association.

Blustein, D. L. (2008). The role of work in psychological health and well-being: A conceptual, historical, and public policy perspective. *American Psychologist, 63,* 228–240. http://dx.doi.org/10.1037/0003-066X.63.4.228

Bowlby, J. (1969). *Attachment and loss: Vol. 1. Attachment.* New York, NY: Basic Books.

Bowlby, J. (1988). *A secure base.* New York, NY: Basic Books.

Boyle, P. A., Barnes, L. L., Buchman, A. S., & Bennett, D. A. (2009). Purpose in life is associated with mortality among community-dwelling older persons. *Psychosomatic Medicine, 71,* 574–579. http://dx.doi.org/10.1097/PSY.0b013e3181a5a7c0

Brandstätter, M., Baumann, U., Borasio, G. D., & Fegg, M. J. (2012). Systematic review of meaning in life assessment instruments. *Psycho-Oncology, 21,* 1034–1052. http://dx.doi.org/10.1002/pon.2113

Breitbart, W. S., & Poppito, S. R. (2014a). *Individual meaning-centered psychotherapy for patients with advanced cancer: A treatment manual.* New York, NY: Oxford University Press. http://dx.doi.org/10.1093/med/9780199837243.001.0001

Breitbart, W. S., & Poppito, S. R. (2014b). *Meaning-centered group psychotherapy for patients with advanced cancer: A treatment manual.* New York, NY: Oxford University Press. http://dx.doi.org/10.1093/med/9780199837250.001.0001

Breitbart, W., Poppito, S., Rosenfeld, B., Vickers, A. J., Li, Y., Abbey, J., . . . Cassileth, B. R. (2012). Pilot randomized controlled trial of individual meaning-centered psychotherapy for patients with advanced cancer. *Journal of Clinical Oncology, 30,* 1304–1309. http://dx.doi.org/10.1200/JCO.2011.36.2517

Breitbart, W., Rosenfeld, B., Gibson, C., Pessin, H., Poppito, S., Nelson, C., . . . Olden, M. (2010). Meaning-centered group psychotherapy for patients with advanced cancer: A pilot randomized controlled trial. *Psycho-Oncology, 19,* 21–28. http://dx.doi.org/10.1002/pon.1556

Breitbart, W. S., Rosenfeld, B., Pessin, H., Applebaum, A., Kulikowski, J., & Lichtenthal, W. G. (2015). Meaning-centered group psychotherapy: An effective intervention for improving psychological well-being in patients with advanced cancer. *Clinical Oncology, 33,* 749–754. http://dx.doi.org/10.1200/JCO.2014.57.2198

Brown, S. D., & Lent, R. W. (Eds.). (2005). *Career development and counseling: Putting theory and research to work.* Hoboken, NJ: Wiley.

Brown, S. D., & Lent, R. W. (2016). Vocational psychology: Agency, equity, and well-being. *Annual Review of Psychology, 67,* 541–565. http://dx.doi.org/10.1146/annurev-psych-122414-033237

Camus, A. (2004). The myth of Sisyphus. In G. Marino (Ed.), *Basic writings of existentialism* (pp. 441–492). New York, NY: Random House. (Original work published 1942)

Cartwright, R., & Lamberg, L. (1992). *Crisis dreaming.* New York, NY: Harper Collins.

Carver, C. S., & Scheier, M. F. (1998). *On the self-regulation of behavior.* Cambridge, England: Cambridge University Press. http://dx.doi.org/10.1017/CBO9781139174794

Cashdan, S. (1988). *Object relations therapy.* New York, NY: Norton.

Castonguay, L., & Hill, C. E. (Eds.). (2007). *Insight in psychotherapy.* Washington, DC: America Psychological Association. http://dx.doi.org/10.1037/11532-000

Castonguay, L., & Hill, C. E. (Eds.). (2012). *Transformation in psychotherapy: Corrective experiences across cognitive behavioral, humanistic, and psychodynamic approaches.* Washington, DC: American Psychological Association.

Chamberlain, K., Petrie, K., & Azariah, R. (1992). The role of optimism and sense of coherence on predicting recovery following surgery. *Psychology & Health, 7,* 301–310. http://dx.doi.org/10.1080/08870449208403159

Chamberlain, K., & Zika, S. (1988a). Measuring meaning in life: An examination of three scales. *Personality and Individual Differences, 9,* 589–596. http://dx.doi.org/10.1016/0191-8869(88)90157-2

Chamberlain, K., & Zika, S. (1988b). Religiosity, life meaning, and wellbeing: Some relationships in a sample of women. *Journal for the Scientific Study of Religion, 27,* 411–420. http://dx.doi.org/10.2307/1387379

Chao, M. M., & Kesebir, P. (2013). Culture: The grand web of meaning. In J. A. Hicks & C. Routledge (Eds.), *The experience of meaning in life: Classical perspectives, emerging themes, and controversies* (pp. 317–331). New York, NY: Springer. http://dx.doi.org/10.1007/978-94-007-6527-6_24

Chochinov, H. M. (2002, May 1). Dignity-conserving care—A new model for palliative care: Helping the patient feel valued (perspectives on care at the close of life). *JAMA, 287,* 2253–2260. http://dx.doi.org/10.1001/jama.287.17.2253

Chochinov, H. M., Kristjanson, L. J., Breitbart, W., McClement, S., Hack, T. F., Hassard, T., & Harlos, M. (2011, August). Effect of dignity therapy on distress and end-of-life experience in terminally ill patients: A randomised controlled trial. *The Lancet: Oncology, 12,* 753–762. http://dx.doi.org/10.1016/S1470-2045(11)70153-X

Cohen, D., & Gunz, A. (2002). As seen by the other . . . : Perspectives on the self in the memories and emotional perceptions of Easterners and Westerners. *Psychological Science, 13,* 55–59. http://dx.doi.org/10.1111/1467-9280.00409

Comas-Díaz, L. (2012). *Multicultural care: A clinician's guide to cultural competence.* Washington, DC: American Psychological Association. http://dx.doi.org/10.1037/13491-000

Constantino, M. J., Arnkoff, D. B., Glass, C. R., Ametrano, R. M., & Smith, J. Z. (2011). Expectations. *Journal of Clinical Psychology, 67,* 184–192. http://dx.doi.org/10.1002/jclp.20754

Cooper, M. (2015). *Existential psychotherapy and counselling: Contributions to a pluralistic practice.* London, England: Sage.

Courtois, C. A. (2013). *Treatment of complex trauma: A sequenced, relationship-based approach.* New York, NY: Guilford Press.

Crumbaugh, J. C. (1968). Cross-validation of Purpose-in-Life test based on Frankl's concepts. *Journal of Individual Psychology, 24,* 74–81.

Crumbaugh, J. C., & Maholick, L. T. (1964). An experimental study in existentialism: The approach to Frankl's concept of noogenic neurosis. *Journal of Clinical Psychology, 20,* 200–207. http://dx.doi.org/10.1002/1097-4679(196404)20:2<200::AID-JCLP2270200203>3.0.CO;2-U

Duffy, R. D., & Dik, B. J. (2013). Research on calling: What have we learned and where are we going? *Journal of Vocational Behavior, 83,* 428–436. http://dx.doi.org/10.1016/j.jvb.2013.06.006

Elliott, K. P., Westmacott, R., Hunsley, J., Rumstein-McKean, O., & Best, M. (2015). The process of seeking psychotherapy and its impact on therapy expectations and experiences. *Clinical Psychology & Psychotherapy, 22,* 399–408. http://dx.doi.org/10.1002/cpp.1900

Emmons, R. A. (1986). Personal strivings: An approach to personality and subjective well-being. *Journal of Personality and Social Psychology, 51,* 1058–1068. http://dx.doi.org/10.1037/0022-3514.51.5.1058

Emmons, R. A. (2005). Striving for the sacred: Personal goals, life meaning, and religion. *Journal of Social Issues, 61,* 731–745. http://dx.doi.org/10.1111/j.1540-4560.2005.00429.x

Erikson, E. H. (1950). *Childhood and society.* New York, NY: Norton.

Falk, D. R., & Hill, C. E. (1995). The process and outcome of dream interpretation groups for divorcing women. *Dreaming, 5,* 29–42. http://dx.doi.org/10.1037/h0094421

Fegg, M. J., Kramer, M., L'hoste, S., & Borasio, G. D. (2008). The Schedule for Meaning in Life Evaluation (SMiLE): Validation of a new instrument for meaning-in-life research. *Journal of Pain and Symptom Management, 35,* 356–364. http://dx.doi.org/10.1016/j.jpainsymman.2007.05.007

Frank, J. D., & Frank, J. B. (1991). *Persuasion and healing: A comparative study of psychotherapy* (3rd ed.). Baltimore, MD: Johns Hopkins University.

Frankl, V. (1946). *Man's search for meaning.* New York, NY: Washington Square Press.

Frankl, V. (1959). *Man's search for meaning.* New York, NY: Simon & Schuster.

Frankl, V. (1963). *Man's search for meaning: An introduction to logotherapy.* New York, NY: Washington Square Press.

Frankl, V. E. (1978). *The unheard cry for meaning: Psychotherapy and humanism.* New York, NY: Touchstone Books.

Frankl, V. (1986). *The doctor and the soul: From psychotherapy to logotherapy* (Rev. and expanded). New York, NY: Vintage Books.

Freedman, J. (1978). *Happy people: What happiness is, who has it, and why.* New York, NY: Harcourt, Brace, & Jovanovich.

Fry, P. S. (2000). Religious involvement, spirituality and personal meaning for life: Existential predictors of psychological wellbeing in community-residing and institutional care elders. *Aging & Mental Health, 4,* 375–387. http://dx.doi.org/10.1080/713649965

Garfield, P. (1991). *Women's bodies, women's dreams*. New York, NY: Holt, Rinehart, and Winston.

Gelso, C. J., & Hayes, J. A. (2007). *Countertransference and the therapist's inner experience: Perils and possibilities*. Mahwah, NJ: Erlbaum.

Gendlin, E. T. (1981). *Focusing* (2nd ed.). New York, NY: Bantam Books.

Gendlin, E. T. (1996). *Focusing-oriented psychotherapy: A manual of the experiential method* (2nd ed.). New York, NY: Guilford Press.

George, L. S., & Park, C. L. (2013). Are meaning and purpose distinct? An examination of correlates and predictors. *The Journal of Positive Psychology, 8*, 365–375. http://dx.doi.org/10.1080/17439760.2013.805801

George, L. S., & Park, C. L. (2016). Meaning in life as comprehension, purpose, and mattering: Toward integration and new research questions. *Review of General Psychology, 20*, 205–220. http://dx.doi.org/10.1037/gpr0000077

Greenberg, J. (2012). Terror management theory: From Genesis to Revelations. In P. R. Shaver & M. Mikulincer (Eds.), *Meaning, mortality, and choice* (pp. 17–36). Washington, DC: American Psychological Association. http://dx.doi.org/10.1037/13748-001

Greenberg, L. S. (2015). *Emotion-focused therapy: Coaching clients to work through their feelings* (2nd ed.). Washington, DC: American Psychological Association. http://dx.doi.org/10.1037/14692-000

Halusic, M., & King, L. A. (2013). What makes life meaningful: Positive mood works in a pinch. In K. D. Markman, T. Proulx, & M. J. Lindberg (Eds.), *The psychology of meaning* (pp. 445–464). Washington, DC: American Psychological Association. http://dx.doi.org/10.1037/14040-022

Harlow, L. L., Newcomb, M. D., & Bentler, P. M. (1986). Depression, self-derogation, substance abuse, and suicide ideation: Lack of purpose in life as a mediational factor. *Journal of Clinical Psychology, 42*, 5–21.

Harris, R. (2009). *ACT made simple: A quick-start guide to ACT basics and beyond*. Oakland, CA: New Harbinger.

Hayes, S. C., & Lillis, J. (2012). *Acceptance and commitment therapy*. Washington, DC: American Psychological Association.

Hayes, S. C., Stosahl, K. D., & Wilson, K. G. (1999). *Acceptance and commitment therapy: An experiential approach to behavior change* (Vol. XVI). New York, NY: Guilford Press.

Hays, P. A. (2013). *Connecting across cultures: The helper's toolkit*. Thousand Oaks, CA: Sage.

Hays, P. A. (2016). *Assessing cultural complexities in practice: Assessment, diagnosis, and therapy* (3rd ed.). Washington, DC: American Psychological Association.

Heffner, M., & Eifert, G. H. (2004). *The anorexia handbook: How to accept yourself, heal your suffering, and reclaim your life*. Oakland, CA: New Harbinger.

Heine, S. J., Proulx, T., & Vohs, K. D. (2006). The meaning maintenance model: On the coherence of social motivations. *Personality and Social Psychology Review, 10*, 88–110. http://dx.doi.org/10.1207/s15327957pspr1002_1

Heintzelman, S. J., & King, L. A. (2014). Life is pretty meaningful. *American Psychologist, 69*, 561–574. http://dx.doi.org/10.1037/a0035049

Heintzelman, S. J., Trent, J., & King, L. A. (2013). Encounters with objective coherence and the experience of meaning in life. *Psychological Science, 24*, 991–998. http://dx.doi.org/10.1177/0956797612465878

Heintzelman, S. J., Trent, J., & King, L. A. (2015). Revisiting desirable response bias in well-being reports. *The Journal of Positive Psychology, 10*, 167–178. http://dx.doi.org/10.1080/17439760.2014.927903

Heisel, M. J., & Flett, G. L. (2004). Purpose in life, satisfaction with life, and suicide ideation in a clinical sample. *Journal of Psychopathology and Behavioral Assessment, 26*, 127–135. http://dx.doi.org/10.1023/B:JOBA.0000013660.22413.e0

Hicks, J. A., & King, L. A. (2008). Religious commitment and positive mood as information about meaning in life. *Psychological Science, 24*, 991–998.

Hicks, J. A., & King, L. A. (2009). Positive mood and social relatedness as information about meaning in life. *The Journal of Positive Psychology, 4*, 471–482. http://dx.doi.org/10.1080/17439760903271108

Hicks, J. A., & Routledge, C. (Eds.). (2013). *The experience of meaning in life: Classical perspectives, emerging themes, and controversies*. New York, NY: Springer. http://dx.doi.org/10.1007/978-94-007-6527-6

Hicks, J. A., Schlegel, R. J., & King, L. A. (2010). Social threats, happiness, and the dynamics of meaning in life judgments. *Personality and Social Psychology Bulletin, 36*, 1305–1317. http://dx.doi.org/10.1177/0146167210381650

Hill, C. E. (1984). A personal account of the process of becoming a counseling process researcher. *The Counseling Psychologist, 12*(3), 99–109. https://dx.doi.org/10.1177/0011000084123010

Hill, C. E. (1989). *Therapist techniques and client outcomes: Eight cases of brief psychotherapy*. Newbury Park, CA: Sage.

Hill, C. E. (Ed.). (2004). *Dream work in therapy: Facilitating exploration, insight, and action*. Washington, DC: American Psychological Association. http://dx.doi.org/10.1037/10624-000

Hill, C. E. (2012). *Consensual qualitative research: A practical resource for investigating social science phenomena*. Washington, DC: American Psychological Association.

Hill, C. E. (2014). *Helping skills: Facilitating exploration, insight, and action* (4th ed.). Washington, DC: American Psychological Association. http://dx.doi.org/10.1037/14345-000

Hill, C. E. (2016). Therapists' perspectives about working with meaning in life in psychotherapy: A survey. *Counselling Psychology Quarterly*, 1–19. Advance online publication. https://dx.doi.org/10.1080/09515070.2016.1173014

Hill, C. E., Bowers, G., Costello, A., England, J., Houston-Ludlam, A., Knowlton, G., . . . Thompson, B. J. (2013). What's it all about: A qualitative study of undergraduate students' beliefs about meaning of life. *Journal of Humanistic Psychology, 53*, 386–414. http://dx.doi.org/10.1177/0022167813477733

Hill, C. E., Chui, H., & Baumann, E. (2013). Revisiting and reenvisioning the outcome problem in psychotherapy: An argument to include individualized and qualitative measurement. *Psychotherapy, 50*, 68–76. http://dx.doi.org/10.1037/a0030571

Hill, C. E., Gelso, C. J., Gerstenblith, J., Chui, H., Pudasaini, S., Burgard, J., . . . Huang, T. (2013). The dreamscape of psychodynamic psychotherapy: Dreams, dreamers, dream work, consequences, and case studies. *Dreaming, 23,* 1–45. http://dx.doi.org/10.1037/a0032207

Hill, C. E., Kanazawa, Y., Knox, S., Schauerman, I., Loureiro, D., James, D., . . . Moore, J. (2017). Meaning in life in psychotherapy: The perspective of experienced therapists. *Psychotherapy Research, 27,* 381–396. http://dx.doi.org/10.1080/10503307.2015.1110636

Hill, C. E., Kline, K., Aaron, A., King, S., & Kivlighan, D. M., Jr. (in press). Changes in meaning in life in psychodynamic psychotherapy. *Counselling Psychology Quarterly.* Retrieved from http://dx.doi.org/10.1080/09515070.2017.1340260

Hill, C. E., Kline, K., Bauman, V., Brent, T., Breslin, C., Calderon, M., . . . Knox, S. (2015). What's it all about? A qualitative study of meaning in life for counseling psychology doctoral students. *Counselling Psychology Quarterly, 28,* 1–26. http://dx.doi.org/10.1080/09515070.2014.965660

Hill, C. E., Kline, K., Kivlighan, D. M., Jr. Borkowski, Z., & King, S. (in press). Changes in meaning in life in long-term psychodynamic psychotherapy. *Counselling Psychology Quarterly.* http://dx.doi.org/10.1080/09515070.2017.1340260

Hill, C. E., Kline, K., Miller, M., Marks, E., Pinto-Coelho, K., & Zetzer, H. (2017). *Development of a measure of meaning in life.* Manuscript submitted for publication.

Hill, C. E., & Knox, S. (2009). Processing the therapeutic relationship. *Psychotherapy Research, 19,* 13–29. http://dx.doi.org/10.1080/10503300802621206

Hill, C. E., Knox, S., & Pinto-Coelho, K. G. (in press). Self-disclosure and immediacy. In J. C. Norcross & M. J. Lambert (Eds.), *Psychotherapy relationships that work* (3rd ed.). New York, NY: Oxford University Press.

Hill, C. E., Spangler, P. T., Jackson, J., & Chui, H. (2014). Training undergraduate students to use insight skills: Integrating results across three studies. *The Counseling Psychologist, 42,* 800–820. http://dx.doi.org/10.1177/0011000014542602

Hill, P. L., Burrow, A. L., Sumner, R., & Young, R. K. (2015). Life is pretty meaningful and/or purposeful?: On conflations, contexts, and consequences. *American Psychologist, 70,* 574–575. http://dx.doi.org/10.1037/a0039063

Hines, P. M., & Boyd-Franklin, N. (2005). African American families. In M. McGoldrick, J. Giordano, & N. Garcia-Preto (Eds.), *Ethnicity and family therapy* (3rd ed., pp. 87–100). New York, NY: Guilford Press.

Hobbs, N. (1962). Sources of gain in psychotherapy. *American Psychologist, 17,* 741–748. http://dx.doi.org/10.1037/h0040135

Hook, J. N., Davis, D. E., Owen, J., Worthington, E. L., Jr., & Utsey, S. O. (2013). Cultural humility: Measuring openness to culturally diverse clients. *Journal of Counseling Psychology, 60,* 353–366. http://dx.doi.org/10.1037/a0032595

Hook, J. N., Farrell, J. E., Davis, D. E., DeBlaere, C., Van Tongeren, D. R., & Utsey, S. O. (2016). Cultural humility and racial microaggressions in counseling. *Journal of Counseling Psychology, 63,* 269–277. http://dx.doi.org/10.1037/cou0000114

Horvath, A. O., Del Re, A. C., Fluckiger, C., & Symonds, D. (2011). Alliance in individual psychotherapy. In J. C. Norcross (Ed.), *Psychotherapy relationships that work: Evidence-based responsiveness* (2nd ed., pp. 25–69). New York, NY: Oxford University Press. http://dx.doi.org/10.1093/acprof:oso/9780199737208.003.0002

Janoff-Bulman, R. (2013). Meaning and morality: A natural coupling. In K. D. Markman, T. Proulx, & M. J. Lindberg (Eds.), *The psychology of meaning* (pp. 191–213). Washington, DC: American Psychological Association. http://dx.doi.org/10.1037/14040-010

Janoff-Bulman, R., & Yopyk, D. (2004). Random outcomes and valued commitments: Existential dilemmas and the paradox of meaning. In J. Greenberg, S. L. Koole, & T. Pyszczynski (Eds.), *Handbook of experimental existential psychology* (pp. 122–138). New York, NY: Guilford Press.

Joo, E. S., Hill, C. E., & Kim, Y. H. (2017). Using helping skills with Korean clients: The perspectives of Korean counselors. *Psychotherapy Research*. Advance online publication. http://dx.doi.org/10.1080/10503307.2017.1397795. Manuscript submitted for publication.

Jung, C. G. (1966). *Collected works: The practice of psychotherapy* (Vol. XVI). New York, NY: Pantheon.

Kashdan, T. B., & McKnight, P. E. (2013). Commitment to a purpose in life: An antidote to the suffering by individuals with social anxiety disorder. *Emotion, 13,* 1150–1159. http://dx.doi.org/10.1037/a0033278

Kay, A. C., Laurin, K., Fitzsimons, G. M., & Landau, M. J. (2014). A functional basis for structure-seeking: Exposure to structure promotes willingness to engage in motivated action. *Journal of Experimental Psychology: General, 143,* 486–491. http://dx.doi.org/10.1037/a0034462

King, L. A. (2012). Meaning: Ubiquitous and effortless. In P. R. Shaver & M. Mikulincer (Eds.), *Meaning, mortality, and choice* (pp. 129–144). Washington, DC: American Psychological Association.

King, L. A., Heintzelman, S. J., & Ward, S. J. (2016). Beyond the search for meaning: A contemporary science of the experience of meaning in life. *Current Directions in Psychological Science, 25,* 211–216. http://dx.doi.org/10.1177/0963721416656354

King, L. A., & Hicks, J. A. (2012). Positive affect and meaning in life. In P. T. P. Wong (Ed.), *The human quest for meaning* (2nd ed., pp. 125–141). New York, NY: Routledge/Taylor & Francis.

King, L. A., Hicks, J. A., Krull, J. L., & Del Gaiso, A. K. (2006). Positive affect and the experience of meaning in life. *Journal of Personality and Social Psychology, 90,* 179–196. http://dx.doi.org/10.1037/0022-3514.90.1.179

Kitayama, S., & Markus, H. R. (2000). The pursuit of happiness and realization of sympathy: Cultural patterns of self, social relations, and well-being. In E. Diener & E. M. Suh (Eds.), *Culture and subjective well-being* (pp. 113–161). Cambridge, MA: MIT Press.

Klinger, E. (1977). *Meaning and void: Inner experiences and the incentives in people's lives.* Minneapolis, MN: University of Minnesota Press.

Knapp, S., Youngren, J. N., VanderCreek, L., Harris, E., & Martin, J. N. (2015). *Assessing and managing risk in psychological practice: An individualized approach* (2nd ed.). Rockville, MD: The Trust.

Konrad, M., & Jobes, D. A. (Eds.). (2011). *Building a therapeutic alliance with the suicidal patient.* Washington, DC: American Psychological Association.

Korotkov, D. (1998). The sense of coherence: Making sense out of chaos. In P. T. P. Wong & P. S. Fry (Eds.), *The human quest for meaning: A handbook of psychological research and clinical application* (pp. 237–259). Mahwah, NJ: Erlbaum.

Krug, O. (2017). Existential, humanistic, and experiential therapies in historical perspective. In A. J. Consoli, L. E. Beutler, & B. Bonger (Eds.), *Comprehensive textbook of psychotherapy: Theory and practice* (pp. 106–120). New York, NY: Oxford University Press.

Lambert, N. M., Stillman, T. F., Baumeister, R. F., Fincham, F. D., Hicks, J. A., & Graham, S. M. (2010). Family as a salient source of meaning in young adulthood. *The Journal of Positive Psychology, 5,* 367–376. http://dx.doi.org/10.1080/17439760.2010.516616

Lambert, N. M., Stillman, T. F., Hicks, J. A., Kamble, S., Baumeister, R. F., & Fincham, F. D. (2013). To belong is to matter: Sense of belonging enhances meaning in life. *Personality and Social Psychology Bulletin, 39,* 1418–1427. http://dx.doi.org/10.1177/0146167213499186

Lazar, S. G. (2010). Psychotherapy in the treatment of depression. In S. G. Lazar (Ed.), *Psychotherapy is worth it: A comprehensive review of its cost effectiveness* (pp. 175–226). Arlington, VA: American Psychiatric Press.

Lethborg, C., Schofield, P., & Kissane, D. (2012). The advanced cancer patient experience of undertaking meaning and purpose (MaP) therapy. *Palliative & Supportive Care, 10,* 177–188. http://dx.doi.org/10.1017/S147895151100085X

Levant, R. F., & Wong, Y. J. (Eds.). (2017). *The psychology of men and masculinities.* Washington, DC: American Psychological Association. http://dx.doi.org/10.1037/0000023-000

Linehan, M. M. (2015). *DBT skills training manual* (2nd ed.). New York, NY: Guilford Press.

Little, B. R. (1999). Personality and motivation: Personal action and the conative evolution. In L. A. Pervin & O. P. John (Eds.), *Handbook of personality: Theory and research* (2nd ed., pp. 501–524). New York, NY: Guilford Press.

Maddi, S. R. (1967). The existential neuroses. *Journal of Abnormal Psychology, 72,* 311–325. http://dx.doi.org/10.1037/h0020103

Maddi, S. R. (1970). The search for meaning. In M. Page (Ed.), *Nebraska Symposium on Motivation* (pp. 137–186). Lincoln: University of Nebraska Press.

Mains, J. A., & Scogin, F. R. (2003). The effectiveness of self-administered treatments: A practice-friendly review of the research. *Journal of Clinical Psychology, 59,* 237–246. http://dx.doi.org/10.1002/jclp.10145

Markman, K. D., Proulx, T., & Lindberg, M. J. (Eds.). (2013). *The psychology of meaning.* Washington, DC: American Psychological Association. http://dx.doi.org/10.1037/14040-000

Martela, F., Ryan, R. M., & Steger, M. F. (2017). Meaningfulness as satisfaction of autonomy, competence, relatedness, and beneficence: Comparing the four satisfactions and positive affect as predictors of meaning in life. *Journal of Happiness Studies,* 1–22. Advance online publication. https://dx.doi.org/10.1007/s10902-017-9869-7

Martela, F., & Steger, M. F. (2016). The three meanings of meaning in life: Distinguishing coherence, purpose, and significance. *The Journal of Positive Psychology, 11,* 531–545. http://dx.doi.org/10.1080/17439760.2015.1137623

Mascaro, N., & Rosen, D. H. (2005). Existential meaning's role in the enhancement of hope and prevention of depressive symptoms. *Journal of Personality, 73,* 985–1014. http://dx.doi.org/10.1111/j.1467-6494.2005.00336.x

Maslow, A. (1970). *Motivation and personality* (rev. ed.). New York, NY: Harper & Row.

Matsumoto, D., & Ekman, P. (1989). American–Japanese cultural differences in intensity ratings of facial expressions of emotion. *Motivation and Emotion, 13,* 143–157. http://dx.doi.org/10.1007/BF00992959

Matsumoto, D., & Willingham, B. (2006). The thrill of victory and the agony of defeat: Spontaneous expressions of medal winners of the 2004 Athens Olympic Games. *Journal of Personality and Social Psychology, 91,* 568–581. http://dx.doi.org/10.1037/0022-3514.91.3.568

Matsumoto, D., Yoo, S. H., & Fontaine, J. (2008). Mapping expressive differences around the world: The relationship between emotional display rules and individualism versus collectivism. *Journal of Cross-Cultural Psychology, 39,* 55–74. http://dx.doi.org/10.1177/0022022107311854

Matthews, K. A., Owens, J. F., Edmundowicz, D., Lee, L., & Kuller, L. H. (2006). Positive and negative attributes and risk for coronary and aortic calcification in healthy women. *Psychosomatic Medicine, 68,* 355–361. http://dx.doi.org/10.1097/01.psy.0000221274.21709.d0

McAdams, D. P. (2008). Personal narratives and the life story. In O. P. John, R. W. Robins, & L. A. Pervin (Eds.), *Handbook of personality: Theory and research* (3rd ed., pp. 242–262). New York, NY: Guilford Press.

McAdams, D. P. (2012). Meaning and personality. In P. T. Wong (Ed.), *The human quest for meaning* (2nd ed., pp. 107–123). New York, NY: Routledge/Taylor & Francis.

McAdams, D. P. (2013). How actors, agents, and authors find meaning in life. In K. D. Markman, T. Proulx, & M. J. Lindberg (Eds.), *The psychology of meaning* (pp. 171–190). Washington, DC: American Psychological Association. http://dx.doi.org/10.1037/14040-009

McDonald, M. J., Wong, P. T. P., & Gingras, D. T. (2012). Meaning-in-life measures and development of a brief version of the Personal Meaning Profile. In P. T. P. Wong (Ed.), *The human quest for meaning: Theories, research, and applications* (pp. 357–382). New York, NY: Routledge/Taylor & Francis.

McGoldrick, M. (Ed.). (2008). *Re-visioning family therapy: Race, culture, and gender in clinical practice.* New York, NY: Guilford Press.

McGregor, I., & Little, B. R. (1998). Personal projects, happiness, and meaning: On doing well and being yourself. *Journal of Personality and Social Psychology, 74,* 494–512. http://dx.doi.org/10.1037/0022-3514.74.2.494

McLean, K. C. (2008). The emergence of narrative identity. *Social and Personality Psychology Compass, 2,* 1685–1702. http://dx.doi.org/10.1111/j.1751-9004.2008.00124.x

McWilliams, N. (2004). *Psychoanalytic psychotherapy.* New York, NY: Guilford Press.

McWilliams, N. (2011). *Psychoanalytic diagnosis: Understanding personality structure in the clinical process* (2nd ed.). New York, NY: Guilford Press.

Metz, T. (2013). Meaning in life as the aim of psychotherapy: A hypothesis. In J. A. Hicks & C. Routledge (Eds.), *The experience of meaning in life: Classical perspectives, emerging themes, and controversies* (pp. 405–417). New York, NY: Springer. http://dx.doi.org/10.1007/978-94-007-6527-6_30

Mikulincer, M., & Shaver, P. R. (2013). Attachment orientations and meaning in life. In J. A. Hicks & C. Routledge (Eds.), *The experience of meaning in life: Classical perspectives, emerging themes, and controversies* (pp. 287–304). New York, NY: Springer. http://dx.doi.org/10.1007/978-94-007-6527-6_22

Napier, A. Y., & Whittaker, C. A. (1978). *The family crucible*. New York, NY: Harper & Row.

Neimeyer, R. A. (Ed.). (2001). *Meaning reconstruction and the experience of loss*. Washington, DC: American Psychological Association. http://dx.doi.org/10.1037/10397-000

Neimeyer, R. A. (Ed.). (2016). *Techniques of grief therapy: Assessment and interventions*. New York, NY: Routledge/Taylor & Francis.

O'Donnell, M. B., Shim, Y., Barenz, J. D., & Steger, M. F. (2014). Revisiting the Meaning in Life Questionnaire, Part 1: Psychometrics, health, and special populations. *International Forum for Logotherapy, 38,* 96–105.

O'Neil, J. M. (2015). *Men's gender role conflict: Psychological costs, consequences, and an agenda for change*. Washington, DC: American Psychological Association. http://dx.doi.org/10.1037/14501-000

Park, C. L. (2005). Religion as a meaning-making framework in coping with life stress. *Journal of Social Issues, 61,* 707–729. http://dx.doi.org/10.1111/j.1540-4560.2005.00428.x

Pinquart, M. (2002). Creating and maintaining purpose in life in old age: A meta-analysis. *Ageing International, 27,* 90–114. http://dx.doi.org/10.1007/s12126-002-1004-2

Polone, G. (Producer), & Hallström, L. (Director). (2017). *A dog's purpose* [Motion picture]. United States: Universal Pictures.

Prager, E. (1996). Exploring personal meaning in an age-differentiated Australian sample: Another look at the Sources of Meaning Profile (SOMP). *Journal of Aging Studies, 10,* 117–136. http://dx.doi.org/10.1016/S0890-4065(96)90009-2

Prochaska, J. O., Norcross, J. C., & DiClemente, C. C. (2010). *Changing for good: The revolutionary six-stage program for overcoming bad habits and moving your life positively forward*. New York, NY: HarperCollins.

Proulx, T., Markman, K. D., & Lindberg, M. J. (2013). Introduction: The new science of meaning. In K. D. Markman, T. Proulx, & M. J. Lindberg (Eds.), *The psychology of meaning* (pp. 3–14). Washington, DC: American Psychological Association. http://dx.doi.org/10.1037/14040-001

Rehm, D. (2017). *On my own*. New York, NY: Vintage.

Reker, G. T., Peacock, E. J., & Wong, P. T. (1987). Meaning and purpose in life and well-being: A life-span perspective. *Journal of Gerontology, 42,* 44–49. http://dx.doi.org/10.1093/geronj/42.1.44

Reker, G. T., & Wong, P. T. P. (1988). Aging as an individual process: Toward a theory of personal meaning. In J. E. Birren & V. L. Bengtson (Eds.), *Emergent theories of aging* (pp. 214–246). New York, NY: Springer.

Reker, G. T., & Wong, P. T. P. (2012). Personal meaning in life and psychosocial adaptation in the later years. In P. T. P. Wong (Ed.), *The human quest for meaning* (pp. 433–456). New York, NY: Routledge.

Rogers, C. R. (1951). *Client-centered therapy: Its current practice, implications, and theory*. Boston, MA: Houghton Mifflin.

Rogers, C. R. (1957). The necessary and sufficient conditions of therapeutic personality change. *Journal of Consulting Psychology, 21*, 95–103. http://dx.doi.org/10.1037/h0045357

Rosenberg, M., & McCullough, B. C. (1981). Mattering: Inferred significance to parents and mental health among adolescents. In R. Simmons (Ed.), *Research in community and mental health* (Vol. 2, pp. 163–182). Greenwich, CT: JAI Press.

Routledge, C., Sedikides, C., Wildschut, T., & Juhl, J. (2013). Finding meaning in one's past: Nostalgia as an existential resource. In K. D. Markman, T. Proulx, & M. J. Lindberg (Eds.), *The psychology of meaning* (pp. 297–316). Washington, DC: American Psychological Association. http://dx.doi.org/10.1037/14040-015

Ryan, R. M., & Deci, E. L. (2001). On happiness and human potentials: A review of research on hedonic and eudaimonic well-being. *Annual Review of Psychology, 52*, 141–166. http://dx.doi.org/10.1146/annurev.psych.52.1.141

Ryff, C. D. (1989). Happiness is everything, or is it? Explorations on the meaning of psychological well-being. *Journal of Personality and Social Psychology, 57*, 1069–1081. http://dx.doi.org/10.1037/0022-3514.57.6.1069

Ryff, C. D., & Singer, B. H. (1998). The contours of positive mental health. *Psychological Inquiry, 9*, 1–28. http://dx.doi.org/10.1207/s15327965pli0901_1

Safran, J. D., & Muran, J. C. (2000). *Negotiating the therapeutic alliance: A relational treatment guide*. New York, NY: Guilford Press.

Sammallahti, P. R., Holi, M. J., Komulainen, E. J., & Aalberg, V. A. (1996). Comparing two self-report measures of coping—the Sense of Coherence Scale and the Defense Style Questionnaire. *Journal of Clinical Psychology, 52*, 517–524. http://dx.doi.org/10.1002/(SICI)1097-4679(199609)52:5<517::AID-JCLP4>3.0.CO;2-K

Savickas, M. L. (2012). Life design: A paradigm for career intervention in the 21st century. *Journal of Counseling and Development, 90*, 13–19. http://dx.doi.org/10.1111/j.1556-6676.2012.00002.x

Scheier, M. F., Wrosch, C., Baum, A., Cohen, S., Martire, L. M., Matthews, K. A., . . . Zdaniuk, B. (2006). The Life Engagement Test: Assessing purpose in life. *Journal of Behavioral Medicine, 29*, 291–298. http://dx.doi.org/10.1007/s10865-005-9044-1

Schlossberg, N. K. (2009). *Revitalizing retirement: Reshaping your identity, relationships, and purpose*. Washington, DC: American Psychological Association.

Scogin, F. R., Bynum, J., Stephens, G., & Calhoon, S. (1990). Efficacy of self-administered treatment programs: Meta-analytic review. *Professional Psychology: Research and Practice, 21*, 42–47. http://dx.doi.org/10.1037/0735-7028.21.1.42

Seligman, M. E. (2012). *Flourish: A visionary new understanding of happiness and well-being*. New York, NY: Simon & Schuster.

Shaver, P. R., & Mikulincer, M. (Eds.). (2012). *Meaning, mortality, and choice*. Washington, DC: American Psychological Association.

Sileo, R. J., & Kopala, M. (1993). An A-B-C-D-E worksheet for promoting beneficence when considering ethical values. *Counseling and Values, 37,* 89–95. http://dx.doi.org/10.1002/j.2161-007X.1993.tb00800.x

Smith, B. W., & Zautra, A. J. (2004). The role of purpose in life in recovery from knee surgery. *International Journal of Behavioral Medicine, 11,* 197–202. http://dx.doi.org/10.1207/s15327558ijbm1104_2

Spangler, P. T., Hill, C. E., Dunn, M. G., Hummel, A., Walden, T., Liu, J., Jackson, J., Ganginis, H. V., & Salahuddin, N. (2014). Training undergraduate students to use immediacy. *The Counseling Psychologist, 42,* 729–757. http://dx.doi.org/10.1177/0011000014542835

Steger, M. F. (2007). Structural validity of the Life Regard Index. *Measurement and Evaluation in Counseling and Development, 40,* 97–109.

Steger, M. F. (2012). Experiencing meaning in life: Optimal functioning at the nexus of spirituality, psychopathology, and well-being. In P. T. P. Wong (Ed.), *The human quest for meaning: Theories, research, and applications* (2nd ed., pp. 165–184). New York, NY: Routledge/Taylor & Francis.

Steger, M. F., & Frazier, P. (2005). Meaning in life: One link in the chain from religion to well-being. *Journal of Counseling Psychology, 52,* 574–582. http://dx.doi.org/10.1037/0022-0167.52.4.574

Steger, M. F., Frazier, P., Oishi, S., & Kaler, M. (2006). The Meaning in Life Questionnaire: Assessing the presence of and search for meaning in life. *Journal of Counseling Psychology, 53,* 80–93. http://dx.doi.org/10.1037/0022-0167.53.1.80

Steger, M. F., Kawabata, Y., Shimai, S., & Otake, K. (2008). The meaningful life in Japan and the United States: Levels and correlates of meaning in life. *Journal of Research in Personality, 42,* 660–678. http://dx.doi.org/10.1016/j.jrp.2007.09.003

Steger, M. F., Pickering, N. K., Adams, E., Burnett, J., Shin, J. Y., Dik, B. J., & Stauner, N. (2010). The quest for meaning: Religious affiliation differences in the correlates of religious quest and the search for meaning in life. *Psychology of Religion and Spirituality, 2,* 206–226. http://dx.doi.org/10.1037/a0019122

Stillman, T. F., Baumeister, R. F., Lambert, N. M., Crescioni, A. W., Dewall, C. N., & Fincham, F. D. (2009). Alone and without purpose: Life loses meaning following social exclusion. *Journal of Experimental Social Psychology, 45,* 686–694. http://dx.doi.org/10.1016/j.jesp.2009.03.007

Sue, D. W., Bernier, J. E., Durran, A., Feinberg, L., Pedersen, P., Smith, E. J., & Vasquez-Nuttall, E. (1982). Position paper: Cross-cultural counseling competencies. *The Counseling Psychologist, 10,* 45–52. http://dx.doi.org/10.1177/0011000082102008

Sue, S. (1998). In search of cultural competence in psychotherapy and counseling. *American Psychologist, 53,* 440–448. http://dx.doi.org/10.1037/0003-066X.53.4.440

Swann, W. B., Jr. (1987). Identity negotiation: Where two roads meet. *Journal of Personality and Social Psychology, 53,* 1038–1051. http://dx.doi.org/10.1037/0022-3514.53.6.1038

Swann, W. B., Jr. (2012). Self-verification theory. In P. M. Van Lange, A. W. Kruglanski, & E. Higgins (Eds.), *Handbook of theories of social psychology* (Vol. 2, pp. 23–42). Thousand Oaks, CA: Sage. http://dx.doi.org/10.4135/9781446249222.n27

Swan, W. B., Jr., & Buhrmester, M. D. (2012). Self-verification: The search for coherence. In M. R. Leary & J. Tangney (Eds.), *Handbook of self and identity* (2nd ed., pp. 405–424). New York, NY: Guilford Press.

Thompson, E. H., Jr., & Bennett, K. M. (2015). Measurement of masculinity ideologies: A (critical) review. *Psychology of Men & Masculinity, 16*, 115–133. http://dx.doi.org/10.1037/a0038609

Triandis, H. C. (1989). The self and social behavior in differing cultural contexts. *Psychological Review, 96*, 506–520. http://dx.doi.org/10.1037/0033-295X.96.3.506

Tummala-Narra, P. (2015). Cultural competence as a core emphasis of psychoanalytic psychotherapy. *Psychoanalytic Psychology, 32*, 275–292. http://dx.doi.org/10.1037/a0034041

Tummala-Narra, P. (2016). *Psychoanalytic theory and cultural competence in psychotherapy*. Washington, DC: American Psychological Association. http://dx.doi.org/10.1037/14800-000

Vance, J. D. (2016). *Hillbilly elegy: A memoir of a family and culture in crisis*. New York, NY: HarperCollins.

Vanhooren, S., Leijssen, M., & Dezutter, J. (2015). Loss of meaning as a predictor of distress in prison. *International Journal of Offender Therapy and Comparative Criminology, 61*, 1–22.

Vanhooren, S., Leijssen, M., & Dezutter, J. (2016). Profiles of meaning and search for meaning among prisoners. *The Journal of Positive Psychology, 11*, 622–633. http://dx.doi.org/10.1080/17439760.2015.1137625

Vanhooren, S., Leijssen, M., & Dezutter, J. (2017). Ten prisoners on a search for meaning: A qualitative study of loss and growth during incarceration. *The Humanistic Psychologist, 45*, 162–178. http://dx.doi.org/10.1037/hum0000055

Vos, J., Craig, M., & Cooper, M. (2015). Existential therapies: A meta-analysis of their effects on psychological outcomes. *Journal of Consulting and Clinical Psychology, 83*, 115–128. http://dx.doi.org/10.1037/a0037167

Wachtel, P. L. (2011). *Inside the session: What really happens in psychotherapy*. Washington, DC: American Psychological Association. http://dx.doi.org/10.1037/12321-000

Wampold, B. E., & Imel, Z. E. (2015). *The great psychotherapy debate: The evidence for what makes psychotherapy work*. New York, NY: Routledge.

Ward, S. J., & King, L. A. (2016). Poor but happy? Income, happiness, and experienced and expected meaning in life. *Social Psychological and Personality Science, 7*, 463–470. http://dx.doi.org/10.1177/1948550615627865

Watson, D. L., & Tharp, R. G. (2014). *Self-directed behavior: Self-modification for personal Adjustment* (10th ed.). Belmont, CA: Wadsworth.

Weinreich, P. (1986). The operationalisation of identity theory in racial and ethnic relations. In J. Rex & D. Mason (Eds.), *Theories of race and ethnic relations* (pp. 299–320). Cambridge, England: Cambridge University Press. http://dx.doi.org/10.1017/CBO9780511557828.016

Weinstein, N., Ryan, R. M., & Deci, E. L. (2012). Motivation, meaning, and wellness. In P. T. P. Wong (Ed.), *The human quest for meaning* (2nd ed., pp. 81–106). New York, NY: Routledge/Taylor & Francis.

Wilson, E. O. (2014). *The meaning of human existence*. New York, NY: Norton.

Wilson, K. G., & Murrell, A. R. (2004). Values work in acceptance and commitment therapy: Setting a course for behavioral treatment. In S. C. Hayes, V. M. Follette, & M. Linehan (Eds.), *Mindfulness and acceptance: Expanding the cognitive–behavioral tradition* (pp. 120–151). New York, NY: Guilford Press.

Wilson, T. D., Ndiaye, D. G., Hahn, C., & Gilbert, D. T. (2013). Still a thrill: Meaning making and the pleasures of uncertainty. In K. D. Markman, T. Proulx, & M. J. Lindberg (Eds.), *The psychology of meaning* (pp. 421–443). Washington, DC: American Psychological Association.

Wolman, B. (1975). Principles of interactional psychotherapy. *Psychotherapy: Theory, Research & Practice, 12,* 149–159. http://dx.doi.org/10.1037/h0086419

Wong, P. T. P. (1998). Meaning-centered counseling. In P. T. P. Wong & P. Fry (Eds.), *The quest for human meaning: A handbook of theory, research, and application* (pp. 395–435). Mahwah, NJ: Erlbaum.

Wong, P. T. P. (2010). Meaning therapy: An integrative and positive existential psychotherapy. *Journal of Contemporary Psychotherapy, 40,* 85–93. http://dx.doi.org/10.1007/s10879-009-9132-6

Wong, P. T. P. (2012). From logotherapy to meaning-centered counseling and therapy. In P. T. P. Wong (Ed.), *The human quest for meaning: Theories, research, and applications* (2nd ed., pp. 619–647). New York, NY: Routledge/Taylor & Francis.

Wong, P. T. P., & Fry, P. S. (Eds.). (1998). *The human quest for meaning: A handbook of psychological research and clinical application* (pp. 237–259). Mahwah, NJ: Erlbaum.

Wong, Y. J., Ho, M. R., Wang, S. Y., & Miller, I. S. K. (2017). Meta-analyses of the relationship between conformity to masculine norms and mental health-related outcomes. *Journal of Counseling Psychology, 64,* 80–93. http://dx.doi.org/10.1037/cou0000176

Yalom, I. D. (1980). *Existential psychotherapy*. New York, NY: Basic Books.

Yalom, I. D. (1992). *When Nietzsche wept*. New York, NY: HarperCollins.

Yalom, I. D., & Leszcz, M. (2005). *The theory and practice of group psychotherapy* (5th ed.). New York, NY: Basic Books.

Zadro, L., Williams, K. D., & Richardson, R. (2004). How low can you go? Ostracism by a computer is sufficient to lower self-reported levels of belonging, control, self-esteem, and meaningful existence. *Journal of Experimental Social Psychology, 40,* 560–567. http://dx.doi.org/10.1016/j.jesp.2003.11.006

Zetzer, H. A. (in press). What are you not willing to pay attention to? Meaning in life and ACT. *Psychotherapy Bulletin*.

Zika, S., & Chamberlain, K. (1992). On the relation between meaning in life and psychological well-being. *British Journal of Psychology, 83,* 133–145. http://dx.doi.org/10.1111/j.2044-8295.1992.tb02429.x

Index

About the Author

Clara E. Hill, PhD, earned her doctorate at Southern Illinois University in 1974. She started her career in 1974 as an assistant professor in the Department of Psychology, University of Maryland, and is currently still there as a professor. She has been president of the Society for Psychotherapy Research, editor of the *Journal of Counseling Psychology,* and coeditor of *Psychotherapy Research.* Her awards include the Leona Tyler Award (American Psychological Association [APA] Division 17: Society of Counseling Psychology), the Distinguished Psychologist Award (APA Division 29: Society for the Advancement of Psychotherapy), the Distinguished Research Career Award (Society for Psychotherapy Research), and the Outstanding Lifetime Achievement Award (Section on Counseling and Psychotherapy Process and Outcome Research, Society for Counseling Psychology). Her major research interests are helping skills, psychotherapy process and outcome, training and supervising therapists, dreamwork, meaning in life, and qualitative research. Dr. Hill has published over 220 journal articles, more than 75 book chapters, and 14 books (including *Helping Skills* [1999], *Dream Work in Therapy* [2004], and *Consensual Qualitative Research* [2012]).